The Royal Artillery at War, 1700–1860

The Royal Artillery at War, 1700-1860

British Gunners & Their Guns in the 18th & 19th Centuries

ILLUSTRATED

James Alex. Browne

The Royal Artillery at War, 1700-1860
British Gunners & Their Guns in the 18th & 19th Centuries
by James Alex. Browne

ILLUSTRATED

FIRST EDITION

Leonaur is an imprint of Oakpast Ltd
Copyright in this form © 2022 Oakpast Ltd

ISBN: 978-1-915234-58-2 (hardcover)
ISBN: 978-1-915234-59-9 (softcover)

http://www.leonaur.com

Publisher's Notes

The views expressed in this book are not necessarily those of the publisher.

Contents

Introduction	7
Europe (Gibraltar Excepted), 1700-1782	11
America and the West Indies, 1741-1782	34
Gibraltar	61
The Royal Artillery in the East Indies	83
Wars of the French Revolution	105
Africa—South America—Italy—Walcheren, etc.	123
The Campaigns in the Peninsula, 1808-1809	141
The Campaigns in the Peninsula, 1809-1812	150
The Campaigns in the Peninsula—Operations in Andalusia	170
The Campaigns in the Peninsula, 1813-1814	178
The War with America, 1812-1814	199
The Waterloo Campaign	211
Syria—Kaffraria	226
The War in the Crimea—Field Operations	237
War in the Crimea—Siege of Sebastopol	254
The Royal Artillery in China	271
New Zealand	285

Introduction

The object of the following pages is to make known to services, gallant actions, inventions, discoveries, travels, and adventures of officers and soldiers of the Royal Artillery.

The ubiquity of the British Royal Artillery is indisputable.

Under the tropical sun, in the islands of Africa and the Indian Ocean, British artillerymen will be found; on the northern coast of America, where perished the martyrs of the *Erebus* and *Terror*, their footsteps may be traced. In Egypt, Syria, and the islands of the Spanish main, they have given their lives in upholding their country's honour; even to Spitzbergen they have ventured in the cause of science.

The thunder of their guns has been heard, and the marks of their shot may still be seen in India and China; the Kaffir and the Maori have also felt their power.

It is not only those who have earned their laurels on fields of carnage that we would bring especially to notice, but those who have trodden in the real paths of glory—religion, humanity, science, and civilization.

It is well known that British artillerymen have never sullied their fame, and by far the greater number who have earned distinction must necessarily be those who have fought and bled, aye, and nobly died in their country's cause; but when nation shall have ceased to rise against nation, and the sound of war shall be no more heard, the names of Chesney, Sabine, and Leake will still be remembered, while the bright example exhibited by such eminent Christians as Maitland, Budd, Vandeleur, and Marjouram will have an influence (not in the regiment only, but in the world at large) on generations yet to come.

All soldiers, but especially artillerymen, are generally looked upon as the horrible destroyers of mankind, and Congreve, Shrapnel, and Armstrong noted as monsters by members of the Peace Societies. A little thought, however, together with a common study of history, will convince such that since the introduction of artillery, fewer lives have been sacrificed, and war made less horrible than in the days of bow and spear; and the more improvements made in artillery, the shorter have been the wars; the nearer we approach perfection in armament, the nearer we shall be to that grand consummation so devoutly to be wished for, when the sword shall be turned into a ploughshare and the spear into a pruning-hook.

Hume, in his *History of England*, says:—

> The artillery first framed were so clumsy, and of such difficult management, that men were not immediately sensible of their use and efficacy; and even to the present time, improvements have been continually making in this furious engine, which, though it seemed contrived for the destruction of mankind and the overthrow of empires, has, in the issue, rendered battles less bloody, and has given greater stability to civil societies. Nations, by its means, have been brought more to a level; conquests have been less frequent and rapid; success in war has been reduced nearly to be a matter of calculation; and any nation overmatched by its enemies either yields to their demands, or secures itself by alliances against violence and invasion.

Not only are the inventors of destructive instruments to be found in the ranks of the Royal Artillery; many, among whom are Bell, Viney (improved water-pipes), and Grant (army cooking machines), have devoted their talents to the preservation and comfort of the lives of their fellow-creatures, and earned for themselves the imperishable esteem of all who are acquainted with their inventions. The Royal Artillery is comparatively of modern establishment, and has ever been held in the same high estimation it enjoys at the present time, (1865.)

> The Royal Regiment of Artillery, whether we consider the distinguished skill of the officers, or the exact discipline of the men, who often die in defending their guns with a heroic ardour, may be considered as one of the most respectable, and assuredly the most skilful corps in the service.

The beginning of that noble force, the flower at this moment of the British Army, dates back no further than the reign of George II., while its excellency both in the science of the gunners, and in the mounting, equipment, and horsing of the guns, has been acquired, or at least perfected, within the remembrance of many men still living, (1865.)

Though the officers of the Royal Artillery have distinguished themselves in every part of the globe, their names have seldom been brought prominently before the public, for no other reason than that in time of war they are never invested with a command. General Sir W. F. Williams of Kars is the only exception during the present generation, and he was not appointed to the command of that fortress he so ably and so bravely defended, but, being there in the performance of his duty as commissioner to the Turkish Army in Asia, assumed that responsibility which he saw the Ottoman commanders were incapable of retaining.

The late Captain Brabazon, writing on this subject, says:—

> Anything but an artilleryman, except an engineer, seems our motto in selecting commanders. Foreigners, noting the constant failure of our siege operations, but not observing that they are rarely controlled by scientific officers, have naturally formed no high opinion of our artillery and engineers.

Yet in the Peninsula, the artillery, though coldly encouraged, most brilliantly performed their duties; and at the conclusion of peace, such was our admitted excellence in this arm, that it was held up for a model to the rest of Europe.

★★★★★★★★★★

> "The perfection to which the English artillery has been brought (the knowledge of which fact has been so forcibly and painfully impressed on them) has induced the French to adopt the whole of your artillery practice."—Letter from Paris, Dec. 29, 1828.

★★★★★★★★★★

These remarks are offered as an apology for the introduction of the subject to the public, who we trust will receive it as it is presented, in the hope of preserving the names and deeds of many gallant men who, beyond their own circle, are entirety unknown.

CHAPTER 1

Europe (Gibraltar Excepted), 1700-1782

To trace the history of artillery from the time of Jonathan, and to argue upon the old questions as to whether the Moors, Chinese, or English were the first to use gunpowder, is not the purpose of this work. (An inscription to be found carved upon a stone near Buxted, in Sussex.) Neither is it intended to inquire into the history of Edward's artillery in Scotland (Edward III. was the first to use cannon, which he did against the Scotch in 1327), nor yet to enter into the particulars of William's "train" in Ireland, (we are told; *Book of Mars*, that at the Battle of Aghrim, July 12, 1691, "Captain Logan of the train levelled one of the field-pieces at St. Ruth taking off his head") mere passing mention only can be made of Sir George Carew, Colonel Legge, and Captain Leake, worthy artillerymen of the olden time; for our purpose it is sufficient to begin, with the formation of the "Royal Regiment of Artillery," which took place in the reign of George II., when Colonel Borgard, an officer of great ability, who "understood the economy of the train exceeding well," was appointed to the command.

★★★★★★★★★★

Sir George Carew held different appointments in the Ordnance Department from 1588 to 1620.

Colonel George Legge, afterwards Lord Dartmouth, served with the artillery from 1677 to 1689.

Captain Richard Leake, Master-Gunner of England, distinguished himself while commanding the artillery in several naval actions. Born 1629; died 1686.

★★★★★★★★★★

Albert Borgard was of an ancient and honourable family in Denmark, and was born at Holbech on the 10th November, 1659. He entered the service of his sovereign at the early age of sixteen, as a cadet in the Queen's Regiment of Foot, and served at the siege of Wismar in the same year (1675). In the following year he served on board the fleet at the Battle of Oeland, in the Baltic (11th June), and on land at the sieges and captures of Helsingborg, Landskroom (July), Christianstadt and Halmstadt (August), where the Danes sustained a defeat at the hands of the Swedes.

In September, 1676, he was made a gunner in the Danish artillery, and served as such at the Battle of Lund, in the following December.

In 1677 he served at the battles of Ronneberg and Oddewall, and at the siege of Marstrand, in Norway. In 1678 he went on an expedition to the Isle of Lanterugen, and the following year was promoted to fireworker, and took part in the survey of the island of Zealand. In 1680 he went to Berlin to study the making of fireworks (both warlike and pleasant), and from Berlin to Strasburg (in 1681) to study fortification. In 1682 he went to Holstein as ensign in the Queen's Regiment, and the next year was promoted to lieutenant. He then went as a volunteer to the relief of Vienna, and fought in the battle gained by Sobieski over the Turks (11thSeptember, 1683). In 1684 he assisted in the fortification of Farrell, in Oldenburg, and in 1685 went to Hungary and served at the siege of Niewhanshal and the Battle of Gran. In 1685 he served with the artillery at the siege of Buda, and here he obtained enough plunder to pay all the expenses he had incurred in Hungary as a volunteer.

In 1687 he was appointed lieutenant in the King of Denmark's Drabanten Guards, and was employed as an engineer in the new fortifications at Copenhagen. Being unjustly passed over in his promotion, he challenged his superior officer, and was obliged to fly the kingdom; he then entered the Polish service and served at Budjack, where he captured two Tartars, and was in great danger of losing his life because he would not deliver them up to a Polish officer. He then entered the service of the King of Prussia as lieutenant in the Guards, and served at the action of Nuys, the siege of Keyserswart, and the destruction of Bonn (1689). He commanded two mortars during the bombardment of the last-named city. In 1691 he again went to Hungary, and was present at the Battle of Salankeman. In April, 1692, he went with some volunteers to the siege of Namur, which was taken from the allies on the 20th June.

Borgard, with another volunteer, led the attack, and Louis XIV. presented them each with a thousand crowns, and offered them captains' commissions in his army, which, however, they refused, as they did not like the French service. Thence they repaired to the English camp at Genap, where, on July 1st, Borgard entered the English artillery as firemaster, under Colonel Goor. He served at the Battle of Steenkirk, and was afterwards sent to Ostend to join a detachment under Colonel Sir Martin Beckman.

★★★★★★★★★★

In 1662 Captain Beckman was Engineer-General of Tangier; in 1664 he was Firemaster to the Artillery, and in 1695 (then Colonel and a knight) he commanded the artillery at the bombardments of St. Martin's and Olonna.

★★★★★★★★★★

From Ostend he went to Tournay, and from thence to Dixmude and Ghent. In 1693 he went with a detachment of bombardiers and fireworkers to Liége, and was present at the Battle of Landen.

★★★★★★★★★★

Bombardiers were at this time commissioned officers; indeed, every man who served in the artillery (even the privates) received commissions signed by the Master-General of the Ordnance. The officers' commissions were first signed by the king on the 30th April, 1751, when those for the soldiers were dispensed with.

★★★★★★★★★★

In 1694 he served under Lieut. Col. Brown at the siege of Huy, and at the siege and capture of Namur in the following year. Here he commanded a battery of twelve mortars, and threw a shell into the enemy's magazine in a demi-bastion and destroyed it.

In 1697 all foreigners were discharged from the British service except Borgard and his companion Schlundt, who, being personally known to King William, were retained in the English artillery, and came to England. Here Borgard remained, enjoying (for the first time since he became a soldier) a few years of peaceful life. In 1703 he was promoted to major, and went on the Duke of Ormonde's expedition to Spain as second in command of the artillery. (The artillery on this expedition was commanded by Colonel George Brown.) He directed the bombardment of Fort St. Catherine (Cadiz) from the mortar-boats, and that of Fort Matagorda from the land-mortars. Fort Durand, at Vigo, was also severely bombarded, and the Franco-Spanish, fleet, which had taken refuge under it, destroyed, when the expedition returned to England.

In 1703 Major Borgard volunteered to join the Duke of Marlborough's army in Flanders; he had scarcely arrived there, however, when he was recalled to command the English artillery who were to accompany Charles of Austria to Spain.

The fleet, commanded by Sir George Rooke, accompanied by a body of land forces under the Duke of Schomberg, sailed on the 4th January, 1704. Furious storms had been raging about the coasts for nearly three months, and at this time had not abated; so, after beating about for some days, and sustaining several losses, the fleet was compelled to put back to Spithead, where it remained till the middle of February. Two transports containing artillerymen and ordnance stores were lost in this storm.

On arriving in Portugal, Borgard, now colonel, and commander-in-chief of the allied artillery, was, with his artillerymen, attached to the force under the Conde das Galueas, who, marching into Spain, laid siege to Valencia d'Alcantara, and carried it by assault. While building the batteries before this fortress, Colonel Borgard had his left arm shot to pieces.

The artillery under the Earl of Peterborough was commanded by Major Collier, who, at the siege of Barcelona, was wounded in the shoulder by a musket-ball. A bombardier (Blunt) was killed at Campilio, and such was the dread the Spaniards had of the infection the body of a "heretic" would spread among the corn, that it was some time before he could be buried, and at last he was laid in a very deep grave on a barren spot of ground.

In 1706 the Earl of Galway's army, with Borgard's artillery, besieged and took Alcantara, (here Colonel Borgard received a wound in his left breast), and marched into Madrid; from whence, however, they were obliged to retire through the imbecility and cowardice of the Austrian candidate for the Spanish throne.

From this date the fortunes of the English troops in Spain under the Earl of Galway began to decline. They suffered dreadful privations from want of supplies; and at the Battle of Almanza (14th April, 1707) sustained a terrible defeat, the artillery losing all their guns and baggage, and nearly all the men.

In 1708 the British artillery under Colonel Borgard accompanied the army composed of Spaniards, Italians, and Portuguese, which left Spain for Minorca. They landed on the 26th August, and the garrison of Port Mahon, consisting of 1,000 Spaniards and 600 French marines, surrendered after a short action, and by the 30th September the whole island was in possession of the allies. In 1709, they returned to Spain, and were present at the battles of Villa Nova, Balagner, Almanara, and

Saragossa.

At the last-named battle, which was a complete victory, the enemy losing all their artillery and 12,000 men (7,000 prisoners and 5,000 killed), our artillery suffered fearfully.

The Spanish cavalry under General Mahoni fell furiously on our batteries, killing 80 men and hamstringing above 300 mules, Colonel Borgard received four wounds, and his gallant conduct on the occasion—as indeed that of the whole of the artillery—was borne witness to by General Mahoni himself, who spoke in the highest terms of commendation of their extraordinary courage.

At the Battle of Villa Viciosa (10th December, 1710), where the army of Charles was completely defeated and compelled to surrender, Colonel Borgard received a wound in the left leg with a canon-shot. He was laid up for six months, and at the end of that time was permitted to come to England on parole. He was soon exchanged, however, for a Spanish colonel, but it was a long time before he was able to move without crutches.

The last service he performed in the reign of Queen Anne was to make fireworks on the occasion of the peace of Utrecht (1713).

The reign of George I., whatever its influence may have been on the civil and ecclesiastical institutions of the country, fills but a narrow space in the military history of England, no British force having appeared in the field during the thirteen years he occupied the throne.

✶✶✶✶✶✶✶✶✶✶

Excepting the army which marched into Scotland in 1715, for the purpose of crushing the rebellion. This force, which was commanded by the Duke of Argyle, Colonel Borgard having the direction of the artillery, marched to Leith, Innerleithen, Stirling, Dundee, etc., but were never engaged.

✶✶✶✶✶✶✶✶✶✶

In 1716 Colonel Borgard was consulted by the Board of Ordnance as to the nature of brass and iron guns; the construction of these weapons, and the probability of improvement in the casting of them, having for some time occupied the attention of several persons connected with the Ordnance. Shortly afterwards it was determined to re-cast a great number of brass guns that had been taken by the Duke of Marlborough in his successful campaigns, a, Mr. Bagley being instructed with the operation, which was to take place at the "Foundry" at Windmill Hill, Moorfields, near the spot where the present City-road Wesleyan Chapel is situated. To witness the process temporary galleries were fitted up for spectators, and a great number of noblemen, military officers, and others, anxious to see the conversion of French metal into English guns, were assembled. At the proper time the furnaces were tapped, and out poured the molten metal. In consequence of a latent dampness in the moulds, steam was generated, which occasioned a dreadful explosion. The roof was blown off, liquid fire was scattered in every direction, and twenty-five persons were severely wounded, seventeen of them dying shortly after. Among the persons thus injured was Colonel Borgard, who was wounded in four places.

This catastrophe had been foreseen and predicted by a young man named Schalch, a native of Schaffhausen in Switzerland, and immediately after its occurrence a notice appeared in the papers requesting him to call at the Ordnance Office in the Tower, and suggesting that the interview might prove to his advantage. Schalch accordingly waited on Colonel Armstrong, the Surveyor-General of the Ordnance, who commissioned him in the name of the Government to seek out some spot within twelve miles of the metropolis, to which the whole manufacture of ordnance might be transferred. He fixed on the Warren at Woolwich, where suitable buildings were erected, forming the commencement of the Royal Arsenal. Schalch was appointed general superintendent, and continued in that office for a period of sixty years, during which time not one single accident occurred. He died in 1776, at the advanced age of eighty-four years. (Many of Schalch's descendants served in the Royal Artillery, the last being the present—at time of publication—Major Andrew Archer William Schalch).

In September, 1719, an English squadron, commanded by Lord Cobham, and having onboard some troops (including the artillery under Colonel Borgard), made an attack on Vigo. Colonel Borgard had bombarded this town seventeen years previously; on this occasion he commanded forty-six mortars of his own projection. This expedition was only a ruse to draw the attention of the Spaniards from other quarters, and to put them in dread or a general invasion; and having succeeded, it returned to England.

Borgard now:

Shouldered his crutch,
And showed how fields were won.

His services as a warrior were at an end, but as a public servant he was still greatly valued and respected, and had yet to accomplish that which alone has preserved his name—to establish on a permanent foundation that which had never existed in the British Army, a Royal Regiment of Artillery. He and General Hopkey laid before George I. plans for the formation and establishment of a regular standing regiment, and they were under the consideration of the Board of Ordnance at the time of that monarch's decease.

****

> Colonel John Henry Hopkey commanded the artillery under the Duke of Marlborough in the early years of the eighteenth century, having three companies under his command, the captains being Robert Guyben, Christopher Brissac, and Andrew Bennett.

****

The same proposals had been made to Queen Anne, but were not attended to, and shortly after the accession of George II. Borgard's plans were put into execution, and barracks built at Woolwich for officers and men.

In 1727 Borgard was promoted to major-general, and a few years afterwards to lieut.-general, but his active service was ended; he was never even consulted in anything relative to the artillery after the appointment of Colonel Armstrong to the post of surveyor.

He was a man "mightily beloved for his humane disposition," and greatly respected on account of his abilities.

> He was strictly honest, and declared often that he could safely affirm upon oath that he never made sixpence out of his regiment above what the king allowed, and gave up the clothing of the regiment to the Board of Ordnance that he might not be suspected to have any profit by it. He chose the patterns, but refused to handle the money taking care that it was all laid out upon the men, and likewise that the officers should not wrong them. He would never take a present from any of the men, as a hare, a bird, or fish, which they caught or shot, without paying them the price they sold for in the market.

In 1703 Borgard was married to Barbara Bradshaw, by whom he had several children, all of whom died young. In 1715 he married Catherine Mitchelson, who was niece to his first wife, by whom he had one son and two daughters.

****

> Withers Borgard (Captain R. A.) died in Flanders 1748, aged nineteen. Borgard's eldest daughter, Mary, was married to Captain (afterwards General) James Pattison, R.A.

****

He died at Woolwich on the 7th February, 1751, having reached the great age of ninety-two years.

The officers of the Royal Artillery, from the great respect they bore to his distinguished valour and abilities, caused his portrait (taken from an original painting) to be placed in the Military Repository, *a.d.* 1785. It was afterwards removed to the select committee-room, Grand Depot, and is now in the officers' mess-room at Woolwich.

In the year 1743 the Royal Regiment of Artillery consisted of eight companies, and was distributed as follows;—One company at Gibraltar, one at Minorca, one at Newfoundland, three with the army in Flanders, and two at Woolwich.

From the latter, detachments were sent to the Mediterranean to serve on board the bomb-vessels of Admiral Mathews's fleet. In 1741 the King of Sardinia applied to the admiral to allow these artillerymen to take charge of the most important ports and batteries on his frontiers. One captain, four lieutenants, and twenty-four bombardiers were accordingly landed, and served with distinction at the defence of Montalban and Montleuze. These two fortresses being assaulted and taken by the French and Spaniards in April, the detachments were made prisoners.

The artillery in Flanders were commanded by Colonel Pattison and Major Belford. It is needless to say our artillery at this time was much inferior to that of the French; but the fault was not that of the officers and men composing the regiment, but of the nature of the guns and their ineffective arrangement. When they had to be moved, the peasants of the country, with their horses, were pressed for the purpose; and they very naturally ran off as soon as the guns were unlimbered for action. The artillerymen had consequently to drag them from point to point during a battle, and if the enemy came upon them, were obliged to leave them.

In June, 1744, the Duke of Cumberland came to Woolwich, and inspected the artillery. He was so pleased with the appearance of the corps under Major Lewis, that he ordered that officer, with his company, to join the army in Flanders, of which he was about to assume the command. Nothing was done this year, the army moving without the artillery, a circumstance which drew forth the ridicule of the French. When in winter quarters, a company of comedians from Paris played in the French camp, and among their performances was a pantomime, in which the following dialogue was introduced. An English officer is represented, who is asked by the clown:—

"Where are you going?"

"*Officer.* To the siege of Lisle, which we shall take in five days."

"*Clown.* You have not a sufficient force."

"*Officer.* Don't mind that. One Englishman will beat five French. Huzza, boys!"

"*Clown.* But where is your artillery?"

"*Officer.* Odd so (*scratching his head*); we have forgot it. Let me think—it is at Ostend or Antwerp, if it has escaped the last storm."

At the Battle of Fontenoy (April, 1745), seven guns advanced with the brigade of Guards under Sir John Ligonier, and they quickly silenced the enemy's artillery. This, however, is all that can be said in favour of our artillery; but when it is considered that the French had two hundred and sixty-six pieces of cannon in the field, and that we had only forty-seven, there cannot be much expected on the part of the latter.

Though the English lost neither colours, standards, nor kettle-drums in this action, the guns were left behind for want of horses, the drivers having "run away so early that they reached Brussels the same day."

The artillery lost in the Battle of Fontenoy, Lieutenant Bennet, one sergeant, one gunner, and seven mattrosses.

****

Mattrosses—"Soldiers in the train of artillery next below the gunners; their duty is to assist the gunners in traversing, sponging, loading, and firing of guns, etc. They carry firelocks, and march along with the store-waggons, both as a guard and to help in case a waggon should break down."—*Chalmers' Cyclopaedia.* The rank of mattross was abolished in 1783, when the whole of the private soldiers in the artillery were called gunners.

****

A detachment of three officers and fifty men was sent from Woolwich, in August, to strengthen the garrison of Ostend, then besieged by Count Leivendhal, which held out about fourteen days.

The Pretender having landed in Scotland, and assembled an army, before the end of September he completely routed the English under Sir John Cope, and prepared to march into England.

There were none of the Royal Artillery at the Battle of Prestonpans. Till then, the Highlanders had had a great terror of artillery; from that moment they acquired a contempt of it. The men who served the

TRAIN OF ARTILLERY.
MATROSS.
1685.   1710.

guns were seamen whom Cope had brought from the fleet. They fled at the furious onset of the Gaels, and left the guns in their possession.

At length the Duke of Cumberland arrived from Flanders, and with him the four companies of the Royal Artillery, which were distributed with the several forces in different parts of the kingdom.

On the 8th of December, two companies under the command of Major Lewis marched from Woolwich to Finchley Common, where a force was being assembled under the immediate orders of the king, for the purpose of meeting the rebels who were marching towards London. They having retired northward after reaching Derby, the camp broke up, and the artillery returned to Woolwich on the 11th.

Six 18-pounders were brought to play on the crumbling walls of Carlisle on the 29th December, and on the following day the city surrendered.

On the 3rd January, 1746, Cumberland gave the command of the English troops to General Hawley, and returned to London. Hawley made at once into Scotland, taking with him a portion of the artillery.

On the 15th January, forty-eight gunners and mattrosses marched from Newcastle to join the main body, and on the 16th were followed by sixteen pieces of artillery.

On the 17th January, the English were again defeated at the Battle of Falkirk. This action took place during a great storm of wind and rain, and ended in the total rout of the king's troops. The artillery were not in action, as the guns stuck in a bog and could not be brought up. As soon as the infantry was seen to turn, the drivers ran away, with the horses and limbers, leaving eight guns on the field. One of these was dragged down to the camp by the grenadiers, the other seven fell into the hands of the enemy.

Public attention was now drawn to the inefficient equipment of our field artillery, and the following article appeared in the *Gentleman's Magazine:*—

> 'Tis surprising that, as this is not the first loss of artillery by bad horses, or by the country people going off with their horses, one out of several remedies that might be thought of was not provisioned against suffering again by such defects. With respect to the horses being bad, 'tis certainly difficult, if not impossible, to get horses of strength or in heart to labour in the north, or countries at a great distance from London; but as this is an affair well known, horses of strength ought to be as much bought

up and appropriated to draw a train of artillery (if one must be drawn, though of late not used) as for carrying our troopers or dragoons—and the drivers to be enlisted soldiers under the military oath. For the country farmers are not punishable for preserving themselves and their horses.

Cumberland arrived at Edinburgh on the 30th January, and immediately made arrangements for the prosecution of the campaign. Marching about Scotland for nearly two months, on the 14th April the Royal Army came up with the rebels, who were halting on the "bleak, black heath of Drummossie," hungry and worn out, having fasted and been kept marching during the whole of the previous night.

The action was commenced by the Highlanders, who fired their cannon for a few minutes without being answered by the Royal Artillery.

A few minutes after one o'clock, soon after the Highlanders had opened up their battery, Colonel Belford (who had ten guns under his command, two being placed at each interval of the first line) received orders to commence a cannonade, chiefly with a view to provoke the enemy to advance. The colonel, who was an excellent artilleryman, performed his duty with such effect as to make whole lanes through the ranks of the insurgents, besides tearing up the ground at their feet, and stripping the roofs of the neighbouring cottages in a manner almost as terrific. He also fired two pieces at a body of horse, amongst whom it was believed the prince was stationed; and with such precision did he take his aim, that that personage was bespattered with dirt raised by the balls, and a man holding a led horse by his side was killed.

It was not till the cannonade had continued nearly half an hour, and the Highlanders had seen many of their kinsmen stretched upon the heath, that Charles at last gave way to the necessity of ordering a charge.

Seeing a determined appearance of a rush. Colonel Belford gave orders to load with grape. This repelled them for a time, but at length the Macintoshes succeeded in reaching the front line of the English. Firing their muskets and then flinging them down, they thrust, sword in hand, on Barrel's and Munro's regiments, and cut their way through them. They were received with a murderous fire by the second line; but, being resolved to die rather than retreat, the few of the Macintoshes remaining rushed on, and the last survivor perished at the point of the bayonet.

The onslaught of the Highlanders fell heavy upon Barrel's and Munro's regiments, between which were two guns stationed, but that was the only part of the line they reached; the fearful discharges of grape from our guns preventing their advancing nearer than a hundred yards. At that distance, however, they did great damage with their pistols. The only casualties in the artillery were one gunner and five mattrosses wounded. These, it is supposed, were attached to the guns between Barrel's and Munro's regiments.

The result of the Battle of Culloden is well known: the enemy was dispersed, and the rebellion at an end.

An expedition against Port L'Orient, in Brittany (the land forces being commanded by Lieut.-General St. Clair), sailed from Plymouth on the 14th September. The whole of this undertaking was miserably mismanaged, both soldiers and sailors being in a condition of the loosest discipline, and the sole result was the burning of some villages, which was a disgrace rather than a glory to England, The Ordnance Department was in dreadful confusion.

Captain Chalmers and his company of artillery were put under the orders of Mr. Thomas Armstrong, the engineer of the force, a person who had never seen service of any kind (and who was at the time extremely afflicted with the gout); the evil consequences of which may be easily imagined, it being very improbable that Captain Chalmers would like to take orders from a civilian. (Armstrong died on the 27th March, 1758, having never been on any expedition excepting this to the coast of France. The Engineers were not commissioned until 1757) There were no horses to draw the guns, and neither the general nor any of his officers had a map, or knew anything of the country they were about to invade.

After wasting two or three days in summoning councils of war and attempting to parley with the enemy, the siege was opened on the morning of the 25th.

On the following afternoon Captain Chalmers reported there were no carcasses or bombs left, and only 150 shot remaining; and that he was positive he could not breach the defences of L'Orient at the distance the battery was placed. Accordingly, on the 27th the siege was raised, and after setting fire to the villages around the port, the army re-embarked and returned to England.

Two companies returned to Flanders, and on this occasion the artillery were for the first time divided among the infantry; two guns, commanded by a lieutenant, being, with a sub-division of the companies, attached to each regiment, and encamped with it.

In 1747 three companies were added to the regiment, the recruits being, for the most part, men who had been discharged from the cavalry. From this period the regiment, improved in appearance and in the size of the men, neither of which had hitherto been much attended to.

Two more companies were sent to Flanders this year, making a total of five. These were under the command of Lieut.-Colonel Belford and Major Borgard Mitchelson, officers to whom the Royal Artillery is much indebted. Their zeal and diligence and their influence during the campaign in Flanders (1747-8) caused the corps to become a recognised body, instead of being looked upon as an auxiliary to the army. By them the regiment was taught the use of small arms and the common drills and exercises of the infantry, and at the end of the war it began to bear a regular military appearance. Great attention was also paid to good order and strict discipline, matters that had been hitherto completely overlooked.

Colonel Belford succeeded to the command of the regiment on the death of Borgard in 1751. He never retired, but remained actively employed till his death, which took place on the 1st July, 1780.

The mob, which at this time, under the pretence of religion, did all in their power to ruin the country by trying to lay its capital and its bank in ashes, meant also to release the convicts and destroy at once the ordnance of Britain by burning the Warren. General Belford had made such dispositions that 40,000 men could not have forced the Arsenal. This important service and despatching trains of artillery to the different camps kept him on horseback day and night.

Such extraordinary fatigue, such unremitting application burst a blood-vessel in his lungs, and brought on a fever which carried him off in a few days. He was seventy years of age, and had taken part in some of the most remarkable events of the eighteenth century, having served his country for upwards of fifty years. He was with Admiral Vernon at Carthagena in 1741, and from that period till his death was ever employed in some military enterprise; the crowning point of his life being the Battle of Culloden, where, "by is spirit and boldness, he checked the vigour of the clans and gave the victory."

Borgard Mitchelson was nephew to General Borgard, and served many years in the Royal Artillery. His first foreign service was at Minorca, where he was stationed for many years, but it was in Flanders that he earned particular distinction. He lost an eye by a musket-ball at the Battle of Fontenoy, which prevented him from taking part in the suppression of the rebellion; but returning to Flanders in 1747, he was appointed major, and second in command of the artillery.

On the establishment of the second battalion io 1757, he was appointed to be colonel-commandant; he died at Portsmouth on the 26th February, 1762, aged fifty-two years. Mitchelson's elder brother, George, was a captain in the Royal Artillery; he served at Minorca, and with the Duke of Cumberland's army in Scotland during the rebellion, and died in Flanders in 1747.

In July, 1747, a detachment was sent from Woolwich to assist in the defence of Bergen-op-Zoom. This fortress, the key of Holland, was taken by the French on the 15th September; the detachment of British artillery having lost fourteen men during the siege.

The war came to an end in 1748 by the treaty of Aix-la-Chapelle, but was renewed with increased vigour by the French in 1755. That England should possess the finest port in the Mediterranean, and so near their own shores, was to them a subject of increasing chagrin. Great preparations were therefore made for an expedition to Minorca, and in May, 1756, a force under the Duke of Richelieu began to besiege Port Mahon.

The English garrison could only muster 3,352 officers and men, including a company of artillery. This company relieved Captain Mace's in 1749; the latter having formed part of the garrison of Minorca from the time that island came into the possession of the British. After a gallant defence of twenty-eight days, the garrison, reduced to 2,755, and worn out with incessant duty and watchings, surrendered on the most honourable terms. During the siege the company of the Royal Artillery had nine men killed and twenty-two wounded, of whom three died. Preparations were being made in England to send troops to the relief of the garrison, and among the new establishments was a company of miners, which was attached to and formed part of the Royal Artillery.

The command of this company was, through the interest of Sir John Ligonier, bestowed upon Lieutenant William Phillips, at the time the youngest of his rank in the regiment. The captain-lieutenants and the senior lieutenants before whom he was preferred were naturally annoyed at being passed over, especially when the only recommendation in Phillips's favour was that he had acted as *aide-de-camp* to Sir John Ligonier. Thinking it merely a temporary appointment, they made no stir in the matter, but the following year the miners were distributed, and the company established as one of the regiment. By this time Phillips was known and respected as an able officer, and his subsequent conduct in Germany and America gained for him the admiration of the whole world. (During the American war of 1813, a general of the American Army, wishing to flatter some of his artillery officers, mentioned them in the despatches as being like the English captains Phillips, Drummond, and Foy).

During this war several descents were made on the coast of France, all of them being more or less miserable blunders. The first was that against Rochfort, under Sir John Mordaunt, in 1757, which was accompanied by a detachment of artillery under Captain James.

The only event worthy of mention that occurred in this expedition was the gallant conduct of Colonel Wolfe, the conqueror of Quebec, it being the first occasion on which that officer attracted attention.

In May, 1758, an expedition under the Duke of Marlborough (junior) embarked at Portsmouth for St Malo, and returned in June, having done nothing except setting fire to a quantity of shipping.

The following month another force under General Bligh destroyed the fortifications of Cherbourg, but they were eventually driven from the French coast in a manner anything but creditable to our army.

Two companies of the Royal Artillery, under Captains Pattison and Brome, took part in these affairs. Of Pattison we shall have frequent occasion to speak. There were two captains in the regiment at this time named Brome—Charles and Joseph (probably brothers). The former left the regiment, or died, about 1760; the latter lived to be a lieut.-general, and is remembered by many old men still living, (1865). He began his service in the Royal Artillery as a drummer about the year 1726, and died on the 24th April, 1706, aged eighty-four years, having been three times commandant of Woolwich garrison. (The exact date of Brome's enlistment cannot be ascertained, but he was made gunner or mattross in 1730).

He was a little man, very attentive to duty, but (probably from a sense of his humble origin, of which he was proud) very reserved, never mixing with the families of the younger officers who had been educated at the Academy. An anecdote is related of him, that on one occasion, while he was commandant, he was entering the Warren, when the guard turned out, presented arms, and the drummer beat two ruffles; little Brome ran up in great displeasure to the drummer, and upbraiding him for his inefficiency in the art of drumming, snatched the drum away, passed the suspending belt over his own neck, and began to rattle away in a very superior style. Finishing with the two ruffles, he exclaimed—"There, you young dog, that's the way I used to beat the drum when I was a drummer." (The Arsenal was originally a rabbit warren. It was called "the Warren" until June, 1805, when, by order of George III., it was named the Royal Arsenal).

In 1761 an expedition under Admiral Keppel embarked for the reduction of Belleisle. The troops were commanded by Major-General Hodgson, and the artillery (three companies) by Lieut.-Colonel Desaguliers. Our batteries opened on the 2nd May, and on the 13th the outer defences were assaulted and taken, the enemy retiring into the citadel. On the 16th new batteries were completed, and the citadel was instantly played upon by forty mortars, ten howitzers, and forty guns of different calibre, while the field-guns were occasionally employed to fire ricochet to dear the enemy's works. On the night of the 20th one of our shells entered a small place in the citadel, made a great explosion, and drove some of the stones into the town with such force that one man was killed and several wounded. The breach began to appear considerable on the 25th, and by the 7th June was large enough to justify an assault.

This was prevented, however, by the enemy, who surrendered the citadel on that day, the British taking possession on the 8th. The island remained in the possession of the British until the peace of the following year, when it was given up in exchange for Minorca.

Colonel Desaguliers was remarkable for his scientific attainments, particularly in the art of war.

In the autumn of 1773. George III. made a special visit to Woolwich to see the effect of some curious smoke-balls invented by General Desaguliers, the intention of which, as exemplified in a mock engagement, was to cover an assailing body when repulsed from a strong position, and thus prevent the enemy from availing themselves of the consequent confusion.

The tangent scale, originally called the Desaguliers, was the invention of this officer.

On the death of Colonel Mitchelson in 1762, Desaguliers was appointed colonel-commandant of the second battalion, still retaining the appointment of chief firemaster, which he had held since 1748. He died (lieut.-general) at London, on the 1st March, 1780.

A large body of British troops embarked for the continent in August, 1758, to co-operate with the allied Hanoverians and Hessians in expelling the French from Germany. Captain Phillips, six lieutenants, and one hundred and twenty non-commissioned officers and men were the only artillerymen who accompanied this force; but in March following a company and a half was sent over to Germany, and a regular brigade of artillery was established, consisting of three companies under Captains Macbean, Drummond, and Foy—the whole under Captain Phillips.

****

Macbean died at Woolwich, November 11, 1800: Lieut. -General and Col.-Commandant of the Invalid Battalion.

Drummond died at Woolwich, June 27, 1805: Lieut. -General and Commandant of the Field Train Department.

Foy died in Canada, April 27, 1779: Secretary to General Haldimand.

****

With the exception of the battles of Minden and Warbourg, the history of this campaign is nothing more than an uninteresting narrative of field manoeuvres and undecisive battles of rare occurrence, which led to nothing.

At the Battle of Minden (1st August, 1759) the British artillery covered themselves with glory.

About seven o'clock a.m. the French began to fire from a battery which raked our column of artillery on its march. The battery erected under the care of Count de la Lippe de Buckebourg, grandmaster of the artillery, contributed greatly to decide the fortune of the day, he having by that battery totally extinguished the fire of the enemy's batteries on their right, and made at the same time great havoc among the Swiss and *Grenadiers de France*. About nine o'clock the enemy began to give way, a general confusion followed, and about ten the whole of the French Army fled in disorder.

Some of the French regiments retired into the old camp, but the British artillery quickly dislodged them, and they were obliged to retire beyond the hills. In the general order published by Prince Ferdinand the day after the battle, particular thanks are given to Captains Phillips, Drummond, and Foy, and on the following day Captain Macbean received an autograph letter from the prince, of which the following is a copy:—

> Sir—It is from a sense of your merit, and a regard for justice, that I do in this manner declare I have reason to be infinitely satisfied with your behaviour, activity, and zeal, which in so conspicuous a manner you made appear at the battle near

Thornhausen on the 1st August. The talents which you possess in your profession did not a little contribute to render our fare superior to that of the enemy; and it is to you and your brigade that I am indebted for having silenced the fire of a battery of the enemy, which extremely galled the troops, and particularly the British infantry. Accept then, sir, from me, the just tribute of my most perfect acknowledgments, accompanied with my most sincere thanks.

I shall be happy in every opportunity of obliging you, desiring only occasions of proving it, being, with the most distinguished esteem, your devoted and entirely affectionate servant,

Ferdinand,
Duke of Brunswick and
Lunenburg.

To Captain Macbean,
of the Royal British Artillery.

Later in the month His Serene Highness sent orders to Monsieur Hedemann, his treasurer, to pay the following officers of the British artillery the undermentioned gratuities, as a testimony of his great satisfaction of their gallant behaviour in the action of the 1st:—

To Captain William Phillips	1000 crowns
" " Forbes Macbean	500 "
" " Duncan Drummond	500 "
" " Edward Foy	500 "

The casualties in the Royal Artillery at the Battle of Minden were two rank and file killed; Lieutenants Robert Rogers (died New York, Feb. 23, 1773), and Richard Harrington (died Minorca, 1768), one sergeant and nine rank and file wounded; Lieutenant John Carden (resigned, 1772), and two rank and file missing.

Among the lieutenants of artillery at the Battle of Minden was Vaughan Lloyd, an officer who served sixty-one years in the regiment. As major he took part in the defence of Gibraltar (1772, etc.), and as lieut.-colonel served in the West Indies during the revolutionary war. He died on the 18th June, 1817 (aged eighty), having been commandant of Woolwich garrison for twenty

At the Battle of Warbourg (31st July, 1760), Captain Phillips brought up the English artillery at a gallop (at that time an unprecedented occurrence, and considered something wonderful), and seconded the attack in a surprising manner, having by a severe cannonade obliged those of the enemy who were formed upon the other side of the River Dymel to retire with the greatest precipitation. Two more companies joined the allied army in the course of the year, and served at Wilhelmstall, etc.

Peace being concluded in November, 1762, in the following January the artillery marched through Holland to Williamstadt and embarked for England.

During the next twenty years our military operations were principally confined to America, the noble defence of Gibraltar being the only event of any consequence which called for the services of our troops in Europe.

In 1781, however, the enemy attacked us on our own shores, a body of the French having landed in Jersey during the night of the 6th January. They entered the capital by surprise before daybreak, and made the governor, Major Moses Corbet, prisoner in a few minutes. He would at once have surrendered the island, but Major Pierson, the second in command, as well as all the subordinate officers, determined to defend it to the last.

The enemy soon made Captain Charlton, of the Royal Artillery, and some townspeople prisoners; they were tied together with ropes and dragged before M. de Ballecourt, the colonel in command of the French, who, when Captain Charlton complained of his treatment as an officer, at once ordered him to be unbound. The capitulation was drawn up, all the prisoners, however, refusing to sign it. The governor, indeed, gave way after various threats, but the officers in the fortress were resolute in their refusal. A body of the enemy advancing to attack the castle, two shots were fired at them, which killed two men and wounded an officer, and compelled them to retire.

In the meantime, Major Pierson made the necessary arrangements for attacking the enemy in the town. The attacking party was formed into two columns; a howitzer was attached to the first, and a six-pounder to the second, which Lieutenant Crozier, of the Invalid Artillery, requested leave to superintend. This service he performed with great judgment, coolness, and intrepidity; and was ably assisted in it by Sergeant Menzies of the artillery, who greatly distinguished himself in action.

As soon as Captain Lumsdaine (commanding the second column) had a complete view of the enemy's main body, he ordered Lieutenant Crozier to fire the gun at the head of the column. It was loaded with grape, and he pointed it so well, that a complete lane was made through the enemy's ranks. This success was repeated several times, and then the infantry poured in a destructive fire, when the enemy fled in all directions.

Major Pierson was shot through the heart at the victorious moment, and instantly expired. The command was then taken by Captain Lumsdaine, to whom the French general and all his troops surrendered themselves prisoners. (General De Rallecourt received four bullet-wounds, one of them having broken his jaw and deprived him of speech, he died the same evening). He then released the governor and asked him for his orders.

On the 1st of May Major Corbet was tried and deprived of his appointment.

Captain George Charlton and Lieut. William Crozier both served as gunners in the Royal Artillery; the former having received his commission as was customary in his time, (in the early history of the regiment the intelligent privates generally received commissions after serving a few years in the ranks), and the latter being promoted from sergeant-major in 1780. They both died at Jersey; Charlton on the 1st September, 1789, and Crozier on the 31st January, 1788.

The capture of Minorca by the allied French and Spaniards was the last event of importance that occurred in Europe before the peace of 1782 (the defence of Gibraltar excepted). Of the three companies of artillery which formed part of the garrison of Minorca, there remained but 125 men at the time of the surrender of Port Phillip, so reduced were they (in common with the other regiments) by putrid fever, scurvy, and dysentery. Scorning to yield to the enemy before them, they sank and died in the batteries.

Port Phillip was besieged from the 19th August, 1781, till the 4th February, 1782, during which the garrison made frequent sorties. Captain Edward Fage, (died, major-general at Greenwich, September 2, 1809), Lieutenants Frederick Irwin (died at Grenada, 1793) and Edward Woodward (died at Hoxton, April 25 1804), of the Royal Artillery, were wounded during this siege, and Captain Bisby Lambert fell one of the many victims to disease on the 23rd December, 1781.

When the garrison surrendered, Captain Jacob Schalch, (died at Plymouth, December 13, 1788), was the senior officer of the Royal Artillery. Perhaps a more noble or a more tragical scene was never exhibited than that of the march of the garrison of Port Phillip through the Spanish and French Armies.

It consisted of no more than 600 old, decrepit soldiers, 200 seamen, 126 of the Royal Artillery, 20 Corsicans, and 25 Greeks. The two armies, consisting of 14,000 men, were drawn up in two lines, and as the noble little force passed through them, many of the foreign officers and soldiers shed tears at the emaciated appearance of our men, who, when they had passed through, laid down their arms—their commander, the brave old General Murray, declaring "they had surrendered them to God alone."

ROYAL ARTILLERY.

1743.   1760.   1815.

CHAPTER 2

America and the West Indies, 1741-1782

The first service of the Royal Artillery in the New World is at the siege and capture of Carthagena in 1741.

Their conduct here, as on all other occasions, reflected great credit on themselves and the army generally, though they had to deplore the loss of their commanding officer, Colonel Jonas Watson—an officer who had distinguished himself in Flanders and at the defence of Gibraltar (1737).

A company was sent to Newfoundland in 1743, and another formed part of the garrison of Louisbourg from 1745 till the peace of 1748, when it was sent to Nova Scotia. On the breaking out of the war in 1754, the following instructions were issued to the commander-in-chief, General Braddock, preparatory to his embarking for America:—

> You are to take under your command as many as you think necessary of the two companies of artillery that are in Nova Scotia and Newfoundland, as soon as the season will allow, taking care to leave enough to defend the last of these places.

Fifty men under Captain Ord were all that could be conveniently spared from these garrisons; all of whom, with the exception of a small detachment which had been sent against Niagara under General Shirley, were cut to pieces at the battle near Fort du Quesne, on the 9th July, 1755. Captain Ord survived to return with the remnant of his detachment (the first of the corps that served in America), and in after years he was appointed colonel-commandant of the first battalion of the regiment sent to that continent. (The fourth battalion, established in 1791. Colonel Ord died at bath, April18, 1777). Two companies under Colonel George Williamson embarked in. February, 1757, for service in the western hemisphere, and they were engaged at the siege and capture of Louisbourg in 1758.

Reinforced by detachments from England, they formed part of the army under General Wolfe, which was assembled in the roadstead of Louisbourg in June, 1759. They rendered great service at the Isle of Orleans, but at the great battle on the plains of Abraham (13th September) there were but fifty artillerymen and one gun (commanded by Capt.-Lieut. Yorke; died at Lisbon, July, 1767), the remainder being encamped on the Point of Levi in readiness to bombard Quebec across the river. This gun played with great success on the enemy's columns, and obliged the French general more than once to make alterations in the disposition of his forces. When the garrison of Quebec surrendered on the 18th, the detachment of the Royal Artillery, with their gun and three companies of grenadiers, under Lieut.-Colonel Murray, marched into and took possession of the upper town, hoisting British colours on the most conspicuous part of the fortification.

Eleanor Job, the wife of a gunner of the Royal Artillery, accompanied her husband through this campaign, and was attached to the army as principal nurse in what was called "the flying hospital."

Her intrepidity and humanity were equally proverbial with the army, for she was often known to rush forward at the cannon's mouth on the field of battle to assist in the dressing of the wounded soldiers, by whom she was held in such regard that she was familiarly known among them by the name of "Good Mother Job."

At the battle on the plains of Abraham she was particularly conspicuous in her heroic exertions to save the wounded. When General Wolfe was killed, she was the person selected to prepare his remains for embalmment.

Her husband having been killed in battle, she returned to her native country, without any adequate provision for her support, and for fifty years she lived as a pauper in the parish of St. Giles's, where she died on the 17th September, 1828, at the advanced age of one hundred and five years.

Previous to the capture of Quebec, a force under General Amherst, including 111 of the Royal Artillery under Major Ord, was sent against Ticonderago and Crown Point. The services rendered by Major Ord in the construction of a rail to carry the heavy ordnance for this expedition are worthy of mention.

A company under Major S. Cleaveland served at Guadaloupe during the struggle for that island in 1759, and with the 63rd regiment garrisoned the citadel of Basseterre after its capture. The French, who were not expelled from the island, kept them in constant expectation of an attack by approaching the citadel in considerable bodies, and sometimes even firing into it.

In order to repel these attacks, Lieut.-Colonel Desbrisay, the governor, ordered the guns to be fired whenever the enemy appeared in force; and to be the more ready for this service, he caused two barrels of gunpowder to be put into the stone sentry-box in the angle of a bastion, to be near at hand when there was occasion to fire the cannon. These barrels, unluckily, had not been properly covered over; and the enemy appearing in a large body, the governor ordered some guns to be fired at them, when a few sparks from, the wadding of one of the guns were observed to blow towards the sentry-box where the powder was lodged.

Colonel Desbrisay being informed of this, sent two bombardiers to cover up the barrels with sheepskins; but unfortunately, another gun was fired before the bombardiers could execute the service they were sent on, and a spark set fire to the gunpowder, causing a dreadful explosion. The governor and the two bombardiers were blown to atoms; two officers, some artillerymen, and several men of the 63rd regiment were killed, and many officers and privates wounded. The enemy, on perceiving this disaster, which they thought was greater than it really was, came down in large bodies, with a design to attack the fort; but receiving a severe fire both from the cannon, and musketry, they were soon convinced of their mistake, and having sustained considerable loss were obliged to retire.

At the capture of Arnonville the British artillery (four 6-pounders and two howitzers) kept up a constant and well-directed fire on the top of the enemy's entrenchments.

The whole island surrendered on the 2nd May.

The success which had attended all our military operations in North America in 1759 induced our commanders steadily to follow up the advantages they had gained, and indeed, if possible, to deprive the French of all their possessions in that part of the world.

For this purpose, in 1760, three expeditions were planned, all of which were to have distinct views in the first part of their operations, but ultimately to form a junction for laying siege to Montreal, by the fall of which an end would be put to the French dominion in America. Detachments of the Royal Artillery accompanied the forces under General Murray and Colonel Haviland, but the main body, under Colonel Williamson, was attached to the army of the commander-in-chief, General Amherst, Oswego being the appointed rendezvous.

On the 10th August all the regulars embarked and proceeded towards the River St, Lawrence. Bad weather obliged General Amherst to put into a small creek at night, and in so doing an artillery boat was lost on the bar at the entrance of it. The weather becoming more moderate, he proceeded, at noon on the 11th, for the River de la Mothe, and on the 12th the army landed.

On the 16th, the advanced guard of the army arrived at Point de Baril, from whence one of the enemy's brigs appeared in sight. The general resolved to attack her with the row-galleys; and Colonel Williamson, of the Royal Artillery, requested leave to lead the attack, to which the general assented. The night being very dark this attack was postponed till the 17th, when the army moved on and soon came up to the enemy's vessel, which was endeavouring to escape up the river. Colonel Williamson, with the five galleys, immediately made towards her. She cannonaded them with great briskness as they advanced. When the galleys got to the proper distance for engaging, the wind died away; this was of great advantage to them, as they were thereby enabled to direct their fire with greater exactness.

Colonel Williamson was rowed in a small boat to the different galleys, and directed the attack. After an action of two hours and a quarter, the vessel struck, and was immediately taken possession of by a party of 300 men. She was called the *Ottawa*; mounted one 18-pounder, seven 12-pounders, and two 8-pounders; and had on board 100 men, commanded by M. la Broquerie. The galleys fired 118 rounds; the brig fired 72. The British had a sergeant of the Royal Artillery killed and a private wounded; the enemy had 3 killed and 12 wounded.

The general was so pleased with the conduct of Colonel Williamson and the Royal Artillery on this occasion that he named the prize the *Williamson*. The army advanced, and on the 19th laid siege to Fort Levis, (situated on Isle Royale), which surrendered on the 25th.

On the 6th September the army reached Montreal, and in the course of the day got up two 12-pounders, five 6-pounders, and five 3-pounders (field-guns). The services of these guns were not required, however, for General Amherst, being joined by General Murray and Colonel Haviland, had a force of about 10,000 men under his command, with which he completely invested the town; and upon sending in his demands, they were complied with by the Marquis de Vandre, the French commandant. Thus, on the 8th September, 1760, not only Montreal, but the whole province of Canada passed into the hands of the British.

The active service of Colonel George Williamson was now ended. On the formation of the third battalion in 1759, he was appointed colonel-commandant; in 1762 he was promoted to major-general, and in 1772 to lieutenant-general. He died at Woolwich, on the 11th November, 1781, aged seventy-seven years.

There were now ten companies of the Royal Artillery in America, including one at Newfoundland. Two of these, under Lieut.-Col. Ord, were with General Monckton at the taking of Martinique (7th February, 1762).

They landed at Cas de Navires, besieged and took Port Royal, and finally obtained possession of the whole island. This was followed by the surrender of St. Vincent, Grenada, and St. Lucia, and the English were masters of the Carribbees. A detachment under Captain Ferguson (died in Nova Scotia, January 13, 1766), was attached to the force which recaptured Newfoundland from the French, in September, 1762, they having surprised the garrison of St. John's and obliged it to capitulate in the preceding June.

The great event of 1762 was the siege and capture of Havannah, in which 377 of the Royal Artillery, under Lieut.-Col. Alexander Leith, played a most conspicuous part. (270 from England—Colonel Leith. 107 from North America—Colonel Cleaveland). After contending with the utmost difficulties in the erection of batteries and bringing up of guns (owing to the rocky nature of the ground), the artillery opened fire on the Moro—the principal fort—on the 1st July. After a severe bombardment of thirty days—during the latter part of which time the artillery, having lost so many men by wounds and sickness, were assisted in the batteries by 500 seamen from the fleet—a mine was sprung, and a narrow breach having been effected, the British troops fought their way through it into the fort, and kept possession of it.

The attack was now on Fort La Punta and the city itself. It was not until the 11th August, however, that the guns of the Moro could be turned against their old masters; but when the fire opened the effect was instantaneous. Within six hours the whole of the Havannah. including all the vessels in the harbour and the country for 180 miles to the westward, were in the possession of the British. The commanding officer of the artillery, Lieut.-Col. Leith, fell while directing the bombardment.

The command of the corps then devolved on Lieut.-Col. Samuel Cleaveland. Captain Samuel Strackey and Lieutenant Bossom were also killed, and Captain Goreham and Lieutenant Benjamin died of wounds. Major Ferron was one of the many victims to the disease which prevailed among the troops during this remarkable siege.

On the 3rd November a general peace was signed between England, France, and Spain; by the terms of which (of the conquests made in the West) we retained Canada, Nova Scotia, and Newfoundland, Tobago, Dominica, St.Vincent, and Grenada; restoring Martinique, St. Lucia, and two other islands to the French, and exchanging Havannah for Florida with the Spaniards.

On the night between the 18th and 19th April, 1775, the first shots were fired by the American colonists in defence of their liberties. The fire being returned by the English soldiers, a sharp engagement ensued, and the great event of the eighteenth century—the American Revolutionary War—had commenced. This affair took place at Lexington, a village of Massachusetts, eleven miles from Boston, and warlike preparations were immediately commenced at the last-named town.

A battery was thrown up on Cope's Hill (an eminence commanding the river and the peninsula of Charlestown), for the security of such of the king's ships as might be required in the river. Lieut.-Col. James, of the Royal Artillery, superintended this work; when finished it was mounted with six 24-pounders from the line-of-battle ships, and called "the Admiral's Battery."

From the day on which the skirmish at Lexington happened all intercourse between the country and the garrison of Boston was cut off, and the town was completely blocked up on the land side.

On the 27th May an affair took place between H.M.'s schooner *Diana* and the Americans; during which the vessel was becalmed, and the enemy brought 2,000 men, with field-pieces, against her. General Gage sent two of our guns to the island facing the enemy, but it was impossible to give the schooner any effectual aid; and the following morning she was abandoned by her crew, who were taken on board the *Britannia* armed sloop, which had been sent to their assistance.

After this disagreeable affair, the great utility of the battery erected by the admiral on Cope's Hill was discovered. The Royal Artillery were ordered to take possession of it, and to arm it with some of their own guns—those belonging to the men-of-war having been returned on board; and as this defence was now considered of some importance, it lost its former name, and obtained that of "Cope's Hill Battery."

At daybreak on the 17th June, the garrison of Boston was alarmed by a heavy cannonade from H.M.'s ship *Lively*, which proceeded from the enemy having taken possession of Bunker's Hill—a height on the peninsula of Charlestown, and which during the preceding night they had fortified with the greatest diligence. They were discovered in the morning erecting a battery to play on the shipping and town of Boston, when General Gage immediately resolved to attack, and, if possible, dislodge them.

At nine in the morning, the *Glasgow* frigate, and a battery of six pieces of heavy ordnance and some howitzers from Cope's Hill opened on the rebels. Shortly afterwards about five regiments of infantry, and Buchanan's and Farrington's companies of the Royal Artillery with field-pieces, were hastily embarked, and landed about noon on Charlestown Point, without opposition, under the protection of the ships of war, and some flat-bottomed lighters with a 12-pounder in each end, served by the Royal Artillery under Colonel James. The latter were engaged during the day in firing across Charlestown Neck, with a view not only to prevent the enemy from marching fresh forces over the isthmus during the action, but also to annoy those who were routed, or to prevent their escape.

The rebels on the heights were in great force and strongly posted. Their centre and left flank were covered, by a breastwork, part of which was cannon-proof; these works reached from the left of their redoubt to the Medford River. About half-past three o'clock the attack was begun by a brisk cannonade from the British artillery, the first and second lines of infantry advancing slowly, and frequently halting to give time for the artillery to fire with, more effect. The infantry now rushed on to assault the breastwork; but the rebels did not return a shot until the assailants were very near, when they poured in a heavy and incessant fire upon them. For some time, they withstood this, but their loss of officers and men becoming very great, the troops recoiled and fell into disorder.

Captain S.O. Huddlestone (died at Woolwich—major-general, February 13, 1814, aged 77), Captain John Lemoine (died at Woolwich—colonel, December 23, 1801), Lieutenant A. Shuttleworth, (invalided as major, 1795, died at Hutherage Hall, near Sheffield, July 9, 1833), Mr. Unance (a volunteer with the artillery), eleven sergeants and eight men of the Royal Artillery were struck down by this murderous fire, though they all escaped death. The enemy being greatly advantaged by the buildings in Charlestown, from whence he directed a severe fire on the British troops, the battery at Cope's Hill received orders to throw carcasses into the town.

These orders were instantly obeyed and had the intended effect. The place was presently in flames; the steeple of the church, being composed of wood, fell full of armed people, and all in a blaze; soon after the rebels were forced to abandon the town.

At this instant the troops renewed the attack, and notwithstanding the various impediments thrown in their way, soon drove the rebels from all their works, and forced them to abandon the peninsula, leaving five guns behind them.

In the autumn of 1775 the Americans, under Arnold and Montgomery, invaded Canada, and having succeeded in capturing Montreal and some of the out-stations without any effusion of blood, they proceeded, in November, to besiege Quebec. General Carleton, afterwards Lord Dorchester, having with him troops escaped from Montreal, took every measure in his power to make as vigorous a defence as possible. A small detachment only of the Royal Artillery being in Quebec, the sailors of His Majesty's ships were landed to work in the batteries. Thus, a formidable regiment of artillery was hastily formed, which performed wonders during the siege.

The Americans appeared before Quebec on the 5th December, and in a few days opened two batteries—one of five mortars, and the other of six guns. These were speedily silenced by our artillerymen and sailors; when Montgomery, the American commander, being very weak in artillery, made preparations for an assault. After making two or three attempts to surprise the garrison, on the 31st December he assaulted it in full force.

Having cut down some palisades which obstructed their way, the Americans pushed on to the next barrier; where as soon as they made their appearance, several guns loaded with grape were discharged with such good aim that Montgomery, his *aide-de-camp*, and many of his men were killed. The American troops, seeing the fate of their commander, turned and fled back up the cliffs. Arnold at the same time was pushing his way through the suburbs of the lower town, having with, him both riflemen and artillery. They assaulted a small but well-defended battery, which they carried, with considerable loss, after about an hour's resistance.

Arnold was severely wounded, and obliged to be carried from the field; and as his successor was about to attack a second battery, he found himself attacked in the rear, and was obliged to surrender, with the loss of 400 men; 100 of whom were killed, and the remainder taken prisoners. Their five mortars and one of their guns were captured and brought into the town. The only loss sustained by the British during the assault consisted of one officer, Lieut. Matthew Anderson, of the navy (who was serving as a captain of artillery), and four men killed, and seven wounded.

Sergeant Anthony Haigh, of the Royal Artillery, whose gallant conduct during the siege was specially mentioned in general orders by General Carleton, was among the wounded. He soon recovered, however, and continued to serve in Canada till 1787, holding many important situations. In April, 1783, he was sent by Colonel Macbean to act as second in command at fort St. John's, taking with him a letter of recommendation to the commandant of the fort, stating that he would be found very useful and deserving of his commander's confidence, and also recommending that he should be furnished with comfortable quarters. He was promoted to sergeant-major of the newly-raised companies of Military Artificers, in 1788, and was stationed at Guernsey, where he exhibited his qualities as a drill-master in the training of the Royal Guernsey Cavalry. In 1806 he received a commission as sub-lieutenant, and died at St. Heliers, Jersey, January 9th, 1836, aged eighty-eight.

The plan of operations in America for the year 1776 was upon a very extensive scale.

The Grand Army in America was under the command of General Howe, and was to act against New York and the middle provinces. The artillery of the Grand Army consisted of six companies under Captains Farrington, Martin, Innes, Buchanan (Sir F. J., invalided July 1779, died at Bath, February 16,1787), and Davies (died at Blackheath, March 16, 1812, colonel-commandant of the 2nd battalion), commanded by Brigadier-General Cleaveland.

A small force, including two companies of artillery, left Ireland in January to serve in the southern provinces under Major-Generals Clinton and Cornwallis.

Another large army, under Major-General Burgoyne, left England in April for Canada with the intention of driving the Americans from that colony, and invading the rebel provinces from the northward. Six companies of the Royal Artillery, under Majors David Hay and Griffith Williams, Captains John Carter, Ellis Walker, Thomas Jones, and William Borthwick, the whole commanded by Major-General Phillips, formed part of this army.

There was a great deal of manoeuvring, but not much severe fighting, in 1776. Charlestown was attacked by Sir Peter Parker and General Clinton in June; and in September, Howe compelled Washington to evacuate New York, and followed him up as far as the Delaware, which was crossed by the Americans in the middle of December. The attack on Charlestown was directed by Colonel James, R.A., who threw some shells at the fort from the *Thunder* bomb. Perceiving that she was placed at too great a distance to be of any service. Colonel James endeavoured to remedy the defect by ordering an additional quantity of powder to each mortar. By this means a few shells reached the fort; but the recoil of the mortars was so much increased that their beds broke down and the vessel became useless for the rest of the day.

This was the last occasion on which Colonel Thomas James commanded the Royal Artillery against an enemy. Having been actively engaged at Gibraltar, on the Continent, in America, and elsewhere for upwards of forty years, he was appointed, on the death of General Belford colonel-commandant of the 1st battalion. He entered the regiment as a private in August, 1737, and died, holding the rank of a field-officer, at Blackheath, on the 6th March, 1782.

The attack was a failure, and the troops joined the mail body under Howe at Sandy Hook. Lieut. William S. Lovel and a sergeant of the Royal Artillery were killed in the engagement at Long Island on the 27th August. (Lieutenant Lovel enlisted in the R.A. in October, 1755, received his commission but a few months before his death). The entire casualties in the regiment during the campaign of 1776, were only one officer, two sergeants, five rank and file killed, one sergeant and seven rank and file wounded. Of these, one sergeant and three privates were drowned in the East River by the oversetting of a boat on the October; the others received their wounds at Long Island Brunk's River, and Fort Washington.

Seldom has Montreal witnessed a scene of higher excitement or more warlike bustle than was presented to the eyes of its inhabitants on the morning of the 8th of June, 1777.

It was on this day that General Burgoyne, having drawn together the whole of his army, was about to open a campaign from which the most brilliant results were expected; but from which, unfortunately, the most disastrous consequences ensued. Major-General Phillips, with his own battery, and those of Lieutenant-Colonel Hay (retired October 12, 1781), Majors Williams and Carter (died in America, March 17, 1779), Captains Jones and Walker, was sent with the commissariat and hospital stores by water to a point near the southern extremity of Lake Champlain, the infantry having marched from Montreal to the same point; Captain Borthwick's company remained in garrison at Quebec. (Borthwick, as major-general, succeeded General Macbean as colonel-commandant of the Invalid Battalion. He died at Greenwich, June 27, 1808).

It was on a beautiful morning, the last in the month of June, that the army began its march. Without recounting the whole of the campaign, suffice it to say the Americans retired before this force until they crossed the Hudson, when, being reinforced, they formed an entrenched camp near Saratoga.

The Hudson was crossed by Burgoyne's army on the 13th and 14th September, and on the 19th, he was attacked by the Americans at Stillwater. A short but severe battle took place, and the British, remaining on the field, claimed the victory; but it was a victory severely won, and far from decisive. It was through the fire of the artillery, however, that the Americans were compelled to retire; for after the first round of grape from the British batteries, they turned about and fled towards their entrenchments. At the Battle of Saratoga (7th October) the British artillery covered themselves with glory.

General Phillips, upon first hearing the firing, moved with Major Williams's battery towards the scene of action. By dint of extraordinary perseverance, he succeeded in making his way through a wood, and came up with the enemy just as the 20th regiment had begun to give way, Phillips seeing this, made haste to remedy the evil. He dashed forward, bringing with him only a few followers, rallied the broken regiment, and led it back in the most magnificent style to the charge; then hurrying away to the right, he brought up his guns to the edge of the wood, from which they opened a tremendous fire of grape and canister upon the enemy's flank.

The guns which rendered this service, however, were left in the field, the horses not only being destroyed, but most of the brave gunners, who had, as usual, under the conduct of Major Williams, displayed the utmost skill and ability in their profession, together with the most undaunted resolution, being all either killed or dangerously wounded, and Major Williams taken prisoner. (Died at Woolwich, March 18, 1790, aged sixty-eight).

Captain Blomefield, R.A., who served as *aide-de-camp* to General Phillips, received a severe wound in the face from a musket-ball.

The other batteries behaved with equal gallantry; the brave Captain Jones, who was unfortunately killed while defending his guns from the assaults of the enemy, was, with his brigade, particularly distinguished.

The artillery of Frazer's division was commanded by Captain Ellis Walker, whose conduct throughout this action is borne testimony to by his commanding officer in the following despatch:—

> In consequence of the death of Brigadier-General Frazer, the command of the advanced corps of General Burgoyne's army devolved on me; and it is with pleasure I acknowledge the defence of my post in that action was principally owing to the conduct of Captain Ellis Walker and his brigade of Royal Artillery, and their services on that evening deserve every encomium that I can bestow.
>
> Earl of Balcarres, Colonel.

★★★★★★★★★★

On the death of Major-General Benjamin Stehelin, Lieut.-Governor of Gentlemen Cadets, Walker became colonel-commandant of the 3rd battalion. He died a general, at Chelsea, on the 14th March, 1820, aged eighty.

★★★★★★★★★★

Though this action terminated in favour of the British, the Americans quitted the field in a most orderly manner, and gave Burgoyne no further hopes of proceeding. Lieutenant Howarth, R.A., was wounded and taken prisoner; and among the men Corporal David Mannings, Bombardier James Dempster, Mattrosses George Fairgreve, David Price, John Powell, and Drummer Francis Harris, were killed; Corporal John Grant, Bombardiers George Yeats and William Whiloe, Mattrosses John Goldie and William Matthews received wounds, from the effects of which they afterwards died; Gunner John Bell lost the use of his left arm through a bullet lodging in his shoulder, and Mattross Edward Froude was shot through the right hand.

Lieutenant Molesworth Clieland was killed during the attack on Skeenborough on the 6th July. This was one of the places the Americans evacuated (after a slight defence) during the advance of Burgoyne's army.

Burgoyne now made preparations for a retreat, but in a few days, he found himself completely surrounded by the Americans, and on the 15th October surrendered himself and the whole of his army as prisoners of war,

Washington having established his winter quarters in the Jerseys, whither he had been followed by a brigade of the British under Earl Cornwallis, frequent skirmishes took place between the outposts and foraging parties; and on one occasion, at Amboy, a gun was brought into play by the British, and its commander, Lieutenant F. Desaguliers, was killed.

In July General Howe left New York with an army, including Brigadier-General Cleaveland and six companies of the Royal Artillery, under Captains Farrington, Traille, Williamson, Standish, Rochfort, and Stewart, and after sailing about the coast for nearly two months, landed on the northern shore of the Elk River, and proceeded towards Philadelphia. (John Stewart was appointed colonel-commandant of the 7th battalion on its formation in 1803. Died at Southampton, January 12, 1807).

On the 11th September General Howe came up with the main body of Washington's army at Brandywine, and after a short battle the Americans fled in confusion, having lost 1,300 men—300 killed, 600 wounded, and 400 prisoners. The Royal Artillery had five men killed in this action Lieutenant Alexander Shand (colonel, 1800, died at Aberdeen, April 7, 1803), two sergeants, and nine rank and file wounded. On the 27th September the British entered Philadelphia, but left the main body of the army at Germantown, ten miles distant. General Howe immediately gave orders for the erection of three batteries to act against any of the enemy's shipping that might approach the town.

These batteries were not finished when two frigates and a number of small armed vessels came up and attacked them. The largest frigate, named the *Delaware*, anchored within five hundred yards of the battery, the other vessels taking their respective stations as they could bring their guns to bear.

About ten in the morning, they began a heavy cannonade upon the town as well as the battery, but the tide ebbing, the *Delaware* grounded; upon which four guns, which had been brought to bear upon her, did such execution that in a short time she struck her colours, and was boarded and taken by the marines.

Cleaveland, who attended the batteries in person, seeing the effect of these guns upon the *Delaware*, turned the direction of his fire to the smaller vessels, and forced all of them, except a schooner that was disabled and driven, on shore, to return to their former stations under the protection of the fort.

Lieutenant George Wilson, who commanded one of the guns engaged with the frigate, having left his post for the purpose of communicating with General Cleaveland, was tried for cowardice. He was honourably acquitted, however, but received a reprimand for leaving the gun.

On the 4th October Washington attacked Germantown, but after a sharp engagement was compelled to fall back on his camp at Shippach, a distance of twenty miles.

Lieutenant James Frost (died at Woolwich, April 27, 1783), and fourteen men of the Royal Artillery were wounded on this occasion. On the 21st October a detachment of 12,000 Hessians, under Count Donop, attacked the American fort at Red Bank, and were repulsed with great loss. The only British officer present on this occasion was Captain Francis Downman, R.A. This distinguished officer served on the coast of France in 1758, at St. Malo, Cherbourg, etc., and commanded the only two guns that were on shore at Fort Cas. He served in the West Indies from 1758 to 1763, at the captures of Martinique, Guadaloupe, and St. Domingo; and after the capture of Pensacola in 1764 (at which he was present) he remained there three years. After distinguishing himself on various occasions during the American devolution, he served again in the West Indies in 1778, at St. Lucia and Grenada. He died at West Maling, Kent, on the 16th August, 1825.

Colonel Ord having died in the early part of 1777, the command of the 4th battalion devolved on Colonel James Pattison, who immediately went to America and assumed that active command which his predecessor had (through illness) been incapable of retaining. Brigadier-General Cleaveland, who had directed the operations of the artillery in the absence of Colonel Ord, now returned to England. This officer, who had served in all the active operations in the West since 1762, was appointed colonel-commandant of the 3rd battalion in 1781, and died at Lymington on the 28th August, 1794.

Colonel Pattison, with his staff-officers S. P. Adye (died at Jersey, March 24, 1794), and Edward Williams (died in London, January 16, 1798), joined the army at Philadelphia on the 26th November.

Howe's army now settled down at Philadelphia, and, excepting the affair at White Marsh on the 5th December, remained peacefully in their quarters during the whole of the winter. There were now eight companies of the Royal Artillery with this army. Two of these were quartered in the public schoolhouse, another in an adjacent building, and the remaining five with the headquarters of the regiment in the State House.

It was in the State House that the Declaration of Independence was adopted by the American Congress, on the 4th July, 1776, and was publicly proclaimed from the steps the same day.

A portion of the step upon which Washington stood on this occasion is still preserved as a relic by the Americans.

From the commencement of this rebellion the American cause had received the sympathy of France. Jealous of British power, and hating the British nation, she had watched the progress of events with, evident satisfaction. Burgoyne's defeat, establishing as it did the supremacy of the rebel arms, was the signal for war on the part of the French, and on the 6th February, 1778, a treaty of alliance between France and America was signed at Paris. Vast fleets were immediately fitted out—one of them, under D'Estaing, proceeding at once to the assistance of the Americans.

In May, 1778, Sir W. Howe left the army, and General Clinton succeeded to the command.

As the French fleet was daily expected, it was thought advisable to withdraw the army from Philadelphia to New York, and accordingly on the 18th June the former city was evacuated. Washington lost no time in following up the British, and on the 28th a portion of his army came up with them at Freehold, in New Jersey; here, however, having been driven back by the infantry, and sustained a severe cannonading from four batteries (under Captains Williamson, Standish, Scott, and Shand), they made a halt, and suffered the British to proceed to New York without further molestation. Lieut. T. L. Vaughan, R.A., was killed in this action. The alliance of the French and Americans having rendered Halifax of more importance, Captain Farrington's company was sent to that station; three non-commissioned officers and twenty-five men under Lieut. Gillespie being the only artillerymen in that garrison since 1775. (Lieut. Robert Gillespie died at Weatherstone, in Essex, November 19, 1790).

Captain (afterwards General) Sir Anthony Farrington, was the son of Lieut.-Colonel Charles Farrington, who entered the Royal Artillery as a private in April, 1733, and died at Woolwich as second commandant of the Invalid Battalion on the 23rd February, 1782. He was born February 6th, 1741, and having passed through the Royal Military Academy, he received his commission on the 29th October, 1755. He served in America from 1764 to 1768, and again from 1773 to 1783, and was engaged in most of the actions with the colonists from Bunker's Hill to the capture of Philadelphia. He commanded the

Royal Artillery at Plymouth in 1788-9, at Gibraltar 1790-1, at Woolwich 1794-7 (during which time he was sorely tried by the breaking out of a mutiny in the garrison), and in Holland in 1799.

He was a D.C.L. of Oxford, and in consideration of his long and valued services he was created a baronet on the 3rd October, 1818. He served faithfully in three reigns, for the long period of sixty-eight years, being at the time of his death the oldest officer in the British service, retaining the use of his faculties and performing the functions of his office to the last. He died at Blackheath on the 3rd November, 1823. His second son, Henry Maturin, a lieut.-colonel in the Royal Artillery, succeeded to the baronetcy on the death of his nephew, the second baronet; he died at Heavitree, October 4th, 1834.

When the French fleet arrived off New York they captured a number of trading vessels and other small craft, and among them the tender of the *Carcass* bomb, with a detachment of the Royal Artillery on board. When the commander (Lieut. Garstin, R.A.) observed that the tender was drifting, he at once put off in a boat to report the circumstance to the admiral. By so doing he escaped the fate of his detachment, but lost all his effects.

In July, 1778, the Americans laid siege to Newport, Rhode Island, which was garrisoned by 5,000 British, including a company of artillery under Lieut.-Colonel John Innes. (Died at Woolwich, May 30, 1788. His son, who served as lieutenant in the Royal Artillery during this campaign, resigned in 1785). During this siege, which lasted a month, the Royal Artillery gained great honour by their distinguished bravery, especially on the 30th August, when the Americans, having raised the siege, were attacked by the garrison, and compelled to quit the island. The casualties in the Royal Artillery were about thirty-three killed and wounded, including Lieut. William Pemble, who had his left arm shattered, and was obliged to suffer amputation.

This officer was promoted into the line.

Early in September Major-General Grey, with a body of troops, sailed for Bedford, a noted port for privateers, and arriving thereon the 5th, destroyed the place, and re-embarked by noon on the 6th. The fort, mounting eleven guns, was blown up by Captain Scott, (died in Newfoundland, September 24, 1779), commanding officer of the Royal Artillery, and thus the only defence the Americans had on the Accushnet River was destroyed.

In November a body of troops under Colonel Campbell, with a detachment of artillery under Lieut. Ralph Wilson (invalided May 21,

1790, died at Greenwich, February 19,1805), escorted by some ships of war, sailed from New York against Savannah in Georgia. This expedition was a complete success. Savannah was attacked, carried, and the whole province speedily reduced.

Lieut.-Colonel Alexander Innes, an officer who greatly distinguished himself during those operations, and was appointed governor of Savannah when it was captured (and afterwards sent home with the despatches—on delivering the despatches, he was presented to the king, who graciously received him, and presented him with 500*l.* to buy a sword), began his career in the army as a private in the Royal Artillery. He received a commission as lieutenant-fireworker in 1759, and five years afterwards was promoted into a line regiment.

The troops composing Burgoyne's army were not sent to England according to the terms of the convention, but were kept confined and treated in a shameful manner by the Americans. They were marched into Virginia in the autumn of 1778, escorted by a guard of Continental troops. Crossing the Hudson River at Fishkiln, a bombardier and twelve men of the Royal Artillery, with many others of the army, contrived to make their escape, and at the peril of their lives reached New York in safety. They were in a dreadful ragged state, having received no clothing for two years.

Some of the officers were exchanged for those of the American Army who had fallen into our hands; by this means Major-General Phillips, Captain Blomefield, Lieuts. Richard Dysart, John H. York, and George Reid, of the Royal Artillery, were restored to their corps.

****

Lieut. Dysart was sent to Canada in 1781; being promoted, he was again sent to New York, and commanded the detachment on board the *Vesuvius* bomb. He was invalided home in 1793, and died February 5, 1797.

Lieut. Reid Retired in September, 1787.

****

Promotion being very slow in the Royal Artillery, it had been customary for officers who had distinguished themselves to solicit and obtain promotion into the line. Many promising young officers were thus lost to the regiment, no fewer than fourteen having availed themselves of the privilege since the commencement of the American war.

****

Among these were Lieut. Alex. Macbean, son of Colonel Macbean, R.A., Lieut. Burrard, afterwards Sir Harry Burrard, and Lieut. P. Harman Black. This last-named officer served as a volunteer (private) in

1777; he received his commission the following year, and was shortly afterwards promoted into the Irish volunteers; in December, 1779, he was restored to his rank in the Royal Artillery, and died in America in 1782.

★★★★★★★★★★

Accordingly, in January, 1779, an order was issued prohibiting any officers from being promoted out of the corps.

The campaign of 1779 opened in Georgia, where the artillery was commanded by Captain Fairlamb (died at Charlton, October 24, 1800): two most successful actions were fought in March, the Americans being compelled to retire, and the British enabled to advance into South Carolina. Sir Henry Clinton sent out various expeditions to destroy the stores and magazines the Americans had amassed in Virginia, and these having swept the whole of the lower Chesapeake with the besom of destruction, a formidable expedition was prepared under Clinton himself, the headquarters and some companies of the Royal Artillery being included.

The object of this expedition was to reduce the works the Americans had erected at Stoney Point and Verplanks, on the River Hudson. The transports, with the troops on board, sailed up the river on the 30th May, and on the following morning Major-General Vaughan landed, with a considerable body of troops and Captain Rochfort's company of Royal Artillery, eight miles below Verplanks; while General Clinton, with four regiments and Captain Traille's company of artillery, proceeded within three miles of Stoney Point.

These troops Clinton placed under the command of Major-General Pattison, R.A., and ordered them to disembark and act in conjunction with the troops already landed—himself commanding the whole, and directing the attack. The enemy abandoned his works on the heights of Stoney Point directly our troops landed, and after a bombardment of two days Fort La Fayette, the principal work on Verplanks, capitulated—the garrison surrendering themselves prisoners of war. Leaving garrisons in these newly-captured works, Clinton returned to New York.

Captain Traille commanded the artillery at Stoney Point, and Lieutenant Douglas at Verplanks. On the night of the 15th July the Americans succeeded in surprising the garrison at Stoney Point, and after a short struggle became masters of the place, the British being compelled to surrender themselves prisoners of war.

Captain Traille, R.A., had that morning left Stoney Point on account of his health, and the command of the Royal Artillery fell upon Captain Tiffin (invalided in 1782; died at Reading, August 30, 1794), who, with Lieutenant Horndon (who resigned in November, 1800), and his men, was captured by the Americans, Lieutenant John Roberts ran to the shore, and plunging into the river, swam to the *Vulture* sloop-of-war (distant about a mile), and thus escaped the fate of his companions, (he died in Barbadoes, November 6, 1793).

The Americans at once commenced firing across the river, as Clinton had done, into Fort La Fayette; while another force invested it on the land side. Lieutenant-Colonel Webster, the commandant, directed Lieutenant Douglas to keep his men at their post, but not to return the enemy's fire. By this conduct the Americans were induced to believe the garrison was destitute of guns, and therefore put their own into a galley to be transported up the river. No sooner had the Americans shipped their guns than Lieutenant Douglas opened upon the galley an 18-pounder—the only piece of heavy ordnance in the fort; and his shot was so well aimed, and raked the galley with such effect, that to prevent her sinking the crew ran her ashore, and there set her on fire. In the meantime, Clinton despatched a relieving force, and the Americans no sooner saw the transports than they retreated. Lieutenant Robert Douglas received the special thanks of Sir Henry Clinton for his meritorious conduct on this occasion.

★★★★★★★★★★

> Lieutenant Douglas was appointed commandant of the corps of artillery drivers on their establishment in 1795, and retained the appointment until the breaking up of the corps in 1817. He died at Woolwich, April 4, 1827, aged seventy-three.

★★★★★★★★★★

The concluding event of the year was the glorious defence of Savannah—the British, under General Prevost, withstanding a siege and repulsing an assault made by the combined armies of France and America, with a loss of only fifty-five men; the allies, in the meantime, having had nine hundred killed and wounded.

Major-General Pattison was now commandant of New York, in which situation he rendered himself extremely popular, bestowing his attention equally on the troops, the loyal citizens and prisoners of war, meting out justice to all; he also interested himself in all charitable institutions, schools, etc., and founded a temporary asylum for the orphans of soldiers killed during the war.

On Tuesday, the 18th January, 1780, being His Majesty's birthday, the usual salutes were fired from all the batteries in and about New York, and from all the ships in the harbour; and in the evening a splendid ball was given by the general, field and staff-officers of the army, which was opened by General Pattison and Madame de Reidesel.

Early this year Sir H. Clinton sailed with a powerful army for the siege of Charlestown. The weather at sea proved very tempestuous, and the ships were driven about for some weeks. Many of the transports were lost, some of them were taken by the enemy, and one vessel, the *Russia Merchant*, having on board the heavy ordnance and Captain Collins's detachment of Royal Artillery, foundered at sea. The crew and artillerymen, however, were saved by the *Lady Dunmore* privateer, and carried into Bermuda.

They afterwards joined the army before Charlestown. Clinton landed his troops on St. John's Island, about thirty miles from Charlestown, on the 11th February, but it was not till the 1st April that he broke ground before the city. It was well defended, and an open communication kept by the American field troops; but our batteries opened on the 10th, and they were so well managed by our artillery under Captain Traille that they soon acquired a superiority over those of the enemy; and the works were pushed forward with great vigour and assiduity.

The enemy's cavalry and field troops having been defeated by a force under Lieut.-Colonel Webster, the enemy's communication was effectually cut off, and Charlestown completely invested. Before opening the new batteries, which had been erected within one hundred yards of the place, on the 8th May, Clinton summoned the American general, Lincoln, to surrender. His demands not being complied with, the batteries were opened, and so destructive a fire poured into the city that it surrendered on the 11th, and the whole garrison, amounting to upwards of six thousand men, were made prisoners.

An unfortunate accident happened a few days after the surrender of Charlestown that greatly increased our loss. A storehouse, in which there were thirty barrels of powder, was appointed for the reception of the rebel army, and many of the drivers and others being employed to throw them in, it is supposed that one of the muskets was loaded, and went off, as the magazine blew up. By this sad catastrophe Captain Collins, Lieutenant Gordon, and fourteen men of the Royal Artillery, besides eleven artificers and other soldiers, lost their lives, and several were badly wounded.

The next affair of any consequence that happened this year was the victory of Camden, which Lord Cornwallis, with 2,000 men, achieved over Gates's army of 6,000 (16th August).

The British had but four guns in the field, manned by two sergeants and fifteen rank and file of the Royal Artillery, and commanded by two lieutenants—one of whom, William Marquois, was severely wounded, and died from the effects of his wounds on the 15th October following. Major-General Pattison, worn out with continued service, and bowed down by years, felt himself unable to retain his command, and on the 1st September, 1780, he left New York for England, being accompanied to the waterside by Sir H. Clinton and his staff.

General James Pattison was born in 1733. He received his commission as lieut.-fireworker in the Royal Artillery on the 1st April, 1740, and advanced a step in promotion each year till he was appointed captain-lieutenant, which rank he retained till 1747, from which time he was ever prominent as a commanding officer of artillery.

On the coast of France, in Portugal, and in America he appeared as a warrior; while in 1769 he was employed at Venice superintending the organisation of the Italian artillery.

He was the originator of many inventions useful in his profession, among which may he mentioned a light piece of artillery, constructed on a most convenient plan, so that both the gun and carriage might be transported on men's shoulders to places impracticable to the usual modes of draught.

He was twice commandant of Woolwich garrison, and was also governor of the Royal Military Academy. He died in London on the 1st March, 1805, and was buried in the family vault in Plumstead churchyard.

The command of the artillery in America devolved on Lieutenant-Colonel William Martin, who had hitherto commanded the companies in New York.

The campaign of 1781 was opened by General Arnold (he who at the commencement of the war had taken so active a part on the American side, but who in 1780 declared himself disgusted with the rebellion, and offered his services to the English), who, with a small force, ravaged the American stores in Virginia. Soon after, Arnold was superseded in the chief command by General Phillips, R.A., who, having been exchanged for the American General Lincoln, had resumed his duty with the army. On the 26th March this army ascended James River, took and destroyed much property in Williamsburg and Yorktown, and ravaged the country round.

On the 27th April they marched to Chesterfield Courthouse, where they were attacked by a number of American vessels of about twenty-six guns each, and a body of between two hundred and three hundred militia.

Notwithstanding this formidable force, the effect of the fire from the British artillery, directed by Captain Fage and Lieutenant Rogers, was such that the ships were soon obliged to strike their colours, and the militia were driven from the opposite shore. Fortunately, not a man of the king's troops was hurt; but the loss of men on the side of the enemy must have been very considerable, as they were quite exposed to the well-directed fire of the British artillery. On the 1st May the army marched to Bermuda Hundred, and here General Phillips was unfortunately seized with a fever, which deprived the army of his abilities, and was a great loss to the public service.

He continued with the army, however, and though too ill to mount a horse, a postchaise was procured for him, in which he travelled from Brandon to Petersburgh, where a number of American and French officers of La Fayette's army were taken. Unfortunately for his country, General Phillips's disorder proved too strong for the skill of the physician to remove, and he breathed his last on the 13th May. In him the king and the nation lost a most excellent officer. His services at the Battle of Minden and elsewhere are given in Chapter 1. An active warfare had also been going on in North Carolina during the early months of 1781. On the 17th January a small body of troops under Colonel Tarleton were defeated by the Americans at Cowpens, or Ninety-six. Our guns (two 3-pounders) fell into their hands, but not until all the artillerymen were disabled.

Earl Cornwallis, in his despatch, says:

No terror could induce the artillerymen to abandon their guns, and they were all killed or wounded in defence of them.

Cornwallis, with his army, now marched and countermarched at least twelve thousand miles, through a country every part of which was hostile to his progress; and with invincible patience and firmness surmounted the impediments which nature had thrown in his way till the 15th March, when he brought the Americans to an engagement at Guildford. This was the hottest and most glorious battle throughout the war. The numbers of the British had been reduced, by various causes, to 1,610 men, which included but half a company of the Royal Artillery under Lieutenant John Macleod (afterwards Sir John

Macleod); while the enemy mustered at least 9,000. Notwithstanding this disparity of numbers, the British, after a hard-fought action, were left masters of the field. The enemy lost their cannon, and afterwards regained them; but finally, they fell into the hands of the British.

Lord Cornwallis was highly pleased with the conduct of the Royal Artillery in this action, and became for ever afterwards the firm friend of Lieutenant Macleod. Lieutenant O'Hara and one gunner were killed, and four men wounded. Of the remainder of the detachment very few survived the hardships and fatigues they had undergone in fording rivers and creeks, dragging the guns through almost impassable defiles, without tents, and very often without provisions; all this told fearfully on this brave band, whose invincible patience manifested their ardent zeal for the honour and interests of their sovereign and country.

Among the victims to fatigue was Lieutenant John Pritchard, R.A., who died a few weeks after the Battle of Guilford.

Though they had suffered many reverses, particularly in the surrender of Burgoyne's army, the war up to this time had been in favour of the British. But now the example of France was followed by Spain; and the Dutch, even, were induced to join the league against England. The consequence was that no more troops could be spared from England for the defence of the colonies, and the army in America had to cope with the united forces of France, Spain, and the colonists, as well as to defend the West India Islands, which were surrounded by fleets of either nation. Under these circumstances it became evident the war would soon terminate in favour of the Americans; notwithstanding, the British troops exerted themselves to the utmost, and did all that men could do to bring about a contrary result.

A small army under Major-General Grant, including two companies of artillery (Standish's and Dowmnan's), under Captain Williamson, had sailed from Staten Island in November, 1778, for the West Indies. (Standish was invalided June, 1780; died at Greenwich, June 28, 1813 and Williamson died at Shooter's Hill, October 19, 1794). They made for Dominica, but finding that island had fallen into the possession of the French, they at once proceeded to St. Lucia. They arrived there just in time to prevent that island being taken; as the French had landed a number of troops, which Grant's force at once attacked and defeated: the fleet, meanwhile, compelling the transports with the remainder of the French troops to return to Martinique.

On the 3rd February, 1781, the Dutch islands of St Eustatius, Martin, and Saba were taken by the British.

A small garrison was left in the former, including a detachment of twenty-seven men of the Royal Artillery, commanded by Captain Garstin (resigned September, 1793), and Lieutenant George Lewis. In August, at the desire of the commandant, Lieut.-Col. Cockburn, these two officers rode round the island to inspect the defences and notice where it might be possible for a landing to be effected by any hostile force. They reported that there were two points where an enemy could land, known by the names of "English Quarter" and "Jenkins's Bay." Colonel Cockburn at once ordered a battery to be erected at "English Quarter," but took no steps for the defence of "Jenkins's Bay."

Accordingly, when the French landed there and took possession of the island on the 26th November, Cockburn laid all the blame on two men of the Royal Artillery. In his despatch he said:

> Had the two men posted on the signal hill, which overlooks the place the enemy landed at, done their duty by giving the proper alarm, this misfortune could never have happened; but villains as they were, they quitted their post in the night, and were taken prisoners in the valley, a considerable time after daylight; Corporal Henderson and James Pickering, both of the Royal Artillery, were the two men pitched upon as trusty for that important post.

Fortunately for the honour of the corps, this statement was proved to be a direct falsehood; for when Lieut.-Col. Cockburn was tried (at Chelsea Hospital, in 1783) for the loss of the island, it was stated by Captain Garstin that the duty of the men was to remain in the sentry-box as long as they could distinguish objects at sea, and to return at gunfire in the morning. About five o'clock on the morning of the 26th November, they were called up by the woman of the house where they lodged (distant about a hundred yards from their post), who told them that some soldiers were on the hill, who she supposed were going to steal her sheep. They at once went up, when they were made prisoners by the enemy, who was already in possession of the post. This information was obtained by Captain Garstin from the French officer who took the men, and from the old woman of the house. Colonel Cockburn was cashiered.

In April, 1781, a Spanish Army crossed over from Havannah and laid siege to Pensacola, which was garrisoned by a small force under Major-General Campbell, with a detachment of artillery under Captain William Johnstone and Lieutenant Edward Wilkinson. (Johnstone enlisted in the corps as a private in 1752, and died a lieut.-general, at Plumstead, December 19, 1802; Wilkinson retired, December, 1785). Both officers and men of the Royal Artillery, together with twelve artillerymen of the Waldeck Regiment, were indefatigable in their exertions, and although they were incessantly on duty, so far from suffering their spirits to sink, they became more animated and zealous in the service as the danger of performing it increased.

On the 8th May a shell burst near the door of the magazine of the advanced redoubt, the powder exploded, and the redoubt was in an instant a heap of rubbish. Two flank-works of the redoubt still remained entire, and from these Captain Johnstone and his artillerymen 'kept up such a galling fire upon the enemy, who at once advanced to the assault, that they were repulsed in their first attempt, while our people carried off all their wounded, with two howitzers and three guns. The enemy then brought up their whole army and obliged the British to abandon the advanced works; and two days afterwards the garrison surrendered on honourable terms. The British troops (about 700, including 32 of the Royal Artillery) were sent to New York.

The crowning event of the war (which, however, was favourable to the Americans) was the surrender of Cornwallis and his army at Yorktown, on the 19th October, 1781.

That general having, after the Battle of Guilford, effected a junction with the army of General Phillips (a few days after the death of that officer), at once assumed the command of the whole, amounting to about 7,000 men, and took up his quarters at Yorktown.

He was shortly followed by the united armies of France and America, under Rochambeau and Washington, who appeared before the place on the 28th September.

In the hope of being reinforced by Sir H. Clinton and some troops from New York, the brave little army under Cornwallis held out against the allies (three times their number) for nearly three weeks. That the Royal Artillery (whose loss during the defence was very severe—24 men killed, 21 wounded, 2 missing), did their duty in a manner worthy of their established reputation, is evident from the despatch of Earl Cornwallis, which says:

> Captain Rochfort, who commanded the artillery, and indeed every officer and soldier of that distinguished corps, have merited my highest approbation. (Captain Rochfort died a lieutenant-general at Woolwich, February 24, 1821).

Being disappointed by Clinton, and having failed in an attempt to escape, Cornwallis, seeing his case was hopeless, surrendered; and, with his army, was sent to England, on the terms of not serving again during the war.

Though the independence of the States was not recognised, nor peace established between them and the mother-country till November, 1782, no other event worthy of mention, in which the Royal Artillery was concerned, occurred after the surrender of Yorktown.

During the war of the American Revolution, the Royal Artillery in Canada was distributed among the advanced posts on the frontier in very small detachments, one gunner being frequently the only representative of the corps in a fort or station. The travelling from Quebec and Montreal to these stations was necessarily very dangerous; the extremes of the climate, the traversing of forests and crossing of lakes, together with the vigilance necessary to escape the Indians and scouting parties of the rebels, rendering it a most hazardous service. Nevertheless, it was ably and cheerfully performed by both officers and men of the Royal Artillery, whose conduct during this trying period was most praiseworthy, and reflected great credit on the corps.

On the 20th June, 1780, the army under General Halimand took the field, and from that date till their return to Quebec on the 22nd October, the Royal Artillery (250 strong) had not a man punished; and though they lived on salt pork and peas nearly the whole of the four months, there were never more than four men sick at one time.

The following detail for the month of July, 1778, will show the duty that had to be performed by the Royal Artillery in Canada, while their comrades were engaged with the rebels in the provinces:—

Capt. Borthwick	2 lieutenants, 74 N.C. officers and men		Quebec.
Lieut. J. Barnes*	12	,,	Montreal.
,, R. Dysart	35 .	,,	St. Johns.
,, J. Gleniet†	19	,,	Isle aux Noix.
,, C. S. Colleton	8	,,	Niagara.
,, H. Duvernet‡	7	,,	Detroit.
Corporal Joseph Davidson...	5 gunners & mattrosses§		Carleton Island.
Corpl. Runsiman	4	,,	Chambly.
Bombardier J. Pattison...	1	,,	Michilimakinac.
————	10	,,	Cadaroquoi.
Gunner C. Cuthbertson	......		Oswegatchie.

* Died at Bath (major-general), April 30, 1810.
† To Royal Engineers, 1779.
‡ Died in the West Indies, August 12, 1791.
§ One of these, Mattross Ralph Haynes, was taken prisoner by a party of scouts from the rebel army.

59

These detachments had of course to be relieved occasionally, and during the passage from one post to another accidents frequently occurred,

In August, 1779, Lieutenant Colleton was relieved at Niagara by Lieutenant C. Terrott, and in the following April he was sent, with Lieutenant Charles Flynn and a detachment, to reinforce the artillery at Niagara and Carleton Island. Flynn proceeded at once to Carleton (where he died in 1781), Colleton remaining for a time at Niagara. In October be embarked with Mattross James Bell on board the ship *Ontario*, for passage across the lake, but before it had proceeded far the vessel foundered, and all on board perished.

In 1782 the Royal Artillery in Canada was reinforced by the companies from New York, and in the following year, upon the establishment of peace, two (Abbott's and Frost's) were sent to the West Indies, and three (Borthwick's, Barnes's, and Fage's) returned to England.

★★★★★★★★★★

The senior lieutenant of Abbott's company was Samuel Rimington, who was born of humble parents at Burton, Kent, in 1740, and was in early life apprenticed to a blacksmith. He enlisted as a mattross in the Royal Artillery at Maidstone, in January, 1757. In less than fifteen years he had so far advanced in the regiment that, on the establishment of the 4th battalion in 1771, he was presented with a commission as second lieutenant. He served actively till 1802, when, as lieut.-colonel, he was transferred to the Invalid Battalion. He died at Woolwich, January 23, 1826, having reached the rank of lieut.-general, and the great age of eighty-six years.

★★★★★★★★★★

CHAPTER 3

Gibraltar

Important as the services of the Royal Artillery have been in all parts of the world, there is no one spot where their bravery and general conduct have shone conspicuously as at Gibraltar.

Upon the final cession of this fortress to Great Britain at the treaty of Utrecht, 1711, the garrison was reinforced by a company of the Royal Artillery, which remained in it till 1749.

The Spaniards having on several occasions entered into fruitless negotiations with the English for the surrender of Gibraltar, resolved once more to besiege it, and early in 1727 their forces were observed making preparations for the attack. The garrison accordingly prepared for a vigorous defence.

On the 22nd February the enemy broke ground by commencing a battery on the western beach, which attracted the notice of General Clayton, the acting governor of Gibraltar. He at once communicated with the commander of the Spanish forces, informing him that, notwithstanding there had been no declaration of war, if he persisted in erecting works so near the fortress, necessary measures would be taken. Receiving an insolent reply, and finding that the works continued, General Clayton ordered the guns at the old mole and Willis's batteries to commence firing. Most of the ordnance in Gibraltar was old and worn-out, and more casualties occurred during the siege from the bursting of the guns than from the enemy's fire.

On the 10th March a 32-pounder burst in Britain's battery, killing a gunner; and on the 19th a gun burst in the same battery, which dismounted another and broke a gunner's leg. On the 2nd May an 18-pounder burst in Willis's, and killed the gunner who fired it.

The first officer killed was Captain-Lieutenant Holman, of the artillery; he fell in the Royal Battery, on Sunday, 5th March.

The Spaniards erected many important works and approached to

GIBRALTAR
From the New Mole Fort looking North

within musket-shot of the fortress, but the garrison being reinforced on several occasions, was not in the least dismayed.

On the 7th April the *Torbay* arrived from England, bringing two infantry regiments and a detachment of the Royal Artillery, under Colonel Jonas Watson, who at once assumed the command of the corps.

During the first week in May, the enemy having completed four gigantic batteries, armed with the finest brass artillery, a terrific fire was opened all along the line. So magnificent was the bombardment—previously unequalled in the history of artillery—that, "for some time," says an eye-witness, "we seemed to live in flames." For fourteen days, 700 shots per hour were thrown into the fortress, and 92 guns and 72 mortars were in constant play.

Though the garrison could only oppose 60 guns to this formidable armament, the Spaniards were soon compelled to cease firing. Their brass guns drooped at the muzzle, and their iron ordnance in many instances burst.

The governor now employed the garrison day and night, restoring the shattered defences and mounting new guns. While the English had thus successfully met the crushing bombardment (which had been expected to command a surrender), and were preparing for a final struggle, the Spaniards had shot their last bolt, and found themselves in a position of the greatest difficulty and danger.

Observing their embarrassment, the governor harassed them with a fire which almost equalled the terrible bombardment of the enemy. A supply of ammunition opportunely arrived from England, and by the end of May the guns of the garrison had gained a complete ascendancy over the besiegers.

Another crushing fire being opened from our batteries, the Spaniards were at last compelled to seek an armistice, which was granted by the governor on the 23rd June, though the articles of peace were not signed till the following March.

The loss sustained by the company of Royal Artillery during this siege was, one officer and eight men killed; sixteen wounded; two died of wounds; one died of sickness.

About six o'clock in the evening of the 4th September, as the men of the artillery were at work driving fuses, one caught fire and set light to the composition; this communicating to the powder in the room, the laboratory was at once blown up, and three men were killed.

Until the middle of the last century, no free market was established in Gibraltar; the garrison was supplied exclusively by contractors, who were under the orders of the governor. This system led to gross abuses: the governor received his provisions gratis, and no person was permitted to purchase anything until the field officers were served.

The officers of the Royal Artillery were the first to petition against this injustice. The first petition, dated August, 1744, entreats Captain Lytton Leslie, commanding the company of Royal Artillery, to intercede with the governor, "that he will be pleased to allow all persons the liberty to import from Barbary all manner of provisions, and that they may sell, and that we may buy them, in a free and open manner."

This petition was looked upon as a symptom of mutiny, and treated as such. Fortunately, however, the affair became known in England, where it was taken serious notice of.

Accordingly, when a second memorial was presented, drawn up by Lieutenant James Butler, R.A. (with the approved consent of his captain, Alexander Leith), and signed by nearly all the officers in the garrison, it was politely received by Colonel Herbert, the governor, who established a free market (about 1748).

****

> Lieutenant Butler entered the army as surgeon in 1742; he became a lieutenant in March, 1747; and in January, 1768 (then captain), he entered the service of the East India Company.
>
> The other officers of the company of artillery were Captain-Lieut. Thomas James, Lieuts. Henry Tovey, Baylie Bryden, George Anderson (died at Plymouth, Dec. 5, 1793). and Robert Hind. The last-named officer commanded. a company on the Belleisle expedition in 1761, and the following year proceeded to Portugal, where he died, March 5, 1763.

****

After the capture of Minorca by the French in 1756, it was feared that they would secure the alliance of Spain against England, and reinforcements including an additional company of artillery, were hastily despatched to Gibraltar,

On the occasion of the next declaration of war against Spain, in 1762, Gibraltar was reinforced by three more companies of artillery, since which time there has never been less than four, or more than eight companies in that fortress.

In 1777, when Spain allied herself with France and America, there were five companies of the Royal Artillery in Gibraltar. Expecting an attack on that fortress. General Elliott, the governor, sent the following message to the Secretary for War;—

In case of service, the garrison must be increased considerably more than double the present number, *especially artillerymen.*

Notwithstanding this timely warning, no additional artillerymen were sent for two years, and then one company was all that could be spared for this service.

Colonel Godwin was the officer in command of the artillery when the Spaniards appeared before the fortress in July, 1779.

He was present at a council of war convened by General Elliott on the 11th September, when it was resolved to open fire upon the enemy, with the intention of impeding their works. Accordingly, on the following morning at daybreak the guns in the fortress broke silence. The first gun, was discharged by the wife of an officer. General Elliott, who was standing by, gave the words, "Britons, strike home!" as the signal. During the following week the firing continued, but was not answered by the Spaniards.'

As it is not our intention to give a full account of this glorious defence, but merely to record the particular services of the artillery, we cannot do better than select the following extracts from Heriot and Drinkwater:—

> Each corps, as it equally participated in the perils and glories of the siege, is entitled to its equal portion of military fame; but none surely will deem it a partial and invidious selection, if the Royal Artillery be deemed deserving of more signal renown. Their duty led them to be constantly in the batteries, and where everything; was effected by the ordnance, their services may be supposed to have been more than generally eminent. Such was the impression which the Duc de Crillon and the combined armies had received of them—such is the just tribute to their military science and gallant conduct, which, not only the present age, but all posterity, must pay.

The year 1780 was not ushered in by any remarkable event. The constantly decreasing stock of provisions was, however, a matter of the greatest importance, and caused the governor much anxiety. The ordinary means of sustenance were almost exhausted, and roots, weeds, thistles, and wild onions were greedily sought after and devoured by the famished inhabitants. On the 13th January all the field officers assembled to inquire into the condition and quantity of the remaining supplies. The result of this conference was the immediate reduction of the soldiers' rations, already barely sufficient to support life. A few weeks afterwards the British fleet under Admiral Rodney captured a considerable convoy laden with provisions, which, after defeating the Spanish fleet in the bay, he sent into Gibraltar.

The same evening, the enemy's batteries having opened, Lieutenant Boag, of the Royal Artillery, was wounded. (Boag enlisted as a mattross, August, 1758; reached the rank of lieut.-colonel, 1800; retired, September 1, 1803; died soon after.) In the evening of the 2nd May a shell from the garrison fell upon the eastern traverse in the St. Carlos battery, under which was the magazine, and communicating with the powder, blew it up. The explosion was not loud, but the damage done was so very considerable, that their guns were silent for several days.

Our artillery annoyed the enemy greatly during their confusion.

The day following. Lieutenant Willington, R.A., was wounded at Willis. (He was commander of the artillery at Gibraltar on the occasion of the mutiny, 1802; afterwards assistant director-general of Field-train Department, died at Woolwich, October 16, 1823, aged sixty-eight).

On the 27th July our batteries were attacked for the second time by the gun and mortar boats of the enemy. Nine shot and fifty-eight shells were returned by the garrison, and by the shrieks and piteous cries heard, it was conjectured that they did great execution.

In this attack a wounded mattross in the hospital was killed by a shell. He had sometime previously had his thigh broken, and being a man of great spirit, he ill brooked the confinement which his case demanded, and exerted himself to get abroad, that he might enjoy the benefit of the fresh air in the court of the hospital. Unfortunately, in one of his playful moments he fell, and was obliged to take to his bed again.

He was in this situation when a shell from the mortar-boats fell into the ward, and rebounding, lodged upon him. The convalescent and sick in the same room instantly summoned up strength to crawl out on hands and knees while the fuse was burning; but this wretched victim was kept down by the weight of the shell, which after some seconds burst, took off both his legs, and scorched him in a dreadful manner; but what was still more horrid, he survived the explosion, and was sensible to the very moment that death relieved him from his misery. His last words were expressive of regret that he had not been killed in the batteries.

On the 20th October, the situation of the enemy's battery afforded a more serious appearance than any operations yet undertaken by him. Colonel Abram Tovey, who had succeeded to the command of the artillery on the promotion of Colonel Godwin, therefore recommended the governor to open upon it, without loss of time, with such heavy guns and howitzers as might be soon brought to bear upon it, assisted at the same time by some 13-inch shells and a few carcasses. (Godwin was promoted to colonel-commandant of the 2nd battalion on the death of General Desaguliers, March, 1780; died at Woolwich, 23rd January, 1786).

The next morning the enemy had almost completed the battery; the governor was therefore induced to comply with the representation of Colonel Tovey, and ordered the upper batteries to he opened on the enemy's works, and to continue to fire as Colonel Tovey should directs. About four o'clock in the afternoon of the 22nd the firing commenced, and was continued with unremitting spirit and regularity the remainder of the evening and during the night. The enemy, in turn, discharged repeated volleys from their lines, but to little purpose; our artillery soon drove them from the battery, which was frequently set on fire by the carcasses. Nevertheless, the enemy had masked five of their embrasures with sand-bags, and at noon of the 23rd our firing was ordered to cease, 1,596 shot, 530 shells, 10 carcasses, and two light balls having been expended.

The new year (1781) was ushered in with the most gloomy prospects; no tidings of relief reached the expectant garrison, and the few provisions that remained were bad in quality, and having been kept too long, were decomposed and unfit for food.

The enemy's batteries having assumed, in spite of the fire of our artillery, a stupendous and formidable appearance, and a Mr. Booth having expressed to Lieutenant Seward, R.A., his opinion of the practicability of a sortie, that officer mentioned the circumstance to General Boyd, who, after consulting with Mr. Booth, suggested it to General Elliott. (Seward died at Cheltenham as a lieutenant-general, 17th January, 1831). The idea was accordingly carried into execution on the night of the 26th November.

One captain, three lieutenants, ten non-commissioned officers, and one hundred men of the Royal Artillery accompanied the sortie. Their exertions were truly wonderful. The enemy's batteries were soon in a state for the fire-faggots to operate, and the flames spread with astonishing rapidity into every part; the column of fire which rolled from the works beautifully illuminated the troops and neighbouring objects, forming altogether a *coup d'oeil* impossible to describe.

Two Spanish officers were taken prisoners; one, a lieutenant, was taken in the middle of the battery by Captain Witham, of the Royal Artillery, who commanded the detachment of the corps out upon this service. The Spanish officer was armed with a drawn sword, when Captain Witham, with a firebrand only in his hand, seized him by the sword-arm, and in Spanish demanded the key of the magazine of that battery. The lieutenant, Don Vincente Friza, replied, "*Todos es bombas*" (the whole is a magazine), and gave up his sword.

The other Spanish officer taken prisoner was Baron Von Helmstadt, an ensign in the Walloon Guards. He had been severely wounded by a musket-ball in one of his knees, and was found lying upon the platform of the St. Carlos battery, by Gunners Campbell and Baton, of the Royal Artillery, who, moved with generous compassion at his situation, resolved to preserve him from his impending fate. They took him up in their arms and carried him out of the battery, where he must soon have perished in the flames. Unwilling to leave him helpless on the sands, they determined on carrying him into the garrison. They were executing their noble purpose when they met with Lieutenant Cuppage, of their own corps, who, while he bestowed the warmest encomiums upon his men for their humanity, himself assisted in the generous office which it suggested.

★★★★★★★★★★

Afterwards Lieutenant-General William Cuppage. He was the son of the Rev. Burke Cuppage, rector of Coleraine, Ireland, where he was born in October. 1756. He was a relative of the celebrated Edmund Burke, who obtained for him the nomination to a cadetship in the Royal Military Academy in 1768. He received his commission in 1771, and first appeared before the enemy on the occasion above recorded. After the siege he served his country in many important positions, the principal of which were the command of the artillery in the Kentish district, during the years of the invasion panic, when great zeal and watchfulness were required; with Sir Charles Stuart, at Minorca, in 1798; and as inspector-general of the Royal Carriage Department.

In the details of this department, his combination of economy with efficiency, his reduction of all the subordinate branches, abroad and at home, to the immediate control of the chief at Woolwich, and his application of machinery which enabled the department to prepare and promptly yield such an increase to the issues of military stores at critical periods as were unparalleled in the same service previously, called forth not only the repealed commendations of the Master-General and the Board, but received the gratifying testimony of the official organ of the Ordnance in Parliament, when he moved for the Ordnance Estimates in 1814.

In 1782, Captain Cuppage married the widow of Lieutenant-Colonel Cairnes, of the 36th regiment, with a family of three daughters and two sons, all of whom he adopted and ever treated as his own: (The eldest of the sons was the late Major Cairnes, R.A.) By this marriage he had three sons and one daughter, the eldest of whom is the present (as at 1902) Major-General Cuppage, R.A., who served with his lamented half-brother at the Battle of Waterloo, and is one of the few veterans of that action who are still (1865) doing duty in the service. Lieutenant-General Cuppage died at Shooter's-hill, on the 9th November, 1832, in his seventy-seventh year.

★★★★★★★★★★

With every possible tenderness they conveyed the wounded prisoner to the barriers, where they did not arrive till two hours after the detachment had retired. During this time, they had been exposed to the enemy's fire from their lines, and had been reported in the garrison as lost. Having presented themselves at the barrier, and being admitted, they passed through the different guards amidst the mingled admiration and applause of the whole, till they reached the garrison hospital, where they deposited the baron. On such an instance of humanity the mind dwells with applauding rapture: while strongly characteristic of the generous disposition of the British soldier towards a vanquished enemy, it dignifies human nature and illumines the rugged front of war with the radiant emanations of philanthropy.

The ordnance spiked in the enemy's works amounted to ten 13-inch mortars and eighteen 26-pounders.

Before the detachment returned from the sortie, Lieut.-Colonel Tovey died, and was succeeded in the command of the artillery by Major George Lewis.

The 1st January, 1782, was remarkable for a circumstance worthy of being rescued from oblivion. An officer of artillery at Willis, observing a shell falling towards the place where he stood, got behind a traverse for protection, which he had scarcely done ere it fell into the traverse, and instantly entangled him in the rubbish. One of the guard, named Martin, observing his distress, generously risked his own life in defence of his officer, and ran to extricate him; but finding his own efforts ineffectual, called for assistance, when another of the guard joining him, they relieved the officer from his situation, and almost at the same instant the shell burst and levelled the traverse to the ground. Martin was afterwards promoted and rewarded by the governor, who at the same time declared "he should equally have noticed him for relieving his comrade."

On the 15th February some practice was made from a gun mounted upon a new-constructed depressing carriage, the invention of Lieutenant Koehler, of the Royal Artillery, which was highly approved of by the governor and the other officers present. A description of this carriage is given by Drinkwater, who observes:—

> As to the accuracy of the depressing shot, no further proof need be adduced than that out of thirty rounds twenty-eight shot took place in one traverse in the St. Carlos battery at the distance of 1,400 yards.

Lieutenant Koehler was unfortunately an object of dislike to the general (Elliott); so much so, indeed, that he was directed to send all his communications in writing, personal intercourse being dispensed with. With the generosity which distinguished the gallant Elliott, he now strove to make amends for his past neglect, and placed the young artilleryman on his staff, in which capacity he served with great distinction during the remainder of the siege.

Elliott had now conceived such an affection for Koehler that he took him with him to England in 1786, and afterwards on a visit to the Continent. At this time the Flemings at Ghent were engaged in an attempt to shake off the Austrian yoke. Being greatly in need of a skilful artillery officer, they solicited Elliott, (later Lord Heathfield), through Count Dillon, to grant leave of absence to Lieut. Koehler, to whom they offered the rank of major-general in their service.

The leave was granted, and the position accepted; but in a short time the Flemings had to give up their cause as hopeless, and Koehler returned to England.

On the 9th March, Lieutenant Cuppage was dangerously wounded on the Royal battery from a splinter of a small shell which burst immediately after being discharged from the Bock gun.

From 7 p.m. on the 4th May, to the same hour the next day, both the garrison and the enemy were silent. This was the first twenty-four hours in which there had been no firing for about thirteen months.

On the 7th June our artillery practised from the King's bastion with red-hot shot against the *Irishman* brig, which was stranded at the back of the old mole. During the first round an explosion took place, by which the artilleryman who was putting in the shot was blown from the embrasure in some hundred pieces; two others were also slightly wounded by the unexpected recoil of the carriage. On the 6th July an artilleryman named Hartley was employed in the laboratory filling shells with carcass composition, and driving fuses into 5½ and 6-inch shells; one of them, by some unaccountable accident, took fire in the operation, and although he was surrounded by unfixed fuses, loaded shells, composition, etc., with the most astonishing coolness he carried out the lighted shell, and threw it where it could do little or no harm, and two seconds had scarcely elapsed before it exploded.

Had the shell burst in the laboratory, it is almost certain the whole would have been blown up, and the loss in fixed ammunition, fuses, etc., would have been irreparable, exclusive of the damage which the fortifications would have suffered from the explosion, and the lives that might have been lost. Hartley was handsomely rewarded by the governor for his gallantry and presence of mind.

On the 8th September the red-hot shot was used for the first time against the enemy, and the effect exceeded the most sanguine expectations. In a few hours the Mahon battery and works adjoining wore completely destroyed and consumed by the fire. While the enemy's loss was enormous, the garrison had two or three killed and several wounded. Lieutenant Boag, of the Royal Artillery, was of the latter number. He had been wounded before; on this occasion he was pointing a gun from the Hanover battery, when a shell fell close to him. He had barely time to throw himself down in an embrasure when the shell burst and fired the gun, under the muzzle of which he lay. The report deprived him of hearing, and it was some time before he recovered a tolerable use of that faculty.

Major Martin had likewise a very fortunate escape from a 26-pounder, which shot away the cock of his hat close to the crown. He was considerably stunned with the wind of the shot, but experienced little further injury. (Philip Martin died a lieutenant-general and colonel-commandant of the 6th battalion, at Leeds Castle, near Maidstone, 5th October, 1821).

On the 10th Major Lewis was wounded. The confinement of this active officer at this critical juncture might have been highly prejudicial to the service, had not his seconds been of confirmed ability and experience; but, owing to their united exertions, the several duties connected with the artillery were conducted with harmony and success.

****

The following is a copy of the letter received by Major Lewis from the Board of Ordnance, in answer to his application for a pension for wounds:—

Whitehall, Feb. 18th, 1788.

Sir,—I have laid before the king your memorial, together with the strong recommendations of your services by General Elliott, and have the pleasure to acquaint you that His Majesty has seen with great satisfaction such effectual proofs of the bravery, seal, and skill by which you and the Royal Artillery under your command at Gibraltar have so eminently distinguished yourselves during the siege, and particularly in setting fire to and destroying all the floating batteries of the combined forces of France and Spain on the 18th September last; and that, as a reward for this service and the very dangerous wound which you received on that occasion, his majesty has been graciously pleased to grant you an allowance of 20s. per day.

I most sincerely hope for your speedy recovery, and have the honour to be, with the highest esteem and regard, your most obedient humble servant,

(Signed) Richmond
Master-General of the Ordnance.

Major Lewis lived only long enough to reach the rank of colonel. He died at Chislehurst, on the 22nd February, 1791.

****

Early in the morning of the 13th September the enormous floating batteries, which had been prepared at an almost inconceivable expense by the allies, approached the rock. They were armed with 212 new brass guns, many of which spoke that day for the first and last time.

The whole host of besiegers, both, by land and sea, commenced almost simultaneously the bold attack, The incessant cannonade so regularly commenced and sustained by the besiegers, was as regularly answered by the defenders. About two in the afternoon that awful cannonade of red-hot balls was showered upon the grand armament of France and Spain. Vessel after vessel exploded or took fire; and, about one in the morning, the flames ascending from them were terrific in the extreme.

The generous nature of the British was then conspicuous. Volunteers from every regiment accompanied Brigadier Curtis, who went in boats to save the helpless enemy, and, in the midst of burning vessels, succeeded in rescuing about 340 Spaniards and twelve Frenchmen. Kindness and compassion were as warm towards the conquered as had been the fire of the artillery against them. All those terrible engines of destruction which the Spanish admiral D'Arcon had declared to be impregnable were destroyed.

The exertions and activity of the brave artillery in this well-fought contest deserve the highest commendation. To their skill, perseverance, and courage, with the assistance of the line, was Gibraltar indebted for its safety against the combined powers, by sea and land, of France and Spain.

During this eventful day. Captain Reeves, Lieutenant Grumley, and five men of the Royal Artillery were killed; Captain Groves, Captain Seward, Lieutenant Godfrey, and twenty-one men, wounded.

★★★★★★★★★★

Captain Reeves Began his services as a mattross.
Lieutenant Grumley was a volunteer belonging to Gibralter.
Captain Groves died at Greenwich, 9th July, 1785.
Lieutenant Godfrey resigned 1798; died at Purfleet, 1831

★★★★★★★★★★

By the evening of the 14th the bay was cleared of all the shattered wrecks, and not a vestige of the formidable armament, which yesterday had been the hope and pride of Spain, remained.

The contest was at an end, and the united strength of two ambitious and powerful nations had been humbled by a straitened garrison of 6,000 effective men.

The garrison expended during this siege 57,163 shot, 129,151 shells, 12,681 grape, 926 carcasses, 679 light-balls, and 8,000 barrels of powder.

On the 3nd February, 1783, the news of the signature of a general peace reached the garrison by a flag of trace; and on the 12th March the gates of the fortress, which had been closed for nearly four years, were once more thrown open. The Duc de Crillon was one of the first to enter, and his expressions of the gallantry of the defenders were most flattering. Being introduced to the officers of the Royal Artillery, through whose courage and ability his brightest hopes of victory had been destroyed, De Crillon met them with praises of their noble conduct, and remarked that "he would rather see them there as friends than in their batteries as enemies, where," he added, "they never spared him."

Spain now abandoned her hopes of ever recovering Gibraltar. The fortress was permitted to remain in the peaceful possession of the English, and the question of its surrender never afterwards agitated.

Since this time very little has occurred at Gibraltar out of the ordinary routine of garrison duty. A few events in connexion with the artillery, however, may perhaps be thought worth recording.

In September, 1797, one of those unfortunate "*affairs of honour*" falsely so called, but too common at that time (and which, we hope, has not a parallel in the history of either corps), took place at Gibraltar, between Captain John Bradbridge, of the Royal Artillery, and Captain Peter Couture, of the Royal Engineers. The latter had served in the Royal Artillery, and while in Canada, in 1780, was transferred, on account of his superior abilities as an engineer, to the corps of Royal Engineers.

It is reported that he and Captain Bradbridge were firm friends until the unfortunate Sunday morning, when, out of the most trifling affair, the most serious quarrel resulted. They were each in command of their respective companies, which were marching together from church, when, on passing through Prince Edward's gate, Couture, without waiting for the artillery to pass straight on to their barracks, gave the word "left wheel," thereby causing the artificers to break through the ranks of Bradbridge's company. The latter took it as a personal insult, and threw his glove to Couture, who instantly picked it up and made arrangements for a hostile meeting. The consequence was that Couture was killed, and Bradbridge dismissed the service.

The latter was the son of Thomas Bradbridge, Esq., of the Royal Ordnance. His younger brother, Thomas, was a lieutenant in the Royal Artillery, and died at St. Domingo on the 30th June, 1794. They were both survived by their mother, who died at Woolwich on the 8th May, 1835, aged 97 years.

On the 24th March, 1802, His Royal Highness the Duke of Kent was appointed governor of Gibraltar, and on the 10th May he arrived and took up his command. He speedily set to work to reform many abuses prevalent in the garrison, the foremost being the disorganised state of the troops through excessive intoxication. By a system as pernicious as it was mistaken, the salary of the governors of Gibraltar had for many years been principally defrayed by the income derived from wine-house licences. To keep up this artificial revenue, every encouragement had been given to the establishment of public-houses, and the sale of wines and spirituous liquors. The Duke of Kent, himself a strict and conscientious soldier, regarded the prevailing evil with alarm, and sought to apply a remedy by striking at the root of the disorder.

Forgetful of his own interests, he endeavoured to suppress the unbridled drunkenness by reducing the number of canteens and spirit shops, while stringent and judicious regulations were put into force for the management of licensed establishments.

Unfortunately, these efforts for reform were not supported by the authorities, either in the garrison or at home. The troops, indignant at the slightest interference with the habits of licentiousness into which they had been silently permitted to lapse, openly defied the orders of the governor, who found himself threatened with a general mutiny.

The artillery on this occasion sustained their character for loyalty and obedience in a manner which reflects the highest honour on the corps.

A field piece having been seized by the mutinous soldiers, and dragged to the convent, where the duke had taken refuge; to prevent its being fired, the officers of the artillery suggested to the men that they should offer their services to the mutineers, and obtaining possession of the gun, bring it back to the park. The linesmen readily accepted the proffered services of the artillerymen, but would not leave them to themselves with the gun. Seeing they hesitated to fire upon the convent, one of the line soldiers seized the portfire, but he was prevented by a gunner from accomplishing his purpose; the latter keeping his thumb upon the vent, suffered it to be burnt to the bone, and was the means of saving the convent from being attacked. The officers of the line had now arrived and restored order among their men, while the governor made his escape from the convent.

A fever of a very malignant character appeared at Gibraltar in September, 1804, and continued its ravages until the close of the year.

It was first noticed by Dr. Kenning, R.A., who reported to Dr. Booth, the chief of the medical department in the garrison, that he had some married people belonging to the corps under his care, whose complaints had assumed an appearance which embarrassed and alarmed him. It was at the same time taken serious notice of by Captains Wright and Dodd, R.A., who reported it to the governor. Sir Thomas Trigge. It was traced to a foreigner, by name Santos, who had arrived in the garrison from Cadiz, where the fever then prevailed.

He kept a grocer's shop, and it was in his shop that the first victim, the wife of Bombardier Fenton, R.A., was taken ill. This was on the 6th September; on the 8th Fenton himself was seized with it, and both he and his wife died on the 12th. Matthew Pole, who was the orderly on Fenton, and Sergeant Shand and his wife, who had visited them, were the next victims. Shand and his wife died on the 22nd, and Pole on the 23rd. By this time, it had spread over the whole of the garrisons the Royal Artillery suffering most severely.

From the 1st September to the end of the year, 462 of the corps were attacked, of whom 201 died.

The companies were stationed as follows:—

Barracks on the Gunner's Parade	Captain R. Wright's*	88 men,	of whom died	28
	„ T. Dodd's	90	„ „	18
Orange Bastion	Major R. Adye's	92	„ „	5
	Captain W. Skyring's‡	91	„ „	13
	„ F. Rey's§	88	„ „	8
Moorish Castle .	Hon. Capt. Gardner's	97	„ „	9

* Died at Edinburgh, October 2, 1823.

‡ Died in London, September 12, 1806.
§ Died in London, November 20, 1833.

The above is independent of the men in the married quarters, who, with their families, were the principal sufferers.

On the 25th September the following General Order appeared:—

The officer commanding the Royal Artillery will order the whole of the guns on the line wall, from the grand battery to the south bastion, to be discharged three times over, as soon as he conveniently can.

This was evidently done for the purpose of clearing the air, but Sir James Fellowes says it was an erroneous idea, and certainly not recommended by a medical officer.

By the beginning of October, the fever had extensively spread; on the 22nd Major Ralph W. Adye died, and in less than a month five other officers of the corps had fallen a prey to the epidemic.

****

This officer served in Egypt in 1800; he was author of the *Little Bombardier* and *Pocket Gunner*, which was published in 1801, a second edition being called for in 1802, In this he was assisted by Captain Alexander Spearman, whose son produced an improved version of the work in 1828, universally known as the *British Gunner*.

The 5 other officers were Lieutenant John Pritchard, October 17; Lieutenant S. H. Halls, October 26; Captain Ralph Lidgerton, November 14; Lieutenants H. F. Ellison and James Wright, November 19.

****

In 1828 another fever broke out at Gibraltar, and though its ravages were very great, the Royal Artillery did not suffer so severely as in 1804. Lieut.-Colonel Payne, the Commanding Officer of the

Artillery, was the only officer who died; Major Gilmour, Captains Bissett and Evans, Lieutenants Burroughs and McCoy were attacked, but recovered.

★★★★★★★★★★

Captain Bissett died at Devonport, April 10, 1840. Captain Evans retired, 1831; died in London, September 18, 1855. Lieutenant Burroughs died, September 27, 1840. Lieutenant McCoy became Colonel McCoy, 12th brigade.

★★★★★★★★★★

There is no place where the Royal Artillery have met with so many accidents, and many of them fatal, as at Gibraltar.

On the second day of 1801, Lieutenant George Nutt fell from the heights, near Willis's battery, and was, of course, killed. Early in 1809 Captain William Holcombe fell down a well near Roscia Bay, and fractured his skull; he died on the 19th February.

The most painful of all accidents, however, was that which occurred in the month of November, 1830. The artillery were practising from one of the batteries on the north front of the rock, which overlooks Spain, when a powder chest in a chamber of one of the highest tiers of the excavations caught fire, and the consequent explosion hurled eight artillerymen out from the mouths of the rock to instant destruction, at the same time killing three men in the battery and injuring many more. The unfortunate soldiers were blown from the embrasures into mid-air, at a height of 800 feet, and scattered on the earth below, burnt and shattered to pieces.

How this fatal accident happened no one knew; many were the suppositions, but nothing certain could be arrived at. Lieutenant Caffin had a fortunate escape. He had requested to be allowed to take his duty that morning in a higher tier of the excavations than that in which the accident occurred, and to which he was directed to attach himself. On hearing the explosion, he at once proceeded, with the men under his charge, towards the passage that led downwards to the fatal spot. He was soon enveloped in thick smoke, through which he groped his way, the light from the embrasures, as he went along, being excluded by the density of the cloud around him, and he could scarcely breathe. (Lieutenant Caffin retired in 1841).

At length, the air becoming clearer, he beheld the miserable wreck which the explosion had left. Here and there lay the wounded, bleeding and scorched, fragments of belts and cartouche-boxes, caps, shoes, and clothes were scattered about the cave, bayonets sticking upright in the earth, while a smoking dead body lay huddled behind a gun carriage in a corner, and on the breast of the dead lay the head of its faithful dog, bleeding and lifeless. It appeared that the animal was not at once killed, but that, while yet living, it had crept to its master's body, where it expired.

On the 11th November, 1844, the troop ship *Apollo*, having on board Captain Gosling's and Stow's companies of the Royal Artillery for Malta and Corfu, arrived at Gibraltar, where it halted to take in provisions and to land Lieutenant Carlyon, R.A. (died there in the following year).

Ten soldiers and a female servant having hired a boat, manned by a man and boy, went on shore to purchase few necessaries for the remainder of the voyage, and while crossing the bay, the boat was unfortunately run down by a Danish *galliot* which had just arrived from Malaga, and was proceeding to its anchorage ground, and, melancholy to relate, six only out of the thirteen in the boat were rescued from a watery grave.

Sergeant Gritton, Gunners Leaver, Bossey, and Latter, of the artillery, perished on this occasion. Sergeant Gritton, who left a wife and five children and one unborn, (who now, 1902, is a non-commissioned officer in the R.A.), had been for many years at Gibraltar, where, besides having raised himself to the rank he held by his exemplary conduct and zealous performance of duty, he was respected and beloved by all who knew him. His father, also in the Royal Artillery, was on duty in the battery at the time of the explosion in 1830.

The *Apollo* had only a few months before taken Captain Dacres' company from Newfoundland to Canada; and, on arriving at Quebec, Bombardier Lawless went on board to see some of his comrades, when, on his return, in descending the gangway to get into the boat, he slipped into the water, and, before assistance could be rendered him, he sank.

★★★★★★★★★★

The year 1844 is remarkable for the number of accidental deaths by which the ranks of the Royal Artillery were thinned. In addition to those above mentioned, two men, gunners, James Norwood and John Cockshane, were smothered in the gravel-pits at Woolwich, in March; Gunner William Carson, servant to Lieutenant Swinton, was drowned by accidentally slipping off the plank when stepping into a boat at Woolwich-pier, in August; and two other gunners, Michael Walker and Alexander Miller, were killed at Portsmouth, in October, by the explosion of a gun from which they were firing a salute to welcome the King of the French, Louis Philippe.

****

Two artillery officers have held the position of governor of Gibraltar—General Sir John Smith, G.C.B., and General Sir Robert William Gardiner, G.C.B., K.C.H. The former entered the corps on the establishment of the fourth battalion in 1771, and two years afterwards was sent to Canada. He was taken prisoner by Arnold's corps, at St. John's, in November, 1775, and in 1777, being exchanged, he joined the army at Rhode Island, and was present in every action during the war, until finally taken with Cornwallis's army at Yorktown.

He served at Gibraltar from 1785 to 1790, and in 1795 went to the West Indies in command of the artillery of Sir Ralph Abercrombie's army. In 1799 he was in Holland with the Duke of York, and he concluded his active service at Gibraltar, serving on that station from 1804 to 1814, first as commanding officer of the artillery, and finally as governor. He died at Charlton on the 2nd July, 1837, aged 83 years.

Sir Robert Gardiner was the youngest son of the late Captain John Gardiner (3rd Buffs), and brother of the late Lieut.-General Sir John Gardiner, colonel of the 61st regiment. He was born May 2, 1781, joined the Royal Military Academy, Woolwich, in 1795, and obtained his commission in the Royal Artillery, April 7, 1797. In October he was sent to Gibraltar, then partially blockaded by the French and Spanish fleets, and remained there till November, 1798, when he embarked with the expedition under Sir Charles Stuart, and was present at the capture of Minorca. In May, 1799, he was appointed on the staff in Minorca as commandant of Mosquito Fort (the point where the Duc de Crillon had landed in 1782), and shortly afterwards became *aide-de-camp* to the general commanding, the Hon. Henry Fox, brother to the great Whig leader.

He returned to England on the evacuation of Minorca at the peace of Amiens in 1802. He became second captain in 1804, and in 1805 commanded twelve guns under Lieut.-General Don, forming the advanced corps of the army destined to serve under Lord Cathcart in the north of Germany, combined with the Russian Army under Count Tolstoy. They advanced as far as Hanover, when the result of the Battle of Austerlitz put an end to the campaign, and the army returned home, their unmolested embarkation being stipulated for by the treaty of Presburg.

He immediately effected an exchange in order to join Sir John Stewart's force employed against the French in Sicily, where he arrived shortly after the Battle of Maida. On Sir John being relieved by General Fox, Captain Gardiner again joined the staff of the latter, and when General Fox returned home, he was appointed *aide-de-camp* to Sir John Moore.

In 1807 the army left Sicily for the purpose of landing in Portugal; but, being detained by contrary winds, only reached Lisbon to find that the Royal family, whose cause they were to have assisted, had sailed for the Brazils, and the force returned to England.

Early in 1808, when Sir John Moore was named to the command of the expedition to Sweden, he repeatedly applied to Lord Chatham, then Master General of the Ordnance, to be allowed to take Captain Gardiner on his personal staff, but the regulations of the corps at that time did not allow of staff employment for artillery officers from home stations. On Sir John's departure for Sweden, Captain Gardiner again exchanged for active service, and joined the army assembling at Cork under Sir Arthur Wellesley. He landed with it at Mondego Bay, and advancing from Lavaos on the 10th August in command of a half-battery, was engaged at Roleia on the 17th, and in the crowning victory over Junot at Vimeira on the 21st, followed by the capture of Lisbon, and convention of Cintra.

Sir John Moore having relieved Sir Arthur Wellesley in Portugal, Captain Gardiner was called to headquarters as brigade-major of artillery, and participated in the prolonged struggle commencing on the 24th December at Benaventi, and ending on the 15th January, 1809, at Liego, called the Corunna retreat. After witnessing the death of his much-loved friend and general, he returned to England, and was immediately appointed brigade-major to the artillery commanded by Brigadier-General John M'Leod, with Lord Chatham's Army of the Scheldt. He was present at the capture of Middleburg and Flushing, and returned with the expedition to England in 1810, having been prostrated by the Walcheren fever.

Three months later he effected a third exchange for active service, and joined the division of the Peninsular Army under Sir Thomas Graham. The monotonous defence of Cadiz was relieved by the expedition to Gibraltar, terminating in the Battle of Barossa, in which his battery bore a conspicuous part.

In November, 1811, he was promoted to first captain, and in February, 1812, proceeded to join the main body of the army under Lord Wellington before Badajoz. He was mentioned in Lord Wellingtons despatches for his services in the trenches, and received a brevet majority in April, 1812. In May he joined a field battery with the first division, and commanded it through the campaign, in the Battle of Salamanca, and at the capture of Madrid. At the siege of Burgos, he volunteered with several of his men for the trenches, and took part in the operations till the siege was raised, when he resumed his field duties throughout the arduous movement and frequent engagements from 28th October to the 19th November, known as the Burgos retreat.

While in winter cantonments he was nominated to the command of E (afterwards D) troop, Royal Horse Artillery (now A battery, B brigade), which he immediately joined, and marched into Spain with Lord Dalhousie's division. In June, 1813, he was attached to the Hussar brigade, and was engaged with them, and mentioned by Lord Wellington, at Morales. The chief actions in, which he took part in the triumphal march through Spain and France were Vittoria, the affairs in the Pyrenees from the 27th to 30th July, Orthes (for which he received a lieutenant-colonelcy), Tarbes, and Toulouse. Proceeding through France, after the peace, he embarked at Calais for England in June, 1814, and was shortly afterwards created Knight Commander of the Bath.

During the corn riots in 1815, Sir Robert Gardiner's troop was stationed in the gardens at Carlton House, and remained there till the mobs dispersed on the news of Napoleon's escape from Elba.

Landing with his troop at Ostend in April, 1815, he was again attached to the Hussar brigade. His troop was most severely pressed in covering the left of the army on the retreat from Quatre Bras on the 17th, and took part in the great battle of the 18th, and in the capture and occupation of Paris.

Returning home in January, 1816, Sir Robert was suddenly called upon to change the life of camps for that of a Court. On the marriage of the Princess Charlotte of Wales with Prince Leopold of Saxe-Coburg, he was selected for the post of principal equerry. On His Royal Highness accepting the throne of Belgium in 1831, Sir Robert continued to reside at Melbourne, on the Claremont estate. He was military *aide-de-camp* to George IV., William IV., and to Her Majesty, until he attained his general's rank in 1841. In 1848 he was appointed governor and commander-in-chief of Gibraltar, and his public service terminated with that appointment in 1855.

He had become colonel-commandant of the 4th battalion Royal Artillery in 1853, and had advanced to the Grand Cross of the Bath in 1855. In 1864 he was gazetted colonel-commandant of B brigade, Royal Horse Artillery. He received the Order of the Guelph for his services in Hanover, and the Russian Order of St. Anne for Waterloo. While at Gibraltar Her Majesty the Queen of Spain sent him the Grand Cross of Carlos III., but the regulations of the service precluded his wearing the decoration. He held a distinguished service pension, and had the gold medal and clasps for Barossa, Salamanca, Vittoria, Orthes, and Toulouse, the silver war medal and clasps for Roleia, Vimeira, and Corunna, and the Waterloo medal.

Sir Robert married in 1816 Caroline, eldest daughter of Lieut.-General Sir John and Lady Emily Macleod, of which marriage two children survive (1865)—Colonel Lynedoch Gardiner, Assistant Adjutant-General, R.A., and Emily, married to Major George Frend. The general died at Claremont, 26th June, 1864.

In April, 1859, a reorganisation of the Royal Artillery took place, and the battalions, now called brigades, moved in bodies instead of detached companies. The 1st brigade, under Colonel Dalton, having, after a severe course of battalion and gun drill, become most efficient as garrison artillery, was sent to Gibraltar, where it has ever since performed all the necessary garrison duties; and is ready, should circumstances require it, to emulate the deeds performed by the old 2nd battalion in 1782.

CHAPTER 4

The Royal Artillery in the East Indies

The want of artillery during the wars on the coast of India from 1746 to 1754, and the impossibility of forming a sufficient number on the spot, induced the Court of Directors of the East India Company to obtain and send out a company of the Royal Artillery; and when the war broke out in 1755, three companies were raised for service in India, and sent out with the reinforcements under Clive to Bombay, and were afterwards distributed among the Presidencies.

The first company that left England for India was commanded by Major John Goodyear, and formed part of the force under Admiral Boscawen, which sailed in November, 1747. Arriving at the Mauritius in June, 1748, preparations were made to attack that island; but the enemy appearing so well prepared to oppose them, the idea was abandoned, and the fleet set sail for the coast of Coromandel. Arrangements were at once made to besiege Pondicherry, the principal settlement of the French in India; and the army being landed, commenced its march towards that fortress on the 8th August.

It was necessary, before reaching Pondicherry, to reduce the fort of Ariancopang, which, unhappily, was found to be of much superior strength than had been reported.

It was attacked, however, and our force was compelled to retreat; but not till they had lost 150 men, and amongst them some of the best officers of the army.

Major Goodyear, of the artillery, commanded in this unfortunate attack, and was mortally wounded, his left leg being taken off by a cannon-ball. This was a loss the army could ill sustain, as he was the person on whom Admiral Boscawen chiefly relied for conducting his operations against Pondicherry.

It was resolved to continue the attack against Ariancopang, and the siege guns were landed from the fleet. The engineers having built a battery, the fire from which had not the least effect upon the enemy's works, the officers of the artillery offered to erect another battery; this they completed in less than twenty-four hours, and opened on the fort with considerable effect.

An explosion took place in the fort on the 20th August, when the enemy retreated to Pondicherry, the British taking possession of the ruins. They sat before Pondicherry on the 30th; and on the 30th September, finding they had made little or no impression on the works, it was determined to raise the siege, and the army began to march back towards Fort St. David.

Forty-three artillerymen died or were killed on this expedition.

Forty men of the Royal Artillery arrived at Madras with the 39th regiment (*Primus in Indus*), and in the arrangements made for retaking Calcutta, after the "Black Hole" massacre in 1756, it was intended that the guns sent from Madras should have been worked by these artillerymen; but the colonel of the 39th regiment, (Aldercon) under whose command they were placed, refused to allow them to go, unless he accompanied them with his regiment. Calcutta was taken, however, after a short cannonade from the shipping, and arrangements were at once made to protect the captured city.

A fortified camp, with outposts around it, was formed about a mile from the town; and towards the end of January, 1757, the artillery arrangements were completed by the arrival of the field artillery under Captain Barker.

****

Captain Barker afterwards Sir Robert Barker: was transferred to the Bengal Artillery in 1762, and was afterwards commander-in-chief of the East India Company. He resigned that post, and returned to England in 1773.

****

Three companies were raised for service in India on the 1st March, 1755, but only two of them (Maitland's and Hislop's) had reached that country, the third having been lost in the *Doddington*. This ill-fitted vessel sailed from England on the 23rd April, 1755, and on the 17th July, when about 230 leagues off the Cape, she struck and foundered; and the whole of the crew and company of artillery, numbering 370 persons, with the exception of 23 who were thrown upon a barren rock, perished. Among the saved there were but three of the Royal Artillery, John Lister, Ralph Smith, and Edward Dysoy, mattrosses. They supported themselves on this rock by picking up relics from the ship, and by fishing, for nearly six months, when, having built a boat, which they named the *Happy Deliverance*, they set sail for the Cape, which they reached in safety in March, 1756.

One of the companies of Royal Artillery, under Captain Tovey, was employed on board the bomb-ketches of Admiral Watson's fleet, which destroyed the forts and ships of the pirate Angria in 1756.

In 1758 the French, under Conflans, were defeated by an army under Colonel Forde, which in the following year captured Masulipatam.

Captain Hislop's company was attached to this army, and was the last of the Royal Artillery who served in Bengal, until the breaking out of the recent mutiny. Hislop died at Woolwich on the 28th December, 1779; but his name, and that of his sons, will ever be remembered in India. The eldest, William, a captain-lieutenant in the Royal Artillery, died of his wounds at Cundapoor on the 13th February, 1783; and the youngest, the late Sir Thomas Hislop, was created a baronet for his services in that country. He died at Charlton in 1843.

On the 9th February, 1759, a force, consisting of 850 Europeans and 1,500 *sepoys*, commanded by Captain Richard Maitland, of the Royal Artillery, embarked at Bombay to proceed against the town and citadel of Surat, held by the Seydees.

Landing at Dentilowry, nine miles from the point of attack, they encamped or several days to make preparations for the siege. The garrison was driven inside the walls of the fortress by the end of February; and on the 4th March the citadel surrendered. Captain Maitland died in India in 1763.

A company of the Royal Artillery, and 30 of the Madras Artillery, commanded by Major Robert Barker, R.A., took part in the expedition against Manilla in 1762. On this occasion the officers of the artillery and engineers exerted themselves in a manner that nothing but their zeal for the public service could have inspired.

By the skill and management of Major Barker, and the officers under him, our guns were served with such accuracy and dexterity, that the twelve pieces the Spaniards had opposed to them were silenced in a few hours, and the men driven from them.

The directors of the East India Company having determined to augment their troops on the Bengal establishment, were desirous of having officers from the King's Artillery to promote their service; and also, cadets from the Woolwich Academy. Many officers of the Royal Artillery were accordingly transferred to command the newly-formed companies of the Bengal Artillery.

The second company of this distinguished corps, raised in 1758, was placed under the command of Captain Broadbridge, R.A. This officer, after distinguishing himself with his company in the operations at Patna, died in 1761.

In 1768 Major T. D. Pearse, of the Royal Artillery, was transferred to the Bengal Artillery as lieut.-colonel, and nominated to command the corps. Owing to some mistake on the part of the authorities, he did not assume the command until the following year, when it was vacated by the death of Colonel N. Kindersley, (October 28, 1769), also an officer from the Royal Artillery.

Colonel Pearse was the first professionally educated artillery officer who entered the Company's service. He entered the Royal Military Academy at Woolwich in his fifteenth year; and in June, 1757, received his commission in the Royal Artillery as lieutenant-worker. He served on the coast of France, at St. Malo, Cherbourg, etc., in 1758, Martinique and Guadaloupe in 1759, Belleisle in 1701, and Havannah in 1762; and, as he states in a letter to a friend, "though not at the head, he was in the heat of every attack."

This distinguished officer held the command of the Bengal Artillery for twenty-one years. He was an intimate friend of Warren Hastings, and was honoured with the confidence of Lord Cornwallis; and to him is mainly due the organisation and efficiency of that honourable and distinguished corps, of which he may justly be styled "the father." Before his time, it was a common practice to make any midshipman who was discontented with his ship an officer of artillery; it was also necessary for an officer in this corps to be what was at that time known as a "gentleman"—that is, in plain terms, a drunkard, a gambler, and a sportsman—in fact, what at the present day (1865) would stamp a man the "blackguard."

It was under such circumstances that Colonel Pearse took the command, and he at once set to work to improve the moral condition of the regiment.

To weed out the inefficient from the officers, to teach the remainder and the new comers their duty, to introduce a proper internal economy and discipline into the ranks, and to obtain proper control over the *matériel* of the regiment, were his first duties. He had a number of young officers from the Royal Artillery transferred to the corps, whose example had a beneficial effect, both on their brother officers and their subordinates.

****

Lieutenants Alexander Leith, Thomas Lee, and Francis Wood were among the officers transferred from the Royal Artillery to the East India Company's service at this time.

****

Steadily did Colonel Pearse pursue his object through difficulties and disappointments, but he was rewarded ere his death by seeing the corps raised to as high a state of discipline and efficiency as any in His Majesty's service. In a letter to General Pattison, dated November, 1774, speaking of the conduct of the corps at a review before General Clavering, he says:

> The performances at the review would not have been a disgrace to dear old Woolwich.

His affection for the old corps was ever undiminished, as the following extract from another letter to General Pattison, dated 21st March, 1783, will show:—

> How happy should I be had I never gone away from your command . . . . At last you are at the head of us—us, I say, for I still claim a right to enrol myself in the Royal Regiment, which, and its commander, God preserve.

Colonel Pearse held a command under Sir Eyre Coote (with whom he was no favourite) in the campaign against Hyder Ali. He was wounded at Cuddalore in June, 1783. In the *British Indian Military Repository* (1823), the services and letters of Colonel Pearse while on this campaign occupy about 300 pages.

Being on duty at a fire in Fort William, Calcutta, on the night of the 9th March, 1789, while under the influence of mercury, it is supposed he was seized with a fatal illness, as none of his correspondence can be found subsequent to the 11th March. He died on the 15th June, and was buried with the highest military honours in the great burial-ground of Calcutta; a handsome pillar, of the Corinthian order, was raised to his memory at Dum-Dum.

In the year 1791 a detachment was raised of volunteers from the battalions of the Royal Artillery, for service in the East Indies. Two companies were thus formed, and a staff, consisting of a major, adjutant, and quartermaster, was appointed to accompany them. Major David Scott was the officer commanding this detachment; Captain T. Ross, Lieutenants R. Clarke, J. Hunter, W. Nicolay, and C. Gold were among the subordinate officers. They left Woolwich early in the year, arriving at Madras in October.

They served under Lord Cornwallis at the defeat of Tippoo Sultan's army, 1792, and at the subsequent of Seringapatam. (The artillery, though present at the capture of Tippoo's fortified camp, on the night of the 6th February, 1792, were without guns. It is not evident in what capacity they served, but most probably as sappers).

While the fortress was being invested the Royal Artillery had to deplore the loss of Major Scott, who died on the 9th February.

A treaty having been concluded with Tippoo, the siege was stopped, and the army dispersed. At this time Lieutenant Gold, assisted by Lieutenant Hunter (died May 18, 1792), made sketches of the principal objects that attracted their attention, particularly of those poor infatuated creatures who, in devotion to their gods, subjected themselves to horrible tortures, such as remaining in painful or ridiculous positions, etc. Happily this is not very prevalent in India at the present day (1865); but at the time of which we are speaking, Christianity had made but little progress in that vast empire.

Neither had these customs been much illustrated in England; so that when Gold (Hunter died May 18, 1792), published these sketches under the title of *Oriental Drawings*, they were considered valuable additions to our knowledge of the Hindoos.

Lieutenant Nicolay had been attached to Lord Cornwallis's staff as an engineer; and in November, 1792, he was transferred as lieutenant to the Royal Engineers. He afterwards served in the West Indies under Sir John Moore and Sir Ralph Abercrombie; and as lieut.-colonel of the staff corps at Vimeira and Corunna.

In 1815 he was at the Battle of Waterloo, and was afterwards appointed governor and commander-in-chief of Dominica and other West India Islands, and lastly of the Mauritius. He died a lieut.-general and a knight, at Cheltenham, on the 2nd September, 1842, aged seventy-one years.

The two companies were present at the siege and capture of Pondicherry in 1793, and at the conquest of Ceylon in. 1795. They went to the Cape in 1796, and from thence returned to England.

Ceylon being now under the British crown, it was determined that three companies of the Royal Artillery should form part of the force in that island; accordingly, in the years 1799-1800 six companies were raised, which, added to the two already established for service in the East Indies, formed the 6th battalion of the regiment.

The first companies sent to Ceylon were commanded by Captains R. E. H. Rogers, P. W. Colebrooke, and E. V. Worsley.

****

Colonel Paulet Welbore Colebrooke died at Shooter's Hill, September 29, 1816, from the effects of disease contracted in the service of his country in Ceylon. He possessed a truly benevolent heart and comprehensive mind, and supported a lingering, painful illness with the greatest firmness, never shrinking from his duty.

Edward Vaughan Worsley lived to be a lieutenant-general and colonel-commandant of the 5th battalion. He died at Cheltenham, August 14, 1850.

****

It was in Captain Rogers's company that Alexander Alexander, whose adventurous though miserable life was published by Blackwood in 1830, served the greater part of his time. Being rather better educated than most of his companions, he does not appear to have been, able to suit himself to their society, but to have passed the most miserable existence possible, fancying every duty a degradation, and every non-commissioned officer a bear. His services in the Royal Artillery are not worth mentioning; but he gives an insight into the way a company passed its time in Ceylon, and a few words about the officers composing it.

> Captain Rogers, though a severe disciplinarian, was very fond of his company, and did all in his power for their comfort. He was a very active officer, whose whole mind was bent on the good of the service. He lost his wife and two children at Ceylon in 1804, and obtained leave to go to England to recruit his health and spirits; but he reached no further than Madras, where he took the fever and died, on the 6th June, 1804.

> The command of the company then devolved (temporarily) on Lieutenant C. G. Alms, who, according to Alexander, knew not the names of half a dozen men of his company, though he served with them upwards of ten years. (Lieutenant C. G. Alms died at Jersey, 29th December, 1832).

> At the end of six months the company was taken over by Captain C. F. Napier—a smart, active man, of strict and correct principles—who did all in his power for the encouragement of morality and the suppression of vice. Captain Napier was promoted to major in January, 1813; and died, while on his passage home from Ceylon, on the 21st March following.

In 1806 two companies, under Lieut.-Colonel Colebrooke, were attached to the brigade under General Maitland, that was sent from Ceylon to quell the mutiny which had arisen among the soldiers of the company at Vellore.

This was the last time the Royal Artillery served on the mainland, until the breaking out of the recent mutiny.

In 1811, detachments of the Royal Artillery, under Captains Byers and W. Colebrooke, were sent from Ceylon to Java, and served with distinction in the batteries erected against Corneilius.

The fire commenced on the 24th August, but was not very successful. Three or four guns were dismounted in our batteries; and Lieutenant Patton and several artillerymen killed. As the commander-in-chief was proceeding to the front during the cannonade, he met an artilleryman going to the rear by himself, with only one arm, the other having been carried off by a cannon-shot. This noble fellow stopped when he came abreast of the general, and deliberately saluted him with his remaining arm.

On the 25th our superiority of fire became evident; and the place was soon afterwards assaulted and captured.

They afterwards served at the siege and capture of Jokjakarta (Djocjocarta). The following extract from the despatches is sufficient to show the services of the artillery on this occasion:—

Captain Byers, with the Royal Artillery, Captain Rudyerd, and the Horse Artillery (Madras) were all conspicuous for the same gallantry and zeal; and the commander of the forces communicates his thanks to Captain Byers for his active exertions in joining Lieut.-Colonel Macleod's detachment with the ordnance stores; and the same approbation is also due to Captain Colebrooke of the Royal Artillery, whose activity has more than once been noticed. Captain Byers and Lieutenant Black rendered effectual assistance to Lieut.-Colonel Macleod in blowing open the Prince's Gate with one of the Horse Artillery This valuable corps is always conspicuous when its services are required.

★★★★★★★★★★

Captain Colebrooke later Sir William Colebrooke. This officer served many years In the East. Besides the expeditions above mentioned, he was engaged in the campaigns of 1817-18-19 in Southern India, and was also present at the capture of the Arab fortresses, Ras-el-Kyma and Zaya, which were taken by a small force, under Sir W. G. Keir, in 1819-20.

~~~~~~~~~~

The following year saw this company of the Royal Artillery engaged at Palembang, in Sumatra. This was the last service of the corps in Polynesia.

At the end of the war the artillery force in Ceylon was reduced to two companies, and eventually to one; and this was the only portion of the Royal Artillery stationed in the East.

In November, 1834, while Colonel J. A. Clement, with two companies under Major Moore and Captain Scott, was in Ceylon, a fearful hurricane passed over the island, doing considerable damage, especially in the Colombo district. Heavy rains also set in, and the rivers overflowed, destroying whole villages, and desolating the country for miles round. One village, four miles from Colombo, was completely deluged, the inhabitants being obliged to erect scaffolds and climb the highest trees, to save themselves from drowning; and to subsist on the produce of the trees and what they chanced to take with them.

A bridge of boats, called "the Grand Pass," that crosses the river near this village, was under the superintendence of Corporal Wilson, R.A., who, in his exertions to save the bridge, was struck on the leg by a raft of timber, and very much hurt. Colonel Clement, hearing of the disaster, at once sent Gunner R. Martin to assist him. Going by the road for three miles, Martin came to the water, and was about to swim to the bridge, when he was prevented by an officer of the Ceylon Rifles, who obtained for him a canoe and two natives to assist him. They soon reached the side of the river, which at the time was running out at the rate of ten miles an hour. The night was very dark and wet, and having no hopes of finding the bridge till daylight, they lashed the canoe to a cocoa-nut tree, and remained all night in the storm.

On arriving at the bridge early in the morning, Martin found Corporal Wilson very ill; he would not leave his post, however, but remained in one of the boats giving his orders. The water was rising rapidly. The bridge being composed of forty-two boats, a native was placed in each to assist with the planks, while Martin took charge of those at each end, letting out the moorings as required. This continued for nine days during the most violent hurricane, the waters increasing meanwhile.

On the 9th November, twenty-seven of the Cingalese who had taken refuge in the trees were rescued and placed in the boats; where, after remaining three days (during which the flood abated), they were landed and supplied with food by the governor, the whole of their dwellings and property having been destroyed. The artillerymen, fortunately, had seven days' provisions with them, or they must have suffered equally with the natives; whose shrieks, when they began to be oppressed by hunger, were most painful to hear.

The officers of the Royal Artillery who rendered assistance to the natives during this catastrophe were Lieut.-Colonel Clement, Lieutenants Dechamps and Williams, (later Sir W. F. Williams of Kars).

During the time that Moore's and Scott's companies were in Ceylon they suffered fearfully from cholera and dysentery.

Captain George Jones and Lieutenant Edward Tindal both died at Trincomalee—the former on the 25th April 1829, and the latter on the 26th March, 1831. These officers, with twenty-two men of Scott's company, one sergeant, thirty-two rank and file, and two drummers of Moore's, made, with Lieut.-Colonel Clement, who died on the 10th June, 1838, a total of sixty of the Royal Artillery who fell victims to the pernicious effects of the climate of Ceylon.

Sunday, the 10th May, 1857, will never cease to be remembered in India.

An outbreak, for some time contemplated, broke out at Meerut in the afternoon of that day. The grievance of the greased cartridges was indeed urged; but a combination had been for some time forming, and the name of the King of Delhi, over eighty years of age, was imagined to be a tower of strength in the endeavour about to be made to restore the supremacy of the Mogul dynasty. Scenes of the most heartrending description occurred, and officers, ladies, and even children, fell victims to the brutality of the *sepoys*.

Outbreaks occurred at Allahabad, Jhansi, Lucknow, Cawnpore, and other places; the European women and children in many of large cities were cruelly used and murdered, while the several mutinous regiments all made for Delhi, hastening thither, as a central point, from all quarters, and committing the greatest outrages by the way. The whole of the available troops were immediately collected and marched to Delhi, which withstood a siege of upwards of three months before it fell into the hands of the British.

The Royal Artillery took no part in this remarkable siege, but their gallant comrades of the Indian service, now of the Royal Artillery, earned for themselves imperishable fame.

The garrison of Lucknow being hemmed in and besieged by another army of the mutineers, a force was hastily collected by Brigadier-General Havelock, whose efforts to relieve the beleaguered garrison will be a glorious page in England's annals till the end of time. None of the Company's artillery being obtainable for this force, orders were suddenly despatched to Ceylon for the only company of Royal Artillery in the East Indies, that branch of Her Majesty's army having for years past ceased to do duty on the mainland.

Captain F. C. Maude, Lieutenant Maitland, four sergeants, nine corporals, thirty-nine gunners, and one trumpeter were accordingly despatched to the scene of action. They embarked on board the *Semiramis*, at Trincomalee, on the 7th June, and arrived at Allahabad in time to take the field early in July.

★★★★★★★★★★

The whole of Havelock's force did not exceed 1,400 men. It was composed of artillery (including 22 of the Bengal Artillery) 77; Madras Fusiliers, 376; 64th regiment, 435; 78th Highlanders, 284; 84th regiment, 190; and Volunteer Cavalry, 20.

★★★★★★★★★★

The mutineers, numbering about 3,500, occupied a strong position at Futtehpore, which was reached by Havelock's force on the 12th July. Pushing forward two of their guns, the enemy commenced a cannonade on the British front, while a body of infantry and cavalry threatened the flanks. They found our troops ready to receive them. Astonished by the precision of the guns under Captain Maude, and the deadly aim of the Enfield rifles, they fell back upon Futtehpore in disorder, leaving three of their cannon. They were eventually compelled to take flight, abandoning twelve guns.

Havelock continued his march upon Cawnpore, and on the 15th July was twice engaged with the mutineers, first at the village of Aong, and next at the bridge over the Pandoo Nudee. Successful in both instances, the column pushed on, and on the following day defeated Nana Sahib in his final stand before Cawnpore. When this miscreant saw that nothing could withstand the advance of the avenging column, he gave directions on the 17th for the massacre of all the English women and children, in his power, and with a savage barbarity caused their bodies to be thrown down a well.

Early on that morning a heavy explosion was heard, caused by the enemy setting fire to the magazine of Cawnpore, when Nana Sahib was withdrawing thence upon Bithoor.

Cawnpore was at once occupied, and the troops were horrified on discovering traces of the late massacre. The capture of the *Nana's* palace at Bithoor was effected without firing a shot, and twenty guns were taken. The British column crossed the Ganges on the 25th July, and on the 29th they encountered and defeated the rebels at Onao and Busheergunje.

Cholera having broken out amongst his troops, Havelock was obliged to fall back upon Cawnpore. Before he reached that city, however, he was engaged with the rebels on three occasions—twice at Busheergunje and once at Bithoor—each time defeating them with great slaughter. Having had the benefit of a month's rest, and being reinforced by Sir James Outram with the 5th Fusiliers, 90th regiment, two batteries of the Bengal Artillery, and the 12th Native Irregular Cavalry, Havelock again advanced on the 21st September, once more defeating the enemy in his old position at Numghowar.

On the 22nd the troops marched fifteen miles in a perfect deluge of rain, and continued their advance on the following day, till they came up with the enemy strongly posted at the Alumbagh, an isolated building to the southeast of Lucknow, from which they were driven and pursued nearly to the canal of the city.

Our troops halted on the 24th, and marched to the assault of Lucknow on the following morning.

Across a bridge, the entrance to the city, the enemy established a battery of four guns, including one or more heavy ones, and the houses behind it were loopholed and full of riflemen. For a while Maude's light field battery, posted on the road, endeavoured to silence the enemy's guns, but after a number of his gunners had fallen, it was found necessary that the infantry should advance. For his services on this occasion Captain Maude was decorated with the Victoria Cross. Havelock, in his despatch, says:

> This officer steadily and cheerily pushed on with his men, and bore down the desperate opposition of the enemy, though with the loss of one-third of the artillerymen.

Sir James Outram adds:

> That this attack appeared to him to indicate no reckless or foolhardy daring, but the calm heroism of a true soldier, who fully appreciates the difficulties and dangers of the task he has undertaken; and that but for Captain Maude's nerve and coolness on this occasion, the army could not have advanced.

From one of Maude's guns nearly all the gunners were shot away; their places, however, were quickly supplied by volunteers, among whom was conspicuous Private Joel Holmes, of the 84th regiment, his noble bearing and gallant conduct, under a murderous fire, winning for him the admiration of the whole army, and subsequently the Victoria Cross from his sovereign.

The enemy's battery was taken, the guns thrown into the canal, and the column fought its way through the streets, and the enemy's batteries, to the Residency, where H-M.'s 32nd regiment was valiantly defending the English women and children who had taken refuge there.

Havelock's army, however, was not able to relieve the beleaguered garrison; and the addition of his troops to the exhausted defenders, however necessary in a military point of view, was most inopportune, as the provisions in the Residency were already insufficient to sustain the lives of those within it for many weeks longer.

In the passage through the city the force had been compelled to abandon several ammunition-waggons which could not be dragged along. The carriage of one of our small howitzers also having been broken, it was abandoned; but another, taken from the enemy, was substituted by Captain Maude.

On the 29th three sorties were made against the surrounding batteries of the enemy. The enemy could be seen in one spot firing heavily from the ground-floor of a mosque, where they were protected by intervening buildings from our fire. Lieutenant Maitland, Royal Artillery, placed a 9-pounder in position, and with admirable precision (in three shots, at a distance of 400 yards) brought down both the minarets of the mosque, which fell in ruins on the head of the enemy.

During this time the cry for help had reached England, from whence troops were hastily despatched in great numbers. A considerable force of artillery, under Major-General J. E. Dupuis, including four troops of the Royal Horse Artillery under Colonel D. Wood, was among these reinforcements.

Two companies of the Royal Artillery were sent to India from China as soon as the news of the rebellion reached that country; Colonel Crawford, with his adjutant, Major Barry, and detachments from the companies under Major Pennycuick, arrived at Calcutta from Hong Kong on the 1st September, and the remainder, under Captains Longden and Middleton, in October. Captain Hardy's company, from the Cape of Good Hope, arrived about the same time; and was quickly followed by Captain Freeth's (under Major Le Mesurier), from the same place.

Great jealousy was exhibited on the arrival of the Royal Artillery in India by nearly everybody except those really concerned—the artillerymen of the Indian service; the English newspapers, especially, tried all in their power to foster an ill feeling between the officers of the Royal Artillery and those of the Bengal, Madras, and Bombay Artilleries. They failed in this, however, the Royal Artillery being received with open arms by their brethren in India, and treated by them with the greatest kindness on all occasions.

The correspondent of the *Illustrated London News* before Delhi, in a letter dated September, 1857, says:—

> The electrifying success of the Royal Artillery under Havelock has called forth mild comments from the sister arm of Bengal, who, with honest rivalry, look forward to the arrival of a branch of the Royal service, hitherto strangers in Hindostan.

(On the departure of Colonel Radcliffe from Calcutta for England, in January, 1859, the officers of the Bengal Artillery gave a ball in his honour.)

The three batteries from China and the Cape joined the army under Sir Colin Campbell, which marched from Cawnpore for the relief of Lucknow on the 9th November. By a rapid march they joined on the same day the column under Brigadier-General Grant, which had been engaged several times with the rebels, and which was also hastening towards Lucknow, when they halted for three days. The remainder of the company of Royal Artillery from Ceylon, commanded by Captain F. J. Travers, was attached to the force under General Grant.

On the 12th November Sir Colin advanced on the Alumbagh, which was captured in the evening, and on the 15th began his remarkable advance into Lucknow.

For three days our troops were making their way through the palaces and gardens of Lucknow (now converted into fortifications) towards their comrades in the Residency, fighting every inch of the road.

In the meanwhile, the garrison within the walls were not inactive. When the advance sounded, the effect was electrical; pent up for six weeks, and subjected to constant attacks, the soldiers felt that the hour of retribution had arrived. It was impossible to withstand them, and in a few minutes the whole of the buildings were in their possession, were armed with cannon, and steadily hold against all attacks.

Maude's men worked at a mortar battery, the shells from which burst well in the buildings occupied by the enemy's riflemen, who were soon dislodged.

The Royal Artillery under Colonel Crawford (died at Rome, March 6, 1862), and the Bengal Horse Artillery under Captain Blunt were most warmly engaged during the advance of the 15th, 16th, and 17th, on which occasion Sir Colin Campbell said:—

> It was highly agreeable to me to be present when the Bengal and Royal Artillery were brought into action together.

Captain Middleton's battery rendered important service during the advance of the 16th, being ordered into action close to the Shah Nujjeef, a building about to be assaulted by the infantry. With loud cheers, the drivers waving their whips, the gunners their caps, they galloped forward through a deadly fire to within pistol-shot of the wall, unlimbered, and poured in round after round of grape. Rockets were afterwards brought into play, which caused the enemy to abandon the post.

Captain Whalley Nicoll Hardy was killed, and Major Pennycuick, Captain Travers, Lieutenants W. D. Milman (died at Calcutta, December 20, 1860), A. Ford, and Surgeon Veale were wounded. Sergeant-Major Hemsley, a deservedly respected non-commissioned officer, received a severe wound on this occasion; he suffered amputation of his leg, and afterwards died on his passage to England, in April, 1858.

The garrison being finally relieved on the 17th, Sir James Outram and Sir Henry Havelock came out to meet Sir Colin Campbell and conduct him into the Residency.

By a series of masterly arrangements, the women and children and the sick and wounded were removed from the Residency unknown to the enemy. A fire was opened on the Kaiserbagh on the 20th, and while the foe was led to believe that an immediate assault was contemplated, the army was being quietly withdrawn. So ably was this movement carried out, that the mutineers were completely deceived, and, instead of following, they commenced firing on the old positions many hours after they had been quitted by the British.

The whole army arrived at the Alumbagh on the 26th, on which day that gallant and beloved soldier, General Havelock, whose duty was now completed, fell a victim to dysentery.

Sir Colin Campbell, leaving a portion of his army in the Alumbagh, under Sir James Outram, including Maude's company of artillery, marched on the 27th November for Cawnpore.

General Windham, who had been left in command of that station, attacked one of the enemy's divisions on the Pandoo Nuddee on the 26th November, routed them, and captured all but one gun. Next morning, however, the enemy being reinforced, they returned to the attack forced the British within their lines at Nuwabgunge, and burnt down the camps of three regiments.

On the 28th the renewed attempts of the enemy were triumphantly defeated.

Major-General Dupuis and the officers of his staff were engaged in these operations. On the 27th, the only battery that could be brought up was a hastily-equipped one of ten pieces, drawn by bullocks, and manned by people of different services and nations, *viz.*, men of the Royal Artillery, seamen of the *Shannon*, Madras and Bengal gunners, and Sikhs. Those manned by the Royal Artillery were brought into action by Lieutenant Oliver; but General Dupuis, noting the extreme youth of that officer, and considering that he had never before been in action, directed his *aide-de-camp*, Captain D. S. Greene, to take command of the battery.

General Dupuis commanded during a part of the action, while General Windham went to inspect, personally, the condition of matters at the entrenchments, upon which the army was subsequently obliged to retire.

It will be evident that the success of the enemy, although they fought well, especially with their artillery, was due rather to their immense superiority in numbers of men and guns than to any other cause.

During the night Colonel Adye, the assistant adjutant-general of the Royal Artillery, with Captains Austin and Bradford, of the Bengal Artillery, volunteered and brought from the centre of the town a 24-pounder, which had been left behind in the retreat, in consequence of its having been jammed in one of the narrow streets.

On the following day Colonel Adye again volunteered and took command of the same gun (manned by a few sailors and Madras gunners), and placed it in a position to protect the canal, where it proved of good service during the day. The fighting on the 28th was very severe; on the left advance the Rifles, supported by Captain Green's battery and part of the 82nd regiment, achieved a complete victory over the enemy, and captured two 18-pounder guns.

The glory of this well-contested fight belongs entirely to the above-named companies and artillery.

Sir Cohn Campbell, having arrived at Cawnpore on the 6th December, attacked the rebels (who had received an addition of four regiments from Oude and the followers of Nana Sahib), and after a severe battle utterly routed them, and compelled them to disperse. The Royal Artillery engaged in this battle were the batteries of Sir Colin Campbell's army under Colonel Crawford, and those at Cawnpore under Major-General Dupuis, with the addition of Captain Smith's battery, newly arrived from England.

During this battle, two batteries under Captain Longden and Lieutenant Millman, both commanded by Captain Middleton, were detached with a force under Major-General Mansfield, for the purpose of taking a position called the Subadar's Tank. They succeeded in silencing the enemy's fire, when he was attacked by the infantry and compelled to retreat.

Brigadier-General Grant, with a body of troops, including Millman's battery, and Remmington's troop of Bengal Horse Artillery, under Captain Middleton, marched on the 8th December to attack a position occupied by the enemy at Serai Ghat, about twenty-five miles from Cawnpore.

The enemy was discovered on the following morning, when General Grant at once ordered up the battery. The road under the banks of the river was of such a dangerous nature, from the quick-sands, that the heavy 9-pounders, drawn by tired horses, ran great risk of being altogether stopped; and it was only through the hard exertions of Captain Middleton, Lieutenant Millman, and the men of the battery, that the guns were got through. A portion of the battery having got over this difficulty, and on to the dry bank of the river, they soon got into position; and, under a very severe fire from thirteen pieces of the rebel artillery, Lieutenant Millman brought his guns into play. Though the fire of grape from the enemy was falling among the artillery like hail, the only casualty in the battery was one horse killed. This was truly marvellous and providential.

The troop, with the remainder of the battery, now came up, and in half an hour's time the enemy was completely silenced and in full retreat, leaving fifteen guns, fifteen waggons, and 1,000 rounds of ammunition in the hands of the British.

In the early part of 1858, the several divisions scattered about the country were employed in dispersing the rebels or forcing them upon Lucknow, with a view of subsequently uniting their forces against that stronghold.

Colonel D. Wood, C.B., with Major Anderson's troop of horse artillery and Lieut.-Colonel Gordon's field battery, was attached to the force in the Allahabad district, under Brigadier W. Campbell. Hearing that the rebels were assembling at Secundra, Brigadier Campbell marched on the 5th January with two regiments and Gordon's battery, for the purpose of dispersing them. The guns, drawn by bullocks, were with difficulty brought into action; and the quick retreat of the rebels on the approach of the infantry left no opportunity for the service of the battery. They followed in pursuit, however, and fired with effect into the village of Syrepore, where many of the rebels were taken.

The army now halted to refresh, when they were joined by the mounted gunners of Major Anderson's troop, who rendered great service as cavalry during this day.

An hour afterwards the enemy, 1,200 strong, advanced to attack Campbell's rear. Gordon's guns were immediately brought into action, while Anderson's troop effectually cut on the enemy's retreat on the left, killing about 150, and driving the remainder on to the guns and infantry. This troop was now divided; a portion, under Colonel Wood, scouring the neighbouring villages to the left, and the remainder, under Major Anderson, was ordered to pursue a force under Naib Nazam, who was making the best of his way to Secundra. They did not overtake the body of this force, but killed about 100 of the enemy who were following in the rear—their own loss being only two horses killed and five wounded.

Major Anderson's troop afterwards joined General Grant's division, and served at the capture of Meangunje on the 23rd February, arriving before Lucknow on the 27th.

Walpole's division, including Gibbon's and Smith's batteries of Royal Artillery, arrived the same day.

The main body, under Sir Colin Campbell, marched from Cawnpore on the 23rd February, and arrived at the Alumbagh on the 1st March. Here they were joined on the 5th by the field force under Brigadier Franks, which had marched 130 miles, during which four actions had been fought at Chanda, Ameerapore, Secundra, and Sultanpore.

Colonel Maberly, with two companies of the Royal Artillery under Captains Middleton and Thring, arrived with this force, making a total of two troops and eight companies of the Royal Artillery before Lucknow.

The whole of the artillery at this siege was under Sir Archdale Wilson of the Indian Artillery—the field batteries being commanded by Colonel D. Wood, and the siege train by Colonel G. R. Barker, of the Royal Artillery.

Royal Horse Artillery, Lieut.-Col. L. D'Aguilar.
- F Troop, Major Anderson.
- E Troop, Captain Yates.

Royal Artillery
- Major Maude .... 3rd Co. 8th Batt.
- „ LeMesurier . 3rd Co. 14th Batt.
- Captain Gibbon .... 5th Co. 12th Batt.
- „ Middleton .. 6th Co. 13th Batt.
- „ Longden ... 5th Co. 13th Batt.
- „ Thring .... 2nd Co. 8th Batt.
- „ Smith .... 7th Co. 14th Batt.
- „ Goodenough . 6th Co. 11th Batt.

Sir James Outram was withdrawn from the Alumbagh, and having crossed to the left bank of the Goomtee on the 6th March, he at once pushed on to turn the first line of works abutting on the river; and on the morning of the 9th attacked the position, driving the enemy before him at all points, until he was enabled to occupy the Fyzabad road, and plant his batteries as to enfilade the works on the canal. The Royal Artillery which crossed the Goomtee consisted of D'Aguilar's (Yates') troop, Gibbon's and Middleton's batteries, and a siege train under Colonel Riddell.

While this attack was made by Outram along the left bank of the river, a very heavy fire was kept up on the "Martiniere," both from the mortars and heavy guns. It was stormed on the morning of the 10th, when the guns were brought up to play on Banks' House, which was also stormed and carried at noon. By means of these buildings, the artillery was enabled to pour a double fire on the Kaiserbagh; Outram attacking it on the right, and Sir Colin on the left.

On the 11th a large block of the palaces, called the "Begum Kotee," was shelled and breached by the batteries, and at 4 p.m. was carried by the infantry. Other buildings, including the Secunderbagh, were taken on the 12th; and on the 14th the Emambara and the Kaiserbagh were carried. Lieutenant Warren, with a detachment of the Royal Artillery, accompanied the infantry into the Kaiserbagh, and turned two of the enemy's guns upon them with good effect.

On the 10th Lieutenant Tracey, of the Royal Artillery, was wounded; and on the 13th Lieutenant Cuthbert particularly distinguished himself by putting out a fin in front of his battery, in a very exposed and dangerous position.

Some loose powder being observed lying about in the Kaiserbagh, after its capture on the 14th, Major Barry, with the assistance of some men of the Royal Artillery, greatly exerted himself in trying to prevent accidents. Unfortunately, however, some of it caught fire, when an explosion took place, and Major Barry, Gunner James Tucker, and others (including Shoeing-smith George Lever, who died from the effects), were severely burnt.

On the 16th a fire was kept up against the Residency until the advance of the infantry, when the howitzers and mortars were moved forward, and a heavy fire was maintained during the night upon the city.

The rebels were now put to flight, pursued on one side by Brigadier Grant, and on the other by Brigadier Campbell; but it was not till the 21st March that Lucknow was completely in our possession.

Several accidents occurred during the occupation of the city by the British; among those by which the Royal Artillery suffered may be mentioned the case of Corporal William Shaw, who accidentally shot himself with his carbine on the 21st, and that of Shoeing-Smith James Farrell, who was killed by the falling of an archway on the 22nd.

This great siege was now at an end, and the troops were dispersed. D'Aguilar's troop. Gibbon's, Maude's, and Goodenough's batteries, remained in Lucknow; Anderson's troop, Longden's and Middleton's batteries, were despatched to the Upper Provinces; Le Mesurier's to Cawnpore, Thring's to Benares, and Smith's to Futteghur.

The last was engaged at Kunhur on the 7th April, on which occasion the only gun the enemy had was taken by Lieutenant F. A. Whinyates, R.A.

While the troops in Bengal were concentrating upon Lucknow, the columns in Madras and Bombay, under Major-General Whitlock and Sir Hugh Rose, were gradually sweeping the country before them, and compelling the mutinous bands to withdraw towards the line of the Jumna, where at Calpee and Gwalior they mustered strongly,

The Royal Artillery, under Sir Hugh Ease, was commanded by Captain Ommanney; and that under General Whitlock by Captain Pulmer. The former served at the assault and capture of Chundaree on the 17th March, and on the 21st arrived before the fortress of Jhansi—a place of great strength, both natural and artificial, and defended by a garrison of about 12,000 men, headed by a determined Amazon, the Ranee of Jhansi. Lieutenant R. Moresby, R.A., was the only officer killed at Chundaree.

Jhansi was stormed and captured on the 3rd April, on which occasion Bombardier Joseph Brennan greatly distinguished himself in bringing up two guns of the Hyderabad contingent, manned by natives, laying each under a heavy fire from the walls, and directing them so accurately as to compel the enemy to abandon his battery. He subsequently received the Victoria Cross.

The column under Major-General Whitlock gained a decisive victory at Banda on the 19th April. This battle, which lasted four hours, was fought in midday, the thermometer rising to 130 degrees in the shade; and of the deaths which occurred on this day more than two-thirds were from sunstroke.

Captain Palmer laid a gun which dislodged the Banda chiefs from their position, and, it was supposed, killed their principal leader, Mahtoob Ali. Captain Palmer's right hand is partially disabled from its long exposure to the sun on that day.

This force, now united with that under Sir Hugh Rose, moved towards Calpee, which they obtained possession of on the 23rd May.

In the meantime, Major-General Roberts, with the artillery under Colonel Price, R.A., had assaulted and captured the town of Kotah, and hunted the rebels in the West Provinces.

During this campaign there were many separate columns, which afforded officers greater opportunities to distinguish themselves than in ordinary cases. So various were the military operations, that it is almost impossible to condense them into one connected whole. We will therefore content ourselves by making mention of those operations conducted by officers of the Royal Artillery.

After the capture of Lucknow, Sir Archdale Wilson left the army, when the whole of the artillery force was placed under the command of Colonel (later Sir David) Wood, K.C.B. When the army was broken up, this officer was appointed to command the station and fort of Allahabad, and carried on successful operations against the rebels in that part of the country.

Colonel (afterwards Sir George Robert) Barker, K.C.B. commanded a column which defeated the rebels at Jano, and subsequently assaulted and took the fort of Birwa. Sir George Barker died at Simla on the 27th July, 1861, aged forty-three years.

Colonel P. P. Faddy, R.A. commanded, as brigadier, the column detached from the Saugor field force, which defeated the rebels at Keutee in Bundelcund on the 4th March, 1859. Captain N. S. K. Bayly commanded a small force (including his company of Royal Artillery temporarily commanded by Captain A. W. Johnson) sent from Kurrachee to reduce a fort on Beyt Island in April 1858. The attack was unsuccessful. Captain Bayly was dangerously wounded, and the casualties in the company of artillery were numerous and severe.

It was taken in 1859 (on which occasion 100 men of the Royal Artillery, under Lieutenant Wortham, were engaged), the captors subsequently securing the neighbouring fortress of Dwarka.

The mutiny may be said to have ended with the capture and execution of Tantia Topee, the rebel leader at Calpee, etc.; but it was not till the summer of 1859 that the last embers of the rebellion were extinguished.

In 1859 the several companies of Royal Artillery in India were formed into three brigades (the 11th, 13th and 14th); and in 1862 the artillery of the East India Army was incorporated into the Royal Artillery, the Bengal, Madras and Bombay regiments of horse artillery becoming respectively the 2nd, 3rd, 4th and 5th horse brigades of Royal Artillery, and the battalions of foot artillery forming from the 16th to the 25th brigades of the Grand Corps.

CHAPTER 5

Wars of the French Revolution

It has been the general policy of England to abstain from interfering in the civil commotions of other countries; but the fierce and ignorant fanatics who, after the execution of Louis XVI., assumed the government of France, proclaimed to the world their purpose of assisting all parties who in any foreign country would imitate their example.

As a measure of self-protection, it became necessary to prepare for war with revolutionary France, whose armies were marching with all possible haste into Germany and Holland; the latter country England being bound by treaty to assist.

The French Convention, with one voice, declared war against England, on 1st February, 1793; when an army under the Duke of York was at once sent to Holland.

The campaigns in Holland and the Netherlands during this and the following years did not bring much glory upon England; but the individual prowess of her soldiers was still the same, and among those who distinguished themselves were many officers and soldiers of the Royal Artillery.

The command of the artillery of the Duke of York's army was bestowed upon Major (afterwards Sir William) Congreve; but the regiment did not move *en masse*, being divided among the infantry;—the guns, properly speaking, were under the officer commanding the regiment to which they were attached; but the immediate control of them was held by a captain or subaltern of the Royal Artillery.

****

Sir William Congreve entered the Royal Artillery as lieutenant-fireworker in 1767. He was remarkable for his scientific attainments, and having for his conduct in the American war received the rank of major, he at once took upon himself to propose many reforms in the professional instruction of both officers and men of the regiment. Among other things, he drew the attention of the Board of Ordnance to the necessity of causing both officers and men to be instructed and practised in the several systems of moving heavy ordnance, such as would be absolutely necessary in the field, and which had been hitherto entirely neglected. Though meeting with much opposition from the subordinates in office, he was fortunate enough to receive the patronage of Lord Townshend, the then master-general, by whom he was introduced to the king. Hence the establishment of the Royal Military Repository.

It was originally in the Arsenal, but in 1804 the model-room was burnt down, and, the ground not being considered convenient for the drill of the men, a piece of ground was shortly afterwards purchased on the side of the common from a Mr. Noble, who leased it under Sir Thomas Wilson, the wealthy proprietor of Charlton parish. Both the Prince of Wales and the Duke of York were greatly attached to Major Congreve, and on the breaking out of the war the latter applied for him to command the artillery of his army. At the conclusion of the war, he was created a baronet, retaining, however, his appointment as superintendent of the Royal Military Repository and comptroller of the Royal Laboratory. He died by his own hand, at Charlton, April 30, 1814, having reached the age of seventy-three years.

The Details of the Rocket System Employed by the British Army During the Napoleonic Wars by William Congreve is republished by Leonaur.

★★★★★★★★★★

The guns attached to the Guards rendered great service during the attack at St. Amand, on the 8th May. They were placed upon the road, and by a well-directed and well-supported fire, kept the battery that was opposed to them in check, and did considerable execution, enabling the Coldstreams to advance. General Dampierre, the French commander, lost his leg by a cannon-ball, and died the next day.

On the 25th May the siege of Valenciennes began—the first battery being opened By Captain G. Cookson. This officer also commanded the artillery in the trenches during the successful storming of the covered way and hornwork, under Sir Ralph Abercrombie, on the 25th July. The garrison surrendered on the 28th, and the Duke of York at once hastened to the assistance of the Prince of Orange at Menin.

Having effected his deliverance, the English Army marched towards Dunkirk, and a desultory sort of warfare continued for the remainder of the campaign. In the action at Lincelles, on the 18th August, where twelve pieces of the enemy's artillery were captured, Lieutenant Depeyster and one gunner were killed, and at Lannoy (October 28th)

Lieutenant Thorton lost his arm.

★★★★★★★★★★

The young officer, Depeyster, received his commission in the Royal Artillery for his voluntary services with the corps during the war in America.

Lieutenant Thorton, afterwards Lieut.-General Sir Charles Wade Thorton, *aide-de-camp* to William IV., lieut.-governor of Hull, etc.; died in London, April 6, 1861, aged ninety.

★★★★★★★★★★

While these events were passing, a fierce conflict was raging at Toulon, that city being held by the British in the name of the royal family of France. Lord Mulgrave arrived in that garrison with troops from Italy, and was shortly afterwards followed by General O'Hara and some reinforcements from Gibraltar, including a company of artillery under Major Koehler. The forts were bravely defended, and the guns were ably manned; but there was a sad deficiency in artillerymen, and seamen from the fleet were landed to assist them. Koehler was seconded by some able officers—Brady, Lemoine, John Duncan, Newhouse, and Alexander Duncan; but an abler one appeared in the French artillery in the person of Napoleon Buonaparte: it was owing to a suggestion of his that the English were at last compelled to quit Toulon.

A severe bombardment was sustained by the garrison from the 15th to the 30th November, during which time the loss in artillerymen was very great. At Fort Mulgrave Lieutenant John Duncan was so essentially useful, that to his exertions and abilities that fort was much indebted for its preservation for so long a time. He was ably assisted not only by his own men, but also by all whose duty led them to this important defence. (He died in London, March 19, 1803).

Private Samuel Myers, of the Military Artificers, was particularly conspicuous in his exertions. At one of the guns all the artillerymen were either killed or disabled, and the gun was consequently silent, though in a position to do much service. Observing this, Myers repaired with some volunteers to the battery and manned the gun. For a considerable time, he laid and fired it himself, with a precision and effect that checked the fierceness of the enemy's cannonade, and attracted the notice of the general.

On the 30th November the garrison made a sortie and spiked a great number of the enemy's guns. They were intercepted by Buonaparte, however, on their return to their batteries; which they did not regain without great loss, particularly that of their commander, General

O'Hara who was wounded and taken prisoner. Buonaparte was himself wounded, as was also the senior lieutenant of the British artillery, Charles J. Brady. The latter died of his wounds on the following day.

By the middle of December, the evacuation of Toulon was decided on. On the 18th the sick and wounded and the field artillery were sent off, and on the following day the troops began to withdraw. The security of the evacuation was effected by Major Koehler and the artillery, who kept up a heavy fire from Fort Mulgrave on the peninsula and after seeing the last man off the shore, spiked all the guns, and effected their own retreat without loss.

The fleet, with the troops, now set sail for Corsica. Major Koehler was sent on with Lieut.-Colonel Moore as a spy to obtain all necessary information as to the state of the island. The artillery was commanded by Lieutenant John Duncan, of whom General Dundas said:

> More zeal ability, and more judgment were never shown by any officer than were displayed by him.

The troops were landed at San Fiorenzo, in Corsica, in February; and in April a force under Captain Nelson, of the navy, laid siege to and captured Bastia, one of the strongholds in possession of the French. In June the remaining fortress, Calvi, was invested by Nelson's force, and after a siege of two months—during which our men suffered greatly from a pestilential fever, and died by hundreds—the French surrendered, and the British became complete masters of the island.

The Royal Artillery took part with Nelson's *Agamemnons* in these sieges; but as there was only the remains of one company on the island, their services were necessarily second to those of the brave seamen. Koehler was promoted to lieut.-colonel, and appointed quarter master-general to the forces in Corsica: the command of the artillery was then assumed by Major William Collier, who died on the island in July, 1796.

Hostilities were resumed in Flanders as soon as the severity of the winter had subsided. On the 17th April a general and successful assault was made on the enemy's positions at Vaux and other places, on which occasion great service was rendered by Captain Boag and Lieutenant Page, and the detachment of artillery under their command. They were thanked in general orders by the Duke of York for the able and spirited manner in which they conducted the battery entrusted to their care.

On the 26tn the British completely defeated the French, who

had taken up their position in the village of Troisvilles, from which they were dislodged by a well-directed fire of 26-pounders under the command of Lieut.-Colonel Congreve. Thirty-five pieces of cannon were the fruits of this victory, with 300 prisoners, including General Chapuy, the French commander.

On the 16th May the whole allied force made a forward movement. They drove the French before them for two days; but on the 18th they made a determined stand, surrounded the British with an overwhelming force, and obliged the Duke of York to resort to the daring alternative of retreating through the enemy's line, which he accomplished, but with great loss. The French hussars charged the battery under Major Wright, captured the guns, and cut down most of the artillerymen. Major Wright himself was killed, and Lieutenants Downman and Boger were wounded and taken prisoners. (Boger died at Ramsgate, September 3, 1851).

The sufferings experienced by our army in Holland during the winter of 1794-5 may be compared to the retreat of the French Army from Moscow. Without shelter, without sufficient food or clothing, and constantly pursued and attacked by the French, during a severe Dutch winter, they were still brave, patient, and enduring. They repeatedly turned during their retreat and drove the enemy back with great slaughter. But on the 11th January Pichegru attacked them in a defile betwixt Arnheim and Nimeguen, with a force of 70,000 men. They fought their way through, however, and succeeded in reaching the Elbe, where they embarked for England.

They suffered greatly in the last engagement, and among the wounded were Lieutenants Legg and Walker. The latter received three wounds—one in the right and above the elbow, another below the elbow, and the other in the right hip. (Later Lieutenant-General Walker, colonel-commandant of the 6th battalion, died February 3, 1857. His son, became the commander of the forces in Scotland, served with distinction in the Crimea, and was severely wounded at the Battle of Inkerman).

During this and the following years the Royal Artillery were employed in the gun and mortar boats which were attached to the fleets sent to annoy the French. In 1801 a detachment under Captain Fyers served at Copenhagen and Boulogne. At Copenhagen Fyers was appointed acting engineer to the force by Sir Hyde Parker, and at Boulogne he was slightly wounded.

****

Captain Peter Fyers was the son of the chief engineer in Scotland, and was born in Edinburgh Castle in 1769. He received his commission in 1793, and was engaged in Holland in the following year. After the above-mentioned services he again served in Holland in 1814, where he greatly distinguished himself. In the action at Merxem, a gun laid by him silenced a battery of several guns of the enemy, which threatened the flank of the 78th, then advancing to drive the French out of the village. For this service he was thanked in general orders and decorated with the C.B. He died major-general, at Charlton, on May 17, 1846, aged seventy-seven.

****

The following is an extract from Nelson's despatch relating to the attack on Boulogne:—

> The officers of artillery threw the shells with great skill, and I am sorry to say that Captain Fyers is slightly wounded in the thigh by the bursting of an enemy's shell. The whole of the affair is of no farther consequence than to show the enemy they cannot with impunity come outside their forts.

As soon as the news of the war reached Barbadoes preparations were made for offensive operations; and as the island of Tobago had been taken from the British in the late war, it was thought now to be a first object to retake it. Accordingly, on the 12th April, 1792, a small force, accompanied by artillery, embarked on board the *Trusty*, and on the 15th, after a short action, took possession of the island. This was the first of the numerous struggles that took place in the West Indies consequent on the declaration of war by the French Convention.

Early in the year 1794 a force under General Sir Charles Grey was despatched against the French islands of Martinique, St. Lucia, and Guadaloupe. The troops landed at Le Cul de Sac Marin, in Martinique, on the 5th March, drove the French back on every point, and established batteries on Mount Mathurin; here two howitzers, served by a party of seamen under Captain Duvernet of the Royal Artillery, demolished the works of the enemy on the Pigeon Isle; when two French companies, after receiving a heavy fire of shot and shell, surrendered. (Duvernet died at Ringmer, in Sussex, October 23,1806). By this success Fort Royal was opened to our fleet.

Prince Edward, the father of Her present Majesty, (1865), held a command in this army. The brigade of guns attached to his division was commanded by Lieutenant Brooke Young—a gallant officer who, at the storming of the Fleur D'Epée, Guadaloupe, took with his own sword an ensign, which he presented to H.R.H. This officer enlisted as a volunteer into the Royal Artillery in April, 1776, and served at Saratoga, where he was wounded and taken prisoner. In 1779 he was exchanged, and returned to England; and on the 17th March, 1780, he was presented with a commission.

At the siege and surrender of Fort Bourbon, Martinique. April 23rd, Lieutenant E. W. Pritchard was wounded by the bursting of a shell, but he recovered in time to take part in the unsuccessful defence of Basse Terre, Guadaloupe, in the following June.

The forts and French capital of St. Domingo surrendered to the British during this summer.

The French had, however, by the end of this year, succeeded in arousing the black population of nearly the whole of the West India Islands to a general revolt against the British. The yellow fever broke out also in most of the islands, and carried off great numbers of the English troops.

In the island of Grenada, the insurrection commenced on the 2nd March, 1795, and so unexpectedly that the governor was made prisoner, and, with more than forty of the English inhabitants, cruelly murdered. The Royal Artillery in this island had suffered dreadfully from the pestilential climate during the last two years. (No fewer than five artillery officers died at this station: Captains Scott and D'Arcy, Lieutenants Swinney, Watkins, and Tomilson); and at the time of the insurrection were but few in number, and were under the command of Captain Joseph Walker of the Royal Irish Artillery. The rebels were complete masters of the island until about the end of June, when they were routed with considerable slaughter.

On the 10th March the Caribs in St. Vincent, at the instigation of the French, who supplied them with arms, ammunition, &c, broke out in open revolt, and on the 13th obtained possession of Dorsetshire Hill, one of the posts in the island. There were at this time but twenty-seven artillerymen in the island, commanded by Captain Lawrence Newton, (died at Woolwich, April 8, 1805). These, however, occupied a post on Sion Hill, annoyed the enemy considerably, and kept them greatly in awe.

A small detachment of three or four, under Sergeant Robert Taylor, (appointed second lieutenant in the Invalid Battalion in 1808), was employed with the inland field force, which routed all the detached parties of the rebels: they were engaged eleven times, and took part in the assault and capture of Duvalle's stronghold, on the 26th April.

Captain Newton, with four 6-pounders and two small mortars, manned by artillerymen and sailors, marched with the division under Lieut.-Colonel Leighton, which captured the port of Vigie, in June. Three months afterwards the French landed in the island, and Colonel Leighton's small force was obliged to retire to Kingstown—the capital.

A reinforcement was at once sent over from Martinique, including a company of artillery under Major Duvernette; and after a sharp contest at the Vigie on the 1st October, the enemy abandoned the post; when the Caribs, deserted by their French allies, were compelled to surrender.

During this year the yellow-fever spread its fearful ravages through the whole of the islands, and carried off no fewer than six officers of the Royal Artillery and a proportionate number of non-commissioned officers and men. Captain Suckling, Lieutenants Mackenzie, Concannon, Le Geyt, Pritchard, and Stackpoole were the officers in 1795.

The latter caught the fever under most painful circumstances. He was stationed at Guadaloupe, where the artillery was particularly affected; and seeing his friend Lieutenant Bingham in a high state of delirium, crying out to be rescued from the flames into which he imagined himself to be cast, caught him in his arms, regardless of his personal danger from contagion, and carried him with all possible speed to a pond, and pitched him in, but as quickly snatching him up again and taking him back to bed.

****

The late Colonel Charles Cox Bingham, father of Captain George Bingham, and Colonel Charles Bingham, the late adjutant-general of artillery, died at Woolwich, June 4, 1835, aged sixty-two. The Binghams are descendants of an ancient family of Melcomb, in Dorsetshire; their pedigree, traced from John de Bingham, knight (reign of Henry I.), is to be found at in Hutchins's *History of Dorsetshire*. The most notable among their ancestry are Robert de Bingham, Bishop of Salisbury, and Sir Richard Bingham, Marshal of Ireland, the conqueror of Brian O'Rourke and MacGuire (1590). He died at Dublin in 1598, and his remains were brought over and interred in Westminster Abbey, where a monument is erected to his memory. It is in the south aisle, near the well-known tomb of Sir Cloudesley Shovel. The father of Colonel C. C. Bingham was colonel of the Dorsetshire Militia, and the late Lieutenant-General Richard Bingham and Sir George Rideout Bingham (who commanded the 2nd battalion of the 53rd regiment during the Peninsular campaigns) were his brothers. Captain George Bingham, R.A., died at Ceylon, November 10, 1850, and Colonel Charles Bingham at Brighton, April 6, 1864. The latter, in his capacity as adjutant-general of artillery, was universally known and equally respected, from the commander-in-chief, to whom he was a most devoted servant to the private soldier, of whom he was a sincere friend.

★★★★★★★★★★

The medical officer having come to see Bingham, now ordered him to be well rubbed from head to foot and covered with blankets. A profuse perspiration was the result, and Bingham's life was saved. Stackpoole's exertions, however, were fatal to himself, for he caught the infection and fell a victim to his friendship.

In 1796 the fever raged with unabated fury, and no fewer than fourteen officers of the Royal Artillery succumbed to its effects, six of whom died in St. Domingo.

★★★★★★★★★★

Officers of the Royal Artillery who died in the West Indies in 1796:— Major S. D. Edwards (on passage home), August 22; Major F. L. Deruvijnes (of wounds), June 12; Captain. John Arbuthnot, October 27; Captain-Lieutenant Mark Pattison (St. Lucia), October 24; Lieutenant Samuel Baker (St. Lucia), October; Lieutenant William Robinson (Martinique) September 2; Lieutenant M. R. Ommanney (St. Kits), November 17; Captain John Rogers (St. Domingo), June 30; Captain-Lieut. Henry Deruvijnes (St. Domingo), June 7; Lieut. Caddy William (St. Domingo), June 17; Lieut. S. S. Carterell (St. Domingo), June 28; Lieut. Francis Worth (St. Domingo), May 9; Lieut. Leonard Arthur (St. Domingo), July 16; Lieut. William Davers (St. Domingo), August 24.

★★★★★★★★★★

Sir Ralph Abercrombie's army, the artillery of which was commanded by Major J. Smith, was now scouring the whole of the West Indies; and at the end of the campaign, we held the islands Martinique, St. Domingo, Trinidad, St. Lucia, Guadaloupe, Tobago, and Curaçoa, all of them having been taken from the French; at the same time retaining our own islands—Jamaica, Barbadoes, St. Vincent, St. Kits, Grenada, Antigua, Dominica, etc. etc.

In 1801, being then at war with Holland, we took the Dutch islands of St. Eustatia, Martin, and Saba. A small force under Colonel Slant, including two guns and a detachment of the Royal Artillery under Lieutenant James Brown, embarked at St. Kits, and effected a landing at St. Eustatia on the 21st April, when immediate possession was taken.

In 1798 a force under Sir Eyre Coote was sent to Ostend to destroy the ships and sluices of Bruges Canal, the object being to prevent the embarkation of the French Army which threatened to invade England at that port.

Two companies of the Royal Artillery, under Captains W. H. Walker and W. Wilson, embarked on this expedition, and were distributed on board the fleet as follows:—

Captain William Hood Walker as commanding officer, and Lieutenant C. C. Clifton as *aide-de-camp* to Sir Eyre Coote, with the headquarters on board the *Expedition*.

Captain Wilson, Lieutenant James Simpson—one 6-pounder, one 5½-inch howitzer, and detachment on board the *Circe*.

Captain Charles Godfrey—one 8-inch howitzer and detachment; *Vestal*,

Lieutenant William Holcroft—one 6-pounder and detachment; *Druid*,

Lieutenant Philip Hughes, Bombardier Graham—one 6-pounder, one 8-inch howitzer, and detachment; *Ariadne*,

Lieutenant Courtney Ilbert and detachment; *Hebe*,

Bombardiers Levens and Platt—one 6-pounder and ammunition; *Harpy*,

Bombardier Cassie—one *fusee*; *Minerva*,

On the evening of the 18th May the fleet approached the Flemish shore, and before daybreak on the following morning the troops landed on the sand-hills, three miles east of Ostend.

The gates and sluices were destroyed by the enemy, and a speedy retreat to the ships was inevitable; but an overwhelming force from Ghent, Bruges, Dunkirk, and other places prevented this, and the British accordingly took up a position on the defensive.

They passed the night on the sands, exposed to a heavy rain, and at daybreak on the following morning they saw the enemy advancing towards them. A severe action of two hours' duration ensued, during which the artillery behaved well, particularly the detachment under the command of Captain Wilson, (afterwards General Sir Wiltshire Wilson: died at Cheltenham, 1842). Captain Walker was severely wounded, and died at Ostend three days afterwards.

The force was soon overpowered, and the survivors surrendered themselves prisoners of war. The artillery were confined in the garrison of Lisle; all the officers, however, were allowed home on parole, except Captain Godfrey, Lieutenants Clifton and Ilbert, who stayed to see justice done to the men and to take charge of them.

To favour the operations of the Russians and Austrians, who were allied against the common enemy—France—a British Army, under Sir Ralph Abercrombie, was sent to Holland: it landed at the Helder, and being joined by a Russian force, the command was taken by the Duke of York.

In addition to the companies of Royal Artillery under Lieut.-Colonels Whitworth and Smith, a troop of Horse Artillery under Major Thomas Judgson accompanied this expedition; this being the first time any portion of that branch of the regiment was sent on service.

****

Lieut.-Colonel Whitworth, Sir Francis Whitworth, second son of Sir Charles Whitworth, and brother to Lord Whitworth. Died in London, January 26, 1805.

Lieut.-Colonel Smith, afterwards Sir John Smith.

Major Thomas Judgson retired 1805; died June 25, 1814.

****

The utility of a corps of horse artillery, and the advantages to be derived from it having been proved by all the Continental powers, a brigade of four troops was formed in 1793, which was attached to, and indeed formed part of, the Royal Regiment of Artillery.

Judgson's troop is memorable rather for its misfortunes than for its services on this expedition. At the action of Egmont-op-Zee, on the 2nd October, it was charged by the 10th French dragoons, who behaved with astounding bravery. Our guns fired, thinning their ranks; but, undaunted, they dashed on, cutting down our gunners, and carrying off in triumph two of the guns.

But this success was short-lived; for some squadrons of the 7th and 11th Light Dragoons, with Lord Paget at their head, suddenly issuing out from a recess between two sand-hills, charged them at full gallop. The French cavalry, wholly incapable of sustaining the shock, were either cut to pieces or rushed into the sea to avoid the British sabres, A small proportion, favoured by the approaching darkness, effected their escape; leaving, however, not only the captured guns, but others belonging to their own horse artillery.

The allied troops having engaged the French at the Zyp, Bergen, etc., without any satisfactory results, a convention was entered into in October, by which the British left the country and restored 8,000 French and Dutch prisoners then in England. (Lieut. James Simpson,

R.A., wounded at Zyp, died on passage home in October. Lieut. Eligèe, R.A., was wounded and taken prisoner at Bergen).

Towards the end of the year 1708 a military mission was sent from England to co-operate with the Turks against the French, who had by that time gained a strong footing in Egypt. The command of this mission was entrusted to Lieut.-Colonel Koehler, of the Royal Artillery—an officer of great experience in the different branches of military science, and who had been at Constantinople on a former occasion, and made himself acquainted with the language and manners of the Turks.

The local rank of brigadier-general was bestowed on Colonel Koehler; and Majors Hope and Fead, Captain Martin Leake, Dr. Wittman, and thirty non-commissioned officers and men of the Royal Artillery, in addition to Lieut.-Colonel Holloway and other officers of the Engineers, with a number of the Royal Military Artificers, were appointed to act under him.

General Koehler, Major Hope, and Major Fead, in company with Lieut.-Colonel Holloway and others of the mission, left England in December to proceed overland to Constantinople.

Their journey at this inclement season of the year was attended by uncommon severities. In passing over to the Continent they were shipwrecked at the entrance to the Elbe, among shoals of ice, and, to relieve themselves from their perilous situation, were under the necessity of passing over the ice a distance of two miles to gain the shore. They then prosecuted their journey, arriving at Constantinople in March.

Captain Leake, Dr. Wittman, and the main body sailed in the *New Adventure* transport, in April 1799, and arrived at Constantinople on the 14th June, where they were heartily welcomed by those who had preceded them.

The principal object of the mission was to give assistance to the Turks, and to show them the latest improvements in engineering and artillery. Major Fead was ordered to the garrison of St. Jean d'Acre, to which place he proceeded in a Turkish ship of war. Arriving at Cyprus, he was attacked with a malignant fever, and was taken on board Sir Sidney Smith's vessel, *Le Tigre*, and died in that ship on the 13th September.

On the morning of the 19th January, 1800, General Koehler, Captain Leake, and others of the mission, all of them equipped as Tartars, left Constantinople, and proceeded by land to Syria. They returned on the 6th of April, and on the 15th June the entire mission embarked for the seat of war in Syria. While on their passage they landed and surveyed the islands of Patmos and Cyprus, and arrived at Jaffa, the headquarters of the Turkish Army, on the 2nd July. The Grand Vizier being desirous of strengthening the port of Jaffa, General Koehler delivered plans for this purpose, and Colonel Holloway and the engineers at once proceeded to carry them into execution.

The situation of the British while in the Turkish camp was one of extreme peculiarity; they were so jealously watched by the Ottoman soldiers that their lives at times were in danger, and it was not considered safe for any of them to be alone. Notwithstanding, the British artillery had prayers every Sunday in the midst of the Turkish camp, and during the whole time they were attached to that army, were never molested or interrupted.

Staying in the midst of a filthy camp, threatened with every kind of disorder, and in a state of complete inaction, did not suit the British artillery officers, who, finding there was nothing for them to do at Jaffa, paid a visit to Jerusalem and other places sacred to Christians.

General and Mrs. Koehler, Major Hope, Captain Leake, Dr. Wittman, and three civilians composed the party.

In December a putrid fever broke out among the members of the mission.

The first attacked was one of the military artificers; he died on the 10th December. On the 13th Gunner Cowden of the artillery was seized, and died on the 18th. Mrs. Koehler, the wife of the general, was attacked on the 7th, and lingered on in great agony till the 14th, when she also died. So strong was the general's affection for his wife that it was with difficulty he could be separated from her corpse. He was seized in nearly the same manner on the morning of the 26th, when he quitted the encampment and went to Jaffa. The malignance of the fever, added to the melancholy into which he had been plunged by his recent loss, very speedily terminated his earthly career. He died on the evening of the 29th, and was buried on the following afternoon with military honours.

On the 16th the site of the encampment was changed, the British selecting an eminence covered with a white clear sand, and commanding a fine view of the sea. The hospital hut, with Gunner Cowden lying in it ill of the plague, was left at the old encampment. A party of Arabs, fearless of the disease, made an attempt to rob it, and were only prevented by the guard firing at them.

On the 25th February, 1801, to the great relief of the British, the camp at Jaffa was broken up, and the army began its march towards Egypt. On the 19th March the army, then at Gaza, was divided. Captain Leake and a number of the artillery being attached to the advance corps.

****

Captain, afterwards Colonel William Martin Leake, was born in London on the 14th January, 1777. He obtained his commission in the Royal Artillery in 1794, and commenced his professional career in the West Indies. His next service was that above recorded.

After the surrender of Alexandria and the withdrawal of the French, Captain Leake received the directions of Lord Hutchinson to accompany the late Mr. William Richard Hamilton (then private secretary to Lord Elgin) into Upper Egypt, for the purpose of making a general survey of that country, as well in regard to its military and geographical as to its political and commercial state.

The results of these labours were a map of the course of the Nile, from the Cataracts to the sea, a determination of most of the ancient sites, a description of all the monuments of antiquity contained in that space, together with a large collection of observations on the agricultural and commercial state of the country: an account of this journey was published by Mr. Hamilton in 1809. In 1802 Captain Leake revisited Syria, and continued there the researches on which he had been employed in Egypt; and on his return home, having embarked on board the vessel in which Mr. Hamilton was conveying the Elgin Marbles to England, he was wrecked off the island of Cerigo, and narrowly escaped with his life.

The acquaintance with Oriental politics and habits which he had acquired during this service was doubtless the cause of his subsequent selection for an important mission to the European provinces of Turkey. He received orders from His Majesty's Government to undertake a survey of the coasts and interior of that country, to examine its fortresses and means of defence, to point out their deficiencies to the native governors and chiefs, and advise for their improvement; and on that service he repaired in the year 1804.

From 1804 to the winter of 1806 he travelled considerably, in pursuance of his instructions, in Northern Greece and the Morea, and while he performed the important duties of his mission in a manner that gave entire satisfaction to the home authorities, his peculiar tastes and talents for research received full development in a country where every day's journey produced an historical or topographical problem, which it taxed his erudition and critical acumen to solve; and where his thorough knowledge of ancient Greek enabled him to decipher obscure inscriptions, which led to the identification of many a ruined site.

The occurrence of hostilities, at the end of 1806, between England and the Porte prevented him from prosecuting his travels. He was detained as a prisoner at Salonica, whence, however, he escaped; and finding his way to Malta, he proceeded to England for the restoration of his health. Subsequently he was again employed by His Majesty's Government in Greece till 1809; and it was on the observations made with so much keenness and perseverance during these years, from 1804 to 1809, extended by subsequent reflection and study, that were formed those valuable and standard topographical works that appeared so many years later, which, by their well-weighed arguments and accurate observations, have justly caused their author to be termed a *"model geographer"* and from this period also may be dated that partiality for the modern Greek people, that indulgence for their weakness, and that hope for their future, which afterwards inspired many of his lesser writings and coloured his conversation.

In 1814 Lieut.-Colonel Leake was, as an English officer, appointed to attend upon the Army of the Swiss Confederation, under the command of the Archduke John, and was for months at Berne, in that capacity, at the conclusion of the great European war. On his return to England his literary labours commenced, and were continued with little intermission, and but little farther interruption from his more purely professional duties (for he retired from the army in the year 1823), until the day of his death. In the year 1814 were published his *Researches in Greece*, in 1821 his first edition of the *Topography of Athens*, and in 1822 his edition of *Burckhardt's Travels in Nubia, Syria, and Arabia*. In 1824 he narrated the observations he made in Asia Minor twenty-four years previously. In 1826 issued the *Historical Outline of the Greek Revolution*, and in 1829 the *Demi of Attica*.

In 1830 he published one of his greatest and most learned works, accompanied by a valuable map, his *Travels in the Morea*, which in 1835 were succeeded by his *Travels in Northern Greece*, a work of equal research and more extensive proportions, with an accurate map on a considerable scale also; and in 1841 appeared the second edition of the *Topography of Athens*. The latter years of his life were occupied in the production of the *Nunmismata Hellenica*, a most considerable and important work, containing an exact and faithful description of every coin in his extensive collection, enriched by critical and historic notes. This was published in 1854; and in 1856, but a few weeks before his death, a supplement on the same plan as the original work, issued from the press, forming with that a mine of information for the collector, the antiquary, and the historical student, who in turn might find, as Colonel Leake himself had found, that the design on a coin could throw strong light upon many a question of ancient history or topography otherwise obscure or disputed. He died at Brighton on the 6th January, 1860, after a short and sudden illness; his intellect never weakened, his energies scarcely relaxed, notwithstanding the weight of eighty-three

****

Authority was given to Captain Leake to summon the garrison of Tineh and Salabieh, then in the possession French. He had no occasion to use his authority, however, for on their approach the French made a precipitate retreat towards Cairo.

To enable the army to cross the desert with greater facility, all the spare tents, heavy baggage, etc., with Gunner Foster of the Royal Artillery and the whole of the civil artificers, were embarked on board ship at El Arish. Leaving the Turkish Army and the British detachment on their march to Egypt, we must now turn our attention to the British Army under Sir Ralph Abercrombie, which by this time had made a footing in the same country, and was waiting the co-operation of the Grand Vizier.

The artillery of this army was commanded by Brigadier-General Robert Lawson—Colonel Thompson and Major Cookson commanding the divisions. (Brigadier-General Lawson afterwards lieut.-general and colonel-commandant of the 10th battalion. Died at Woolwich, February 25, 1816). The troops landed in the bay of Aboukir on the 8th March, when all the field pieces were landed after a plan of Major Cookson's, never before adopted; by this means they were ready for service, and consequently brought into action, as soon as, if not before, the infantry.

Having landed in spite of the attack of the French, the British proceeded to besiege the castle of Aboukir. The heavy artillery being placed in position, the bombardment commenced under the direction of Major Cookson, and on the 19th March the castle surrendered.

At the Battle of Alexandria, on the 13th March, the Royal Artillery had thirty-two light pieces and two 24-pounders in the field; but they were compelled, from want of draught, to remain almost stationary during the whole of the battle. Had any of our guns been well horsed, it is probable the fate of Alexandria would have been decided on that day. The only horses the artillery had were the refuse of the cavalry, whose best were only a set of hacks from Constantinople.

Lieutenant H. Sturgeon, J. S. Burslem, and D. Campbell were wounded during this action. Preparations were now made to reduce the forts of Rosetta, St. Julian, El Hamed, etc.

✯✯✯✯✯✯✯✯✯✯

Lieutenant H. Sturgeon was promoted into the staff corps
Lieutenant J. S. Burslem lost his right leg by a cannon-shot. Retired 1819; died at Sidmouth, April 24, 1861, aged eighty-one.
Lieutenant D. Campbell died at Edinburgh, July 14, 1849.

✯✯✯✯✯✯✯✯✯✯

On the 18th April a mortar battery erected against Fort St. Julian, under the direction of Captains Lemoine and Duncan, fired some shells with remarkable accuracy; one them pitched on the centre of the roof, and tore away the flagstaff and colours, which the French never dared to erect again. The fort surrendered on the following day.

General Hutchinson, now the commander of the British Army, hastened to join the Grand Vizier; but before he could accomplish this, he had to pass 4,000 French in a fortified camp at Ramanieh. A battle took place on the 9th May, and the French were compelled to take shelter their entrenchments.

During this engagement the British artillery remained firm, maintaining the contest until positive orders were brought them to retreat. An unfortunate chance shot took off the leg of Colonel Thompson as he was riding to the left. He died at Rosetta on the 8th June, exciting universal regret.

Captain Adye, placing his guns on the most eligible points, contended for some time, exposed as he was, with the superior weight of metal and the covered batteries of the French; but as General Hutchinson was not attacking the position. Colonel Stuart directed that Captain Adye should discontinue the cannonade and place his men out of fire. The fortifications at Ramanieh were eventually taken, and the army pushed on for Cairo. The exertions of General Lawson in forwarding the heavy artillery from Rosetta for the siege of Cairo proved most beneficial to the service as well as honourable to himself.

To return to the army of the Grand Vizier. After a troublesome, fatiguing, and hazardous march across the desert, they arrived before Cairo on the 30th April, when the *vizier* sent Major Hope, R.A. (with a view of reconnoitring), to summon the place. He was not admitted into the town, but was civilly treated, dining with the French officer at the outward guard. General Belliard refused to surrender, and the Turkish Army settled down at Elkanah, awaiting the arrival of the British.

On the 15th May the French Army came out of Cairo and attacked the Turks at Elkanah; but after a severe fight, which lasted seven hours, they were compelled to retire within the walls of the city. During this action. Major Holloway, R.E., and Major Hope, R.A., were in attendance upon the Grand Vizier, Captain Lacy, R.E., with, the infantry under Mehemmed Pasha, and Captain Leake, R.A., with the cavalry, under Tahir Pasha, and rendered every assistance in their power.

In the despatch from the British ambassador at Constantinople, the Earl of Elgin, it is stated that in the account which the *vizier* sent of the action to the Porte, His Highness speaks in the highest terms of the artillery, which "Major Hope is well known to be so very capable of directing."

The British Army arrived before Cairo early in June, and on the 4th Captain Adye and other officers went over to the Turkish camp to pay their respects to the *vizier* and to see their old friends of the Royal Artillery. The armies were now united, and the French general, Belliard, seeing that further defence was useless, surrendered Cairo on the 27th June.

Preparations were now made for the siege of Alexandria, the direction of which was entrusted to General Coote, the artillery being commanded by Major Cookson.

In the night of the 18th August, General Coote, with the unremitting exertions of the officers of the Royal Artillery, established two batteries, with mortars and 24-pounders in them, against Fort Mamton, and directed the bombardment to commence. The celerity with which the guns had been brought up was a remarkable instance of zeal, as they had to be carried over almost inaccessible rocks, from which vast quarries were hewn out, as is supposed, for the building of the ancient Alexandria.

On the 22nd August Menou made a final attempt to drive the British from before Alexandria, but having failed, he surrendered on the 27th; and thus the whole of the French Army in Egypt was vanquished and compelled to quit the country.

In General Coote's orders relative to the action of the 22nd August, he says:—

> The brunt of the day fell on the artillery, under the command of Major Cookson, and the advance corps, who used every exertion and showed much discipline.

An English Army of Occupation remained in Egypt until the signing of the treaty of Amiens (25th March, 1802), which closed the war between Great Britain and the French Republic.

CHAPTER 6

Africa—South America—Italy—Walcheren, etc.

As early as 1758 the Royal Artillery set foot in Africa. A detachment of the regiment under the command of Captain Walker accompanied the fleet which captured Senegal and Goree, the only French settlements on that continent. At the peace of 1762 the latter was restored, but Senegal was retained by the British, a detachment of the Royal Artillery remaining in the garrison. Of their particular services at this period, we have no account.

At the capture of the Cape of Good Hope in 1795, the services of the artillery were not very important. But their conduct here, as elsewhere, reflected the highest possible credit on themselves and the army generally. During the mutiny on board the fleet in 1797, their loyalty and their unremitted attention to their duties called forth the highest possible commendation from the commander of the forces. The following is a copy of the letter sent by General Dundas to Colonel York, the commanding officer of the artillery:—

Castle, Cape of Good Hope,
15th November, 1797.

Sir,—The corps of artillery having had the greatest part of the extraordinary duty which the late disturbance on board the fleet has occasioned, and as their alacrity in the discharge of their duty was no less conspicuous than on former occasions when the artillery had been called upon to act, I am desired by Major-General Dundas to express his entire approbation of their conduct,—honourable to themselves and to the service.

Peter Abercrombie, Major.

This colony was surrendered to the Dutch at the peace of Amiens, but in 1806 was again captured by an army under Sir David Baird. Colonel York, having the rank of brigadier-general, was appointed to the command of the artillery of this force, which consisted of three companies under Major William Spicer, (later Lieut.-Colonel, died at Exeter, January 21, 1813), Captain Alex. Watson, and Captain Francis Power (later Lieut.-Colonel, died at' Woolwich).

They embarked at Plymouth on the 1st August, 1S05, and proceeded to join the main body of the expedition at Cork. For the purpose of concealing the object of the expedition, the course of the vessels was shaped for South America, and after a tedious passage they arrived off the coast of Brazil, where, on the 1st November, the *King George* transport, having on board the staff and Captain Power's company of the artillery, ran on a shoal of rocks. The vessel soon became a total wreck, but after great exertion on the part of the crew, twelve chests of dollars were saved. Only three individuals perished, but of these Brigadier-General York was one; his loss at such a moment was severely felt.

Lieutenant James Gray (died a major-general in London, December 21, 1857), of the Royal Artillery greatly distinguished himself on this trying occasion; he saved several lives by his personal exertions, and was the last person taken from the rocks by the boats which had been sent to their aid from the *Leda* frigate.

The companies, now under the command of Major Spicer, arrived at the Cape in time to be present at the Battle of Blue Berg and the capture of the colony in January, 1806. In April, one of them embarked with General Beresford's army for South America. This expedition arrived at Buenos Ayres on 24th June, disembarked on the 25th, and marching against the enemy, who fled at their approach, entered the city on the 27th. The artillery, commanded by Captain J. E. Ogilvie, were only provided with four 6-pounders and two howitzers. The Spaniards, discovering the insignificance of the force which had surprised them, collected in sufficient numbers to make prisoners of them all.

Some fighting took place in the streets of Buenos Ayres before the city was surrendered, in the course of which Captain Ogilvie and his subaltern. Lieutenant Alex. Macdonald, were both wounded. (The former was assassinated while a prisoner of war, in the following January.)

In October a reinforcement arrived from the Cape, the artillery being commanded by Captain Alex. Watson, who had resigned an appointment and volunteered for this service. (He died at Brighton, August 11, 1849, lieut.-general and commandant of the 6th battalion). These troops landed and drove the Spaniards from Maldonada, where they took up their quarters and waited for reinforcements.

In January, 1807, a force under General Achmuty arrived from England, and after a sharp contest with the Spaniards, took possession of Monte Video. The news of the recapture of Buenos Ayres having reached England, an army under General Whitelock, to which was attached a troop of Horse Artillery under Captain (afterwards Sir Augustus) Frazer, sailed in March, 1807, and arrived at Monte Video in May. Upon the arrival of Captain Frazer and his troop, Captain Watson resigned the command of the artillery and served as *aide-de-camp* to Sir William Lumley; and when the troops left the country, he rejoined the company at the Cape. The whole history of this expedition is anything but creditable to those who took part in it. The artillery were hardly engaged at all, as the light guns they had were worse than useless.

A writer in the *United Service Journal* (1836), however, makes a bitter and very unjust attack on the artillery of this army. He first complains that the "officers in garrison had to give up their horses for the use of the artillery, who never fired a shot." We are quite sure that the fact of their not being engaged was more keenly felt by themselves than by any in the army, and it was not their fault if they had not been provided with horses.

He again complains that another officer and himself, with two hundred men, were ordered to assist in getting the guns out of the mud at Ensenada:

> On arriving at the spot, we found the drivers spurring and flogging away at the poor horses, neither accustomed to harness nor the dirty element into which they were forced, and they were repaying the kindness by kicking and plunging, making what footing was had still worse. After some arguments we persuaded these fellows to unharness the unhappy brutes, and we soon, whirled the guns to dry land, although, for any use they were afterwards, they might as well have stayed with the *naiades* of Ensenada.

Not content with hurting the feelings of the corps in general, this bitter, writer insults the memory of one of the most amiable of men and most honourable of officers, who, at the time these remarks were published, had only been dead a year. He proceeds;—

SIR AUGUSTUS WILLIAM FRAZER

Not a bad bit of official pomp attended this manoeuvre; Major Frazer of the artillery sent us a regular letter of thanks, the officer who was with me happening to be his senior.

It is evident that Major Frazer was more of a gentleman than his critic, for if he did not consider it his duty as a soldier to thank those who had assisted him, he knew it was his duty as a man, and acted accordingly.

It is remarkable that this same writer afterwards speaks of the troop as a "competent and well-served artillery."

The useless attack on Buenos Ayres in July, 1807, (here Lieutenant Makonokie was wounded), and the expulsion of the British from the country, are matters too well known. The following extract from the general's despatch is creditable to the commanding officer of the artillery:—

> I cannot sufficiently bring to notice the uncommon exertions of Captain Frazer, commanding the Royal Artillery, whose fertility of mind, zeal, and animation, in all cases left difficulties behind.

England had not yet taken any active measures against the French Empire, busied as she was in endeavours to protect her own shores; but no sooner had Napoleon marched his "Army of England" into the north of Europe, than troops were despatched from our shores to the assistance of the allies.

In October, 1805, a force of 14,000 men, including some companies of artillery under Colonel Cookson, was sent to North Germany. By the desire of Lord Cathcart, Colonel Cookson assumed the command of the allied artillery, when that of the British artillery devolved on Major Brooke Young. (This was the same officer that distinguished himself at Martinique; he died a major-general at Bath, May 19, 1835). The result of the Battle of Austerlitz having baffled the hopes of Austria, Prussia, and England, the British troops returned without striking a blow or seeing an enemy.

Another force under Sir James Craig embarked for the Neapolitan States to join with the Russians in expelling the French. The object of this movement was defeated, and the troops returned to Sicily.

In 1806 Sir John Stuart assumed the command of this army, with which, on the 1st July, he crossed over into Calabria. Three companies of the Royal Artillery, under the command of Lieut.-Colonel Lemoine, were attached to this army. The guns with which they were armed were of light calibre—ten 4-pounders, four 6-pounders, and two howitzers being the only ordnance that could be brought into the field. The French Army, under General Regnier, was drawn up in a strong position near Maida, about ten miles in advance of the British.

On the 4th of July Sir John Stuart marched to the attack, and the enemy, leaving their strong position, advanced to meet him. The French, greatly superior in numbers, came on (covered by the fire of their artillery) with every show of confidence; whilst our troops pressed forward to meet them, not a whit more doubtful as to the result. And now our artillery began to open with an effect which contrasted strongly with that produced by the enemy's cannonade. In general, the French gunners were excellent; but this day their fire was as worthless as any that came from the merest recruits. Not one shot out of fifty took effect; almost all passing over our front line, and falling short of the second. It was not so with our pieces. Light as they were, every shot told, and grape and canister swept away whole sections from the ranks that received it. As each file of Frenchmen fell, our brave fellows raised a shout of triumph; and loud and frequent were the plaudits bestowed upon the gallant blue coats who so ably supported them.

The enemy's attack on the right of the British line was repulsed by one of the most splendid bayonet-charges ever made. He then tried to outflank the left, and for this purpose extended his right wing, drawing all his cavalry to this part; but they were so effectually kept in check by the warm and well-directed fire of the artillery—which was the admiration of the whole army—that they were repulsed in every part.

The artillery were afterwards employed at the sieges of Scylla, Reggio, and Gaeta; the infantry in the meanwhile driving the French into Upper Calabria. Here they were joined by a powerful army under Massena, and the British were forced to give up the pursuit.

The casualties in the Royal Artillery during this campaign were very inconsiderable.

At the Battle of Maida there were only three men wounded, and their loss during the sieges was proportionally small.

Among the wounded at the siege of Scylla Castle was Sergeant John Sparks of Captain Pym's company. This intelligent non-commissioned officer was eighteen years in the Royal Artillery, and having served throughout the Italian campaign of 1806, and in Egypt in 1807 (where he was again wounded at the siege of Rosetta), he was in 1812 promoted to sublieutenant in the Royal Sappers and Miners. He retired from that corps on full pay on the 1st March, 1817, and died at Woolwich on the 12th December, 1864, aged ninety years. He had two sons, John and Edward, educated at Sandhurst, who received commissions in the army, first as ensigns, and afterwards as lieutenants. The former joined the 5th Foot, from which he exchanged into the 95th, and afterwards selling out, obtained a majority in the Canadian Militia during the Papineau rebellion. He perished in October, 1843, in an attempt to reach the shore from a vessel driven in a storm on the coast near Blackpool. The latter served an honourable career in Scinde, etc., in the 2nd Foot, and with a young lieutenant and a military surgeon, was, in 1839, while out shooting, burnt to death by the accidental firing of the jungle.

On the 6th March, 1807, Captain Pym's company embarked at Messina with the small army under General Frazer which set sail for Egypt in the hope of subduing that country. (Captain later Major-General Robert Pym died in London, June 8, 1845).

The capture of Alexandria, the siege of Rosetta, and the subsequent retreat from the country, are matters well known to every military reader. A demi-battalion of the Royal Artillery served in Italy from this period until the termination of the war in 1814. On the 17th February, 1808, the castle of Scylla was evacuated by its commandant, Lieut.-Col. Robertson, and the troops under his command, after having been invested by the French during seven weeks, and battered for six days by fourteen pieces of heavy ordnance. The Royal Artillery casualties from the 4th to 17th February were, three gunners killed, one bombardier and eight gunners wounded.

In 1809 our forces on the Italian coast were met by the active spirit of the new King of Naples, Murat. He seized the opportunity, when the English ships of war were absent, to send troops over to the island or Capri, which soon fell into their hands. The only Englishmen on the island were Lieut.-Col. Hudson Lowe and a corporal and eight men of the Royal Artillery; the other defenders being three weak regiments of Maltese and Corsicans. Our forces captured the islands of Ischia and Procida, and after destroying the forts, sailed away to other parts of the coast.

During all this time our war-ships were scouring the whole of the coasts of southern Italy, capturing every vessel that ventured out, and keeping the French general on shore in constant agitation. In the summer of 1810 a division of mortar-boats, manned by detachments of the Royal Artillery, was added to the fleet. Captain W. D. Jones had command of the artillerymen on board these vessels, and they were engaged in almost daily skirmishes with the batteries and flotilla of Murat. (He died at Bournemouth, Hants, May 20,1857). The defence of Sicily was the principal object in 1811. The artillery in the batteries of the Faro were constantly annoyed by those the French had erected on the opposite coast. On the 2nd October a shot came across the strait which killed Lieutenant John C. Bloomfield. He was the only officer of the Royal Artillery who fell during the whole campaign.

Lieut.-Col. Lemoine remained in command of the artillery in Italy until the end of the war, the last events of which were the captures of Savona, Spezia, and Genoa, in 1814. The headquarters of the artillery were at the last-named city when Pius VII. returned from imprisonment in France. An amusing; anecdote is related of Colonel Lemoine in connexion with the arrival of His Holiness on this occasion. A guard of honour being ordered, as the Pope approached, Colonel Lemoine and the officers advanced to meet him. His Holiness, thinking no doubt the Protestants would not appreciate his customary salute, tendered his *hand* for the heretics to kiss. Lemoine, on seeing the proffered hand, hastened forward and seized it with a sturdy grasp, and giving it a hearty and continued shake, said:—

"How d'ye do, my dear old gentleman? Very glad to see you; welcome to Genoa. You've been d——d ill-used; but never mind, we'll take care of you, we'll make you jolly and comfortable; God bless your old heart!"

Shortly after this, Colonel Lemoine, accompanied by his brigade-major, Captain A. M, Maxwell, Lieutenant George Smith, and two or three other officers stationed in Genoa, paid a visit to Napoleon at Elba.

****

Captain A. M, Maxwell, afterwards promoted into the line, and died colonel of the 36th regiment, at Newcastle-on-Tyne, May 21, 1845. Lieutenant George Smith died at Woolwich, 1833. His youngest son is at present (1865) a sergeant in the Royal Artillery.

****

After being introduced to Count Bertrand, they were taken to General Drouet, the governor, who, having been the commander of Napoleon's artillery, naturally took an interest in the British officers of that arm. They met Buonaparte, well-mounted, accompanied by a small escort, and drew up on one side of the lane by which he must pass; and when he got abreast of them, he pulled up his horse, moved his hat. and with a brisk, military air exclaimed, "*Du quel regiment êtes vous?*"

"*De l'artillerie, sire,*" answered Lemoine.

Napoleon seemed much pleased, and added, "*Anglais?*" which was replied to in the affirmative. He then proceeded to ask Lemoine's rank, adding "*Du quel regiment?*" "*Du quell nombre?*" "*À cheval, ou à pied?*" To these rapid questions Lemoine answered that he commanded the whole of the artillery in the Mediterranean; that the corps formed one entire regiment, numbered off by battalions; and that the Horse Artillery formed a component part of the whole.

After just merely addressing the infantry officers, Buonaparte spoke to Captain Maxwell about the number of our batteries and their equipment. He then came to Lieutenant Smith, and on hearing that he too belonged to the Royal Artillery, he become very animated and exclaimed, "*Ah! vous êtes tous de l'artillerie,*" no doubt remembering that from that corps he had himself sprung.

It was remarked that Lemoine's behaviour on this occasion was very different to all that had been before known of him; he kept interlarding his responses with "sire," "*votre majestie,*" etc., "which," says Maxwell, "I was astonished at from so blunt and rough a soldier, whose manners had been formed in camps instead of courts." Colonel Lemoine retired to Genoa after the war, and died there on the 1st March, 1825.

In 1807 the Government of Denmark, which had hitherto observed a strict neutrality, prohibited, under French influence, all commerce with Great Britain; and an expedition under Lord Cathcart and Admiral Gambier was fitted out to prevent the Danish Navy from passing into the hands of the French. Eight companies of the Royal Artillery, under Major-General Blomefield, accompanied this expedition. The field officers of the Royal Artillery were Lieut.-Cols. Harding, Cookson, Robe, and Major Newhouse; and the captains of companies, Percy Drummond, John May, J. P. Cockburn, and F. Paterson.

★★★★★★★★★★

The officer, J. P. Cockburn, is well known to the public by his excellent sketches of Pompeii, Swiss scenery, route of the Simplon, etc., which he made while on a tour in the south of Europe in 1817, and published on his return to England. He served at the capture of the Cape, 1795, and afterwards in the East Indies. He died at Woolwich, March 18, 1847, aged sixty-eight.

****

After a useless parley, during; which almost every proposition was made to prevent effusion of blood, the troops were landed on the 16th August, and prepared to attack Copenhagen. They were attacked by the enemy's gunboats, but a 9-pounder brigade being brought up by Captain Paterson, the boats (though armed with 24-pounders) were obliged to withdraw. (Captain Paterson died at Woolwich, June 13, 1856). On the 18th the enemy opened a heavy and rather destructive fire of artillery upon our outposts, by which we lost Lieutenant Henry Lyons and several men of what was called the windmill battery, which was our farthest advance at this time.

On the 29th, part of the army, under Sir Arthur Wellesley, marched to Keoge against a body of Danish troops which had strongly fortified themselves there in order to assail the besiegers, who were quickly routed. Major Newhouse commanded the batteries of this part of the army. Copenhagen was bombarded from the 1st September to the 5th, when the town being rendered untenable, an unconditional surrender of the fleet was agreed to, and the expedition returned to England. In consideration of his long and valued services, as well as for his particular conduct on this occasion, a baronetcy was conferred on Major-General Blomefield.

He was the only son of the Rev. Thomas Blomefield, rector of Hartley and Chalk, in Kent. He entered the Royal Military Academy in February, 1758, and on New Year's Day following received his commission in the Royal Artillery as lieutenant-fireworker. He was an officer remarkable for his scientific knowledge and wonderful foresight, and he was consulted in everything relating to improvements in ordnance or the organisation of the regiment.

Serving under General Phillips in America, he received a severe wound in the face at Saratoga, and was afterwards made prisoner with the troops under the Convention. Being exchanged in 1779, he returned to England, when, observing the number of men at Woolwich disabled by wounds from taking part in active service, he recommended the formation of the Invalid Battalion. He also reported on the scarcity of artillery in America, and impressed on the authorities the necessity of augmenting the corps. Two additional companies were thereupon raised in each battalion, and the Invalid Battalion (later the Coast Brigade), consisting of ten companies, was established. Captain Blomefield himself was appointed Inspector of Artillery and of the Brass Foundry, in which position he rendered signal service to his country.

Suspecting the master founder, Mr, Verbrugen, a Dutchman, of casting the guns imperfectly, he ordered a brass cannon to be well cleaned, and particularly to be freed from grease, and then washed with strong vinegar over the whole surface. This having been done, on the following day a vast number of circles of *verdigris*, of different diameters, appeared, dispersed from the muzzle to the breech. Blomefield now directed that the gun should be sawn into two longitudinal sections, when, after washing the bore first with soap and water, and then with vinegar, fifty-six screws were discovered to have been most ingeniously inserted into as many cavities or defects in the casting, many of them having been driven from the inside. Verbrugen lost his contract, his conduct being regarded as fraudulent, and he shortly afterwards died through excessive grief.

Upon the formation of the 9th battalion, on the 1st June, 1806, Colonel Blomefield was appointed colonel-commandant; and on the 25th July, 1810, he was promoted to lieut.-general. He died at Shooter's Hill, the 24th August. 1822, aged seventy-nine years, and was succeeded as baronet by his only son, the late Sir Thomas William Blomefield.

To create a diversion in favour of Austria, who had been well beaten by Napoleon at Abensburg, Landshut, and Eckmul, a formidable expedition was prepared by England in the summer of 1809, for the purpose of invading the French dominions. This was the hapless Walcheren affair, on which no less than sixteen companies of the Royal Artillery were employed. Colonel Macleod had the command of the regiment on this occasion, the subordinate field officers being Colonels Terrot and Cookson; Lieut.-Cols. Franklin, Wood, and Waller; and Majors Gold, Carncross, and Griffiths.

The captains commanding the companies were Adye, Fyers, Gardner, Drummond, Campbell, Younghusband, Webber Smith, Munro, D'Arcy, Birch, Wilmot, Paterson, and Oliver. The main body of the artillery embarked at Gravesend on the 24th July, and on the following day proceeded to Margate. The vessels then anchored in the Downs until the 29th, when they sailed for the Scheldt, at the mouth of which the troops were landed on Sunday, 30th.

On the 1st August the fort of Ter Vier surrendered, and on the following day preparations were commenced for the bombardment of Flushing. The Royal Artillery and Engineers were indefatigable in their exertions during the construction of the different batteries until

HORSE ARTILLERY IN ACTION

they were completed, which was on the 13th of August. The battery; on the right of the line was the most formidable, and was commanded by Lieut.-Colonel Wood; the centre battery was commanded by Lieut.-Colonel Waller, and that on the left by Lieut.-Colonel Franklin. The general fire commenced from all the batteries and gunboats at 1 p.m. on the 13th.

On the 14th the enemy's two-gun battery was attacked, a party of artillerymen, with spikes and hammers, being attached to the assaulting column. They succeeded in spiking the guns, and took fifty prisoners. It was during the bombardment of Flushing that Congreve rockets were first employed against a fortress. Mr. Congreve had accompanied Lord Cochrane to the Basque Roads a few months previously, and directed the fire of his weapons against the French fleet; but their success being very questionable, he took this opportunity of trying them on land. Being the eldest son of Sir William Congreve, of the Royal Artillery, he had had at Woolwich every facility for proving and improving the weapon he had invented; and being honoured with the friendship of the Prince Regent, he received every possible encouragement. On his return from Flushing, he was appointed colonel in the Royal Artillery and *aide-de-camp* to the prince, and received a parliamentary grant of £1,200 *per annum*. He never did duty with the regiment, however, his rank being considered merely honorary.

In 1813 a, troop of Horse Artillery was armed with rockets, and sent to the assistance of the allies in Germany. They were placed under the orders of the Crown Prince of Sweden; and to the success of the rockets in the hands of this troop may be attributed the subsequent popularity of the weapon. The commander of the rocket troop, Captain Richard Bogue, was a great favourite with the Prince Regent, by whom he was frequently invited to the Pavilion. He was strikingly handsome; indeed, so handsome was he, that the Brighton *belles* christened him "Look and die."

He entered upon this service with characteristic activity, little thinking it would be his last. Some Prussian battalions of General Bülow's corps having engaged the enemy at Pounsdorff (Leipsic), 18th October, and obliged them to retire, the Prince Royal directed the rocket brigade to form on the left of a Prussian battalion, and open upon the retiring columns. Congreve's formidable weapon had scarcely succeeded in paralysing a solid square of infantry, which after one fire delivered themselves up (as if panic-struck), when that gallant officer Captain Bogue, alike an ornament to his profession and a loss to his friends and country, received a shot in his head, which deprived the army of his services. Bernadotte sent the order of the "Sword" to his widow, together with an autograph letter of condolence, accompanied by more substantial marks of his royal sympathy.

A detachment of the troop, under Lieutenant Strangways, was sent to assist in the reduction of a fortress (in the possession of the French), which was necessary to the communication of the allies. Having discharged their duty to the satisfaction of the officer in command of the corps to which they were attached, they returned to the main portion of the troop just in time to accompany it into the field.

Lieutenant Strangways at once succeeded to the command, and his men again distinguished themselves on the 19th. Leipsic having surrendered unconditionally, on the same evening the Emperor of Russia, King of Prussia, and the British ambassador (Lord Cathcart) proceeded to the Swedish position to inspect the Rocket Brigade. Strangways was congratulated by all the sovereigns, and received special marks of favour from the Emperor of Russia, who questioned him most minutely as to the *modus operandi* of the force under his command. He bestowed upon him the order of St. Anne, and rewarded the other lieutenants, Wright and Montague, with the fourth class of the order of St. Wladimir. Strangways was appointed captain in the Swedish army, and received the order of the "Sword," and the gold medal for "bravery and good conduct" from the Crown Prince.

The Rocket Brigade afterwards joined Lord Lynedoch's army in Holland, but their success was not the same as at Leipsic. On one occasion they were brought up to destroy a French ship which had dropped down the river with the intention of destroying one of our batteries erected against Antwerp. The rocket that was fired hung for a few seconds above the ship, but returned with the same velocity, falling among some ice a few yards in rear of the spot from whence it was discharged, the shell attached bursting at the same time.

Colonel Congreve received the order of St. Anne for the services of his weapon at the battle of Leipsic, and on the death of his father, whom he succeeded as baronet, he was appointed inspector of the Royal Laboratory at Woolwich. In 1826 he engaged in some mining transactions, which resulted in a suit in Chancery and a decision against him of fraud. This was on May 3rd, 1828, when Sir William hastened to Toulouse, where, eleven days afterwards, he died.

But to return to Walcheren. On the 23rd August a portion of the army was sent to the island of South Beveland, and an unsuccessful attempt was made to proceed to Antwerp. Colonel Cookson commanded the artillery of this force. After the occupation of Flushing, the fever common to the country set in with peculiar virulence, and the Royal Artillery suffered severely. The only officers who died were Captain Thomas Fead and Lieutenant Wm. Miller (died on the passage home, September 17, 1809); but the loss in non-commissioned officers and gunners was enormous. After the arrival of the regiment at home, the hospitals were full of sufferers, and they were buried in great numbers in Woolwich churchyard. Dr. Hargrove mentions cases of Gunners M'Crea, Larkin, and Gondie, who, in 1812, were in the hospital at Island Bridge, Dublin, suffering from the fever which attacked them while in Walcheren, they never having done a day's duty from the time they were seized, three years previously.

Colonel (afterwards Sir John) Macleod, the commander of the artillery in this expedition, was born on the 29th January, 1752, and entered the Royal Military Academy in 1767. He received his commission in 1771, and on the breaking out of the American revolution he was sent with his company to New York. He commanded the artillery at the Battle of Guilford, when he won for himself not only the esteem, but the personal friendship of Lord Cornwallis. On their return from America his lordship introduced Lieutenant Macleod to the king, when he was placed upon the staff of the Master-General; and from this time till his death he was engaged in the most important yet inglorious duties of the organisation of the regiment, and or the arrangement and equipment of the artillery for all the expeditions, of which there were no fewer than eleven, during those years; he holding the appointment successively of Chief of the Ordnance Staff, Deputy Adjutant-General, and Director-General of Artillery.

He frequently applied to be allowed to go on service, but in this one instance only was his application, successful; the Earl of Chatham, who commanded the army, being at the time Master-General. When Lord Cornwallis was appointed Governor-General and Commander-in-Chief in India, he expressed a desire that Captain Macleod should accompany him, but he could not be spared from the important duties he was performing at home; his eldest son, Charles, however, was with Lord Cornwallis when he died—he was the bearer of the despatch to England announcing that melancholy event. (He afterwards served at Copenhagen and in the Peninsula, and was killed while leading the assault on Badajoz in 1812. The officers of his regiment erected a monument to his memory in Westminster Abbey).

In 1793 an expedition was being organised under the Marquis of Hastings, and that officer was pleased to send a secret communication to Captain Macleod, offering him the command of his artillery, which, however, he could not accept. He solicited very earnestly to be allowed to accompany Lord Cornwallis to Ireland during the rebellion of 1798, but His Majesty desired to be pressed no farther on the subject. When Captain Macleod was first appointed to his arduous position the Royal Artillery consisted of four battalions of garrison artillery and eight invalid companies; in 1814 it had been augmented to ten battalions of artillery, one horse brigade, one rocket brigade, and an invalid battalion of twelve companies—the horse artillery and field batteries having been formed and perfected daring that time. In 1820 George IV., desirous of marking his sense of such long and important services, commanded his attendance at the Pavilion at Brighton, where, under circumstances of peculiar kindness and distinction, he conferred on him the honour of knighthood, and invested him with a Grand Cross of the Royal Guelphic Order.

> The leading feature of Sir John Macleod's character was the confidence he inspired in others, and the unbounded trust they reposed in him; and thus, whether called on for counsel or to act under unforeseen or sudden emergencies of service, he was ever ready and prepared to meet its exigencies. His watchfulness seemed never to sleep, but to be in anticipation of what might occur, and to forestall events by securing means to meet them.
>
> ★★★★★★★★★★
>
> In confirmation of this ever-watchfulness of Sir John Macleod, the following anecdote, related, by Colonel Landmann, will be sufficient:— "Crossing Woolwich Common in a post-chaise one night with Lady Emily, a well-mounted highwayman, compelling the driver to stop, presented his pistol in the carriage, demanding money, watches, etc. Lady Emily, feeling very faint, was at that moment refreshing herself by the application of *eau-de-Cologne*. The major at once seized the bottle, and, ramming it in the highwayman's face, declared in a voice of thunder that he would instantly shoot him if he did not take himself off. The highwayman, fancying a pistol was at his head, turned his horse round and galloped off."
>
> ★★★★★★★★★★

'His whole soul,' to use a commonplace expression, 'was in his profession.' Of every soldier he *made* himself the friend. To his equals in rank, he was a brother, to those beneath him a father in kindness and in counsel, and to the private soldier a benefactor, ever watching over his comfort and welfare. Honoured by his sovereign, respected by all ranks of the army, loved by his friends, and revered by his family, his private life afforded an example to all who love goodness, honour, and benevolence, while his professional career ever pointed to the highest and noblest attainments by which we can serve our country.

He died at Woolwich, 26th January, 1833.

Colonel (afterwards General) Terrot died at Newcastle-on-Tyne, on the 23rd September, 1839, being at the time the oldest officer in the regiment. Lieut.-Colonel Thomas Franklin died 4th June, 1851.

Major (afterwards Lieut.-General Sir Joseph) Carncross commanded a division of artillery in the Peninsula from 1811 to the end of the war. He had previously served in the West Indies from 1797 to 1801. He lived to be the senior officer of the regiment, and died at Kildare on the 7th December, 1847.

Major Frederick Griffiths was born in 1768, and educated at Eton, from whence he was removed to the Royal Military Academy in 1782. He remained seven years in the Academy—not that his progress was slow, but the promotion in the corps was so slow that the candidates for commissions were necessarily obliged to wait many years. He served for some years at Gibraltar, and was afterwards appointed to the C troop of Horse Artillery, in which he held consecutively the ranks of lieutenant, second captain, and captain.

At the time of the encampment in 1805, when the king, George III., was present, C troop was quartered at Weymouth, and was noted for its discipline and efficiency; the captain of it not only being commended in the field by the king, but often honoured and complimented by His Majesty's sons, who, at that exciting period, took deep interest in military operations. The troop having returned to headquarters, Captain Griffiths received an appointment in the Royal Arsenal. The expedition to Walcheren induced him to resign the monotonous duties of the garrison (diversified as they were by those of the carriage department) for the more glorious field of warfare, and he therefore *volunteered* his services to accompany his corps to Walcheren.

Actively employed in the previous operations for the attack, he was selected for the command of the battery on the right bank of the Scheldt on the day before, and the morning of the surrender of

Flushing. This campaign having been brought to a close, he returned to England and resumed his duties as assistant inspector of the Royal Carriage Department. On the breaking out of the Luddite disturbances, he was ordered to take command of the northern district, and proceeded to Weedon with half a battalion of artillery. In 1822 Colonel Griffiths returned to Woolwich, and the following year retired from the corps. He died at Southampton on the 19th October, 1846. In the *United Service Magazine* for 1846 the following tribute is paid to his memory:—

> Colonel Griffiths was one who was admired and esteemed for his scientific attainments, upright and honourable conduct, thorough knowledge of all the duties of an artillerist (combining deep-searching theory with that touchstone of ability, practice), throughout the period of his whole life, thus exhibiting the qualities of an accomplished gentleman, energetic and zealous student, and right good soldier.

Captain the Hon. William Gardner was the third son of Admiral Alan Gardner, and was born on the 6th October, 1774. He entered the Royal Artillery in 1793, and served in various parts of the world in garrison; though it was never his fortune to appear before an enemy except at Walcheren. He was appointed colonel-commandant of the 10th battalion on its formation in 1846, and died a lieutenant-general at Bishopteignton in Devonshire, on the 15th December, 1856. He married the third daughter of General Fyers, R.A., by whom he had several children. His eldest son is, (1865), the present Colonel William Bethel Gardner, R.A.

Captain Charles Younghusband died a major-general at the Isle of Man, on the 8th April, 1843.

Captain Joseph D'Arcy served in the West Indies in 1793, and in Sicily in 1806. On his return from Walcheren, he, in company with Captain Henry Stone, was sent on a special mission to Persia. Stone died there on the 7th November, 1812; but the services of D'Arcy in instructing the Persians in the science of artillery were so highly valued by the *Shah*, that he bestowed upon him the orders of the "Lion" and "Sun," and, with the consent of the English Government, retained him for five years in the service of his son. Prince Abbas Mirza. He died at Lymington on the 7th February, 1848, aged sixty-seven years.

Captain Nathaniel Wilmot Oliver died a major-general, at Clifton, 11th January, 1854.

CHAPTER 7

The Campaigns in the Peninsula, 1808-1809

On the 12th May, 1808, a company of the Royal Artillery, commanded by Captains T. S. Hughes and H. T. Fanquier, embarked at Gibraltar to form part of the division under General Brent Spencer, the destination being unknown. The same evening Captain Fanquier was ordered to disembark on account of the state of his health, (he retired July 19, 1808), and Captain Hughes became so alarmed at the heavy responsibility upon him that reason forsook him, and he was placed under medical observation. (He died at Gibraltar six days afterwards, May 18, having forced himself through a window while in delirium of fever). The command of the company was now entrusted to Captain W. Morrison, and the following day the expedition sailed. Many were the rumours as to its destination; the greater number of the troops believed they were for Egypt, until finding themselves in the Atlantic, they were firmly persuaded that South America was to be the scene of their adventures.

All the conjectures, however, were erroneous, for in a few hours they found themselves attached to the blockading force before Cadiz, and remained on board for a month, during which time fresh transports arrived with officers and men of the Royal Artillery, and the following diapositions were made:—

H.M.S. *Atlas*, off Cadiz,
11th June, 1808.

General Order.

Lieutenant-Colonel Ramsay being arrived, he will assume the command of all the artillery.

Captain Lloyd is to act as adjutant, and Lieutenant Mitchell as quartermaster to the Royal Artillery.

One 6-pounder and one light howitzer will be attached to the first brigade, under the charge of Captain F. Smith and Lieutenant Holloway of the artillery.

One 6-pounder and one light howitzer will be attached to the second brigade, under Captain Morrison and Lieutenant Johnstone.

One 6-pounder and one howitzer to the 6th regiment, under Lieutenants A. Thomson and Leathes; and one 6-pounder and one howitzer to the reserve, under Captain Cowley and Lieutenant Festing.

The brigade of 12-pounders will be held in reserve.

****

Lieutenant-Colonel Ramsay died at Canterbury, September 6, 1834.
Captain F. Smith died in London, June 22, 1837.
Lieutenant Holloway died at Gibraltar, October 19, 1813.
Lieutenant A. Thomson died at Leith, July 5, 1828.
Captain Cowley retired 1812.

****

This force was landed in Cadiz, with the exception of the brigade under Captain Smith, which was stationed at Santa Maria.

The victory gained over the French by Castanos at Baylen, rendered these troops unnecessary at Cadiz and accordingly they were re-embarked, and, with the exception of a portion of the Royal Artillery, which was ordered to return to the garrison of Gibraltar, joined the army under Sir Arthur Wellesley, which had arrived from England.

To this army was attached 357 of the Royal Artillery, under the command of Lieut.-Col. Robe, the brigades being commanded by Major Viney, Captains Geary, Elliott, and Lawson; Lieutenant Patten adjutant. (Captain Elliott died near Hastings, August 26, 1855 and Lieutenant Patten at Emsworth, August 28, 1842). They embarked at Cork on the 12th July, and arrived off the coast of Spain on the 20th, and landing at Figuieras, in Mondego Bay, on the 1st August, they were joined by Spencer's division on the 5th.

On the 9th August General Wellesley commenced his march southward in the direction of Lisbon, to encounter Junot, and came up with him on the 16th at Obidos, and on the 17th attacked Roliça, where De Laborde's division of Junot's army was strongly posted. The artillery were not very conspicuously engaged in this action. Colonel Robe, having placed a battery in position, fired two Shrapnel shells upon a visible body of the enemy, to try the effect, it being the first time they were used in action.

****

This shell was an invention of Colonel Shrapnel, of the Royal Artillery, who introduced it into the service about the year 1804, and received a, parliamentary grant of 1200*l. per annum* for the invention. These shells were cast and perfected by Gunner John Henderson, of the Royal Artillery, who had, previous to his enlistment, been employed in the Carron Iron Works. This man was at first unrewarded, almost unnoticed, until, assisted by Dr. M'Culloch and others, he obtained his discharge, and an appointment as master founder in the Royal Arenal, with an allowance of 2*l. per diem*. This he held till his death, which took place on the 16th October, 1826. General Shrapnel died on the 12th March, 1842. Colonel Robe, in a letter to Colonel Shrapnel after the Battle of Vimiera, says—"Your shot is the admiration of the whole army. I should not do my duty to the service were I not to attribute our good fortune to a good use of that weapon with which you have furnished us. I told Sir Arthur Wellesley I meant to write to you, and asked if it might be with his concurrence. His answer was, 'You may say anything you please, you cannot say too much.'"
Sir Arthur himself, in a letter dated October 18th, 1808, says—"I shall have great pleasure in testifying at any time the great benefit which the army lately under my command derived from the use of the spherical case-shot in two actions with the enemy—a benefit which, I am convinced, will be enjoyed wherever they will be judiciously and skilfully used." Of late years the case-shot of General Shrapnel has been greatly depreciated, especially in the Indian service; the Duke of Wellington himself appears to have altered his opinion of the invention before he died, for in 1842 he declined to recommend the family of the deceased general for public favours. But however later improvements may have caused the Shrapnel shell to be lightly thought of, there is no doubt they rendered great service in the Peninsula and elsewhere in the early part of the present century. In 1812 Marmont, before the Battle of Salamanca, being nearly struck by a spent musket-ball, demanded of his *aide-de-camp* "whether the English lines had not been reported above a mile distant?" To the answer that such was the case the marshal rejoined, "How then do you account for this musket-ball?" The phenomenon, although inexplicable at the time, soon became familiar to the French Army, who learned and felt the deadly power of Shrapnel's invention.

****

Being quite satisfied as to the result, he directed the fire upon the enemy's guns, which were pouring a destructive fire of canister upon our attacking columns. These guns now turned their fire upon ours with round shot, and thus the infantry was relieved from the canister.

A brigade of artillery being required in front of the attacking columns, a rush was at once made by two of the batteries disengaged to be first at the post of honour. Captain Geary's battery was, however, the first to cross the small stone bridge over the Columbeira, and the other at once retired. In a short time, the top of the heights was reached by this battery, and the guns were prepared for action.

The French skirmishers advanced to within sixty yards of the guns, and Geary having fired one gun charged with canister, as he pointed the second said, "I'll be properly into them this——" time he would have added, but he raised his left hand half-way to his head and fell to the ground perfectly lifeless. A shot had passed through his head, having entered half an inch above his left eyebrow. Captain Geary left a wife and five children, and had he not been ordered for active service he would have resigned his commission and settled down at his farm in the Isle of Wight, having 800*l*. a year private income. His body was rolled in a sheet and buried by the officers of the artillery and engineers at eight o'clock the same evening, the funeral service being read by Lieutenant Patten.

On the 21st August the British, who were strongly posted in and about the village of Vimiera, were attacked by the French under Junot, and here, as at Roliça, they experienced a signal defeat. In this battle the artillery, though they did great service, did not have an officer killed or wounded. On one occasion the enemy's cavalry were about to turn our right flank, when they received a discharge of spherical case from the 9-pounder battery under Captain Elliott—they at once turned round and effected a hasty retreat.

A column of about 5,000 grenadiers was at one time advancing upon our guns, covered by a swarm of *voltigeurs*, who came to within twenty yards of the guns. The artillery kept up a most destructive fire with round shot and canister, and at every discharge a complete lane was cut through the column from front to rear by the round shot, whilst the canister was committing dreadful carnage on the foremost ranks. At this moment Colonel Robe, turning to Captain Landman of the engineers, said, "If something be not very quickly done, the enemy will in a few minutes have our guns, and we shall all be bayoneted."

Landman then suggested that he should order up his horse and prepare for the worst. "No! no!" exclaimed the gallant Robe, with scorn, "I'll neither leave my guns nor my gunners; I'll share the fate of my brave boys, be it what it may." The French column, however, did not reach our guns by about sixty yards, for it was fired into, charged, and driven into the utmost disorder by the 50th regiment, who, when the broken column turned and fled, chased them for nearly 300 yards.

During the battle the divisions under Generals Acland and Anstruther arrived from England; with them were 379 of the Royal Artillery, amongst whom was Lieutenant William Robe, the eldest son of the colonel. He arrived during the early part of the action, and remained by the side of his father the whole of the day, the old man declaring his happiness complete by having his son with him. He afterwards proved himself a good soldier, as will be seen in the course of the work.

Major-General Sir Harry Burrard was among the reinforcements which landed during the action, and at its close he relieved Sir Arthur Wellesley of the command of the army.

This officer began his military career in the Royal Artillery. He entered the Academy in April, 1768, and received his commission as second lieutenant on the 17th June, 1772. Four years afterwards he resigned his commission in the artillery, and was promoted into the 60th regiment. He died in 1815.

Directly after the Battle of Vimiera, Sir John Moore's army arrived from England, and disembarked at Maceira Bay, Great difficulty and some loss was sustained in getting on shore, an operation only effected by five days of incessant exertion on the part of the navy; the boats were constantly swamped by the surf, and not more than thirty remained fit for service at the conclusion. There were 712 men of the Royal Artillery with this division, under Colonel Harding, the brigades being under Captains Wilmot and Drummond. The artillery lost a number of men by the upsetting of the boats, and many who had landed perished in the attempt to save a drowning comrade.

Foremost in this enterprise of danger was a young Scotch gunner, in Captain Drummond's company, of the name of McNeil. Three times he had returned to land in safety, bearing at each return an exhausted comrade in his arms. Another boat upset in bounding through the dangerous whirlpool. McNeil heard the cry of despair from the crew, and although his strength was subdued by great exertion, threw himself into the raging element, to return alas! no more. The noble fellow had grasped the arm of one of the imploring suppliants, when the prow of a ship's launch, impelled by a heavy sea, struck him a fatal blow upon the head. He sank, and towards evening the tide left his inanimate body on the shore. It was interred the same night, the funeral service being read by one of his own officers.

It was in October Sir John Moore commenced his march from Lisbon into Spain, when he sent the whole of his artillery (twenty-four pieces) by the Talavera road, under an escort commanded by Sir John Hope, taking one battery, under Captain Wilmot, with himself, by Almeida, to try the roads, which were pronounced by the Portuguese to be impracticable for artillery. Sir John soon found however, that he had been misled, and being in great anxiety for the safety of his guns, wrote to Sir John Hope as follows:—

> The road we are now travelling is practicable for artillery; the brigade under Wilmot has already reached Guarda, and, as far as I have seen, the road presents few obstacles, and those easily surmounted this knowledge was, however, only acquired by our own officers.

He then instructed Hope to trust no longer to reports, but seek for himself a shorter route to Salamanca

On the 29th October Sir David Baird arrived at Corunna with a considerable reinforcement, and after some delay he advanced to meet Sir John Moore, leaving a portion of his army at Corunna.

There were 798 artillerymen with this division, under Colonel Cookson, including two troops of Horse Artillery under Captains Dowman and Eveleigh.

★★★★★★★★★★

Colonel George Cookson saw considerable service during his long life. He served in the Royal Navy in the American war, at the alternate captures and defences of the West India Islands, 1773-7. He obtained a commission as lieutenant in the Royal Artillery in 1778; in 1785 he commanded the detachment of the artillery on the unhealthy shores of the Black River on the Spanish Main in South America for nine months. His other services in Holland, Egypt, Hanover, and Copenhagen have been recorded in the preceding chapters. He died a lieutenant-general at Esher, Surrey, on the 12th August, 1837, aged seventy-five years.

Captain Eveleigh died at the Isle of Wight, 24th August, 1859, being at the time the senior officer of the regiment.

★★★★★★★★★★

While these three armies were wandering about Spain in the hopes of being speedily united, Buonaparte was pouring troops into the country by thousands, and by the 4th December he had defeated two Spanish Armies and taken Madrid. He then prepared to drive the "English leopards" from the Peninsula. Fortunately, Moore and Sir John Hope met on the 6th December, and on the 23rd they were joined by Baird at Majorga. On the same day intelligence was received that 100,000 men, headed by Buonaparte himself, were in full march after them. There was no further thought of advancing, but of retreat, before the army was completely surrounded. The weather was very severe, and the marches long, and there were several skirmishes betwixt the British cavalry and the horse of the French, and on every such occasion the British drove them back in confusion and with heavy loss.

On the 29th December a dashing affair took place between the two cavalries at Benevente, on which occasion the French general, Lefébvre, was taken prisoner. The French fled at full speed towards the river (Esla), the British following, sabring the hindermost, until the French squadrons, without breaking their ranks, plunged into the stream and gained the opposite heights; then, like experienced soldiers, they wheeled and seemed inclined to come forward a second time, but when two guns of Downman's troop opened upon them they retired.

Six 3-pounders were abandoned during the retreat. These guns were landed at Corunna without the general's knowledge; they never went beyond Villa Franca, and not being horsed, they were thrown down the rocks when the troops quitted that town.

It speaks well for the conduct of the artillery, that while 2,627 of the infantry and nine of the cavalry strayed away from the army during this retreat, not one artilleryman is reported to have absented himself from his post. (In Sir John Moore's own words, "The artillery consists of particularly well-behaved men."—Cadell).

Early in January, 1809, a gun detachment attached to the rearguard was overtaken by a small band of the French cavalry. Being some distance in rear of the main army, and well knowing that no mercy was to be expected at such a crisis, the non-commissioned officer in charge commanded the men to "stand firm." The gun was instantly wheeled round to face the approaching enemy, and though it contained nothing but a little dust contracted on their journey, the non-commissioned officer stood with a lighted match in his hand as though well prepared to receive them. The ruse succeeded, for the Frenchmen instantly turned about and galloped away as fast as they could, our own fellows as quickly limbering up their gun and hurrying towards their friends in front.

While Napoleon was watching the rear-guard of the retreating army, on the 1st January, 1809, he received despatches which caused him at once to give up the pursuit and return to France. Feeling confident, however, that the doom of the British Army was fixed, he gave the command to Soult, who he conceived had nothing to do but conquer them.

The torrents of rain, the heavy falls of snow, the roads rough with rocks or deep with mud, together with the scarcity of provisions, rendered the retreat very miserable at this period, and caused much disorder in the British Army.

On the 2nd, detachments of the hostile armies met and engaged at Villa Franca. Captain Carthew's battery rendered effectual service in this action, severely handling and eventually staying the progress of a French column.

During these operations a young officer of the artillery. Lieutenant Henry Mussenden Leathes, was wounded. His wound was not of a serious nature, nor were his subsequent services at Waterloo, etc., of a character which calls for a special notice, but he has within a few days passed from among us, and with him his well-known—

Words of friendship, comfort, and assistance.

Descended from the distinguished family of Mussenden (which includes Sir William de Mussenden, Grand Admiral of England, and the founder of Missenden Abbey) in 1848, having some time previously retired from the army, he succeeded to the family estates in Suffolk. He at once became conspicuous in his efforts to do good: his kindness of heart and unbounded charity made him universally respected, and in 1863 the Emperor of the French sent to him the gold medal of honour in appreciation of the services he had so long rendered humanity.

He died at Lowestoft on the 16th December, 1864.

On the 13th January the army came in sight of Corunna and the sea, but great was their consternation not to see the transports in the bay. Sir John, however, quartered his troops in Corunna, and determined to defend it manfully till the transports could get up from Vigo, where they were detained by contrary winds. Here was found abundance of arms and ammunition, so much that, for fear it should fall into the hands of the enemy, care was taken to destroy it. A party under Colonel Cookson, Royal Artillery, blew up two magazines containing twelve thousand barrels of gunpowder, producing a concussion that shook the town like an earthquake.

On the following day, the 14th, the transports hove in sight, and the sick, the horses, and baggage were at once embarked, the army meanwhile preparing for a fight, for Soult was now close upon the town. Fifty pieces of artillery were embarked, and there were only nine guns kept on shore for action. These were commanded by Captains Beane, Drummond, Wilmot, and Carthew. The nature of the ground prevented any movement of the artillery on either side, hence the French columns in their attacks were exposed to a fire of grape, which they could not return because of the distance of their batteries.

That the French were beaten. Sir John Moore killed, and the army embarked during the night of the 14th and morning of 15th, are facts well known by every reader of history.

When rest succeeded to toil, the effect of the over-exertion during the retreat told fearfully on the army, and on no portion so much as the artillery. Lieutenant George Wilson died the day he embarked (13th January), Captain Romer (16th) and Captain Carthew (22nd) died while on the passage, and Lieutenant George Lear died on board the *Norge* directly after her arrival at Plymouth on the 24th. (*Norge*, captured from the Danes at Copenhagen, much used for the conveyance of troops by the British Army during the war. It took Major Munro's company to America in 1814).

The commander of the artillery, Lieut.-Colonel Harding, never recovered from the ill effects of this campaign, but lingered on, doing little or no duty, at Woolwich until his death, which took place on the following 18th of June.

CHAPTER 8

The Campaigns in the Peninsula, 1809-1812

In the meantime, another expedition was prepared in England, and placed under the command of Major-General Sherbrooke. It sailed from Ramsgate on the 10th January, 1809, and after encountering a series of contrary winds and tempestuous weather, proceeded direct for Cadiz, in the hope of securing that important seaport. The Spaniards refusing admittance to the British force, the latter immediately proceeded to the Tagus, and the defence of Portugal then became the primary object of Great Britain.

Sir Arthur Wellesley arrived at Lisbon on the 22nd April as commander-in-chief of the combined British and Portuguese Armies; Sir J. Craddock having the command of the British, and General Beresford of the Portuguese forces. Some of the British artillery were attached to Beresford's army, of which Captain Alexander Dickson had the command, as well as of the Portuguese artillery, in which service he was nominated lieutenant-colonel. The Royal Artillery of the British Army was commanded by Brigadier-General Howarth, Colonel Robe, Lieut.-Cols. Framingham and Fisher. The latter remained at Lisbon, not only as commanding officer of the artillery in that garrison, but in charge of all the ordnance stores, which it was his duty to forward to the army as required.

★★★★★★★★★★

Brigadier-General afterwards Lieut.-General Sir Edward Howarth, K.C.B. Died at Banstead, near Epsom, March 5, 1827.
Lieut.-Colonel Framingham afterwards Major-General Sir Hoylet Framingham, K.C.B. Died at Cheltenham, May 10, 1820, aged fifty-six.

★★★★★★★★★★

Sir A. Wellesley had hardly arrived in Portugal when a forward movement was decided on. The army, amounting to 25,000 men, was concentrated at Coimbra, where it was reviewed by Sir Arthur on the 2nd May. On the 12th May the Douro was crossed and the French driven out of Oporto. Three guns, under Captain Taylor, R.A., attached to General Murray's division, swept a portion of the French position, and contributed in no small degree to the success of the passage of the river.

The British were very deficient of field artillery at the Battle of Talavera (27th and 28th July), as neither horses nor mules could be procured to draw the guns. ("The English guns were few, and of small calibre."—Napier). Brigadier-General Howarth, however, made the best possible disposition of the artillery under his command. Ten guns were placed in a battery on the right of the position, two brigades were with General Hill on the left, and others were distributed on the most favourable points along the line. This force of artillery was composed of English, Spanish, and Portuguese batteries.

There were not more than three British batteries engaged; they were commanded by Captains Campbell, May, and Baynes. The latter received a severe wound in the head, and another officer of the Royal Artillery, Captain John Taylor, was so severely wounded that he was unable to be removed from Talavera, and consequently fell into the hands of the French when they took possession of that place after the disgraceful retreat of Cuesta and the Spaniards on the 3rd August.

★★★★★★★★★★

Captain Campbell, later General Campbell. Died September, 1857.
Captain May, later Major-General Sir John May, K.C.B. This officer took part in the whole of the Peninsular campaigns from January, 1809, to June, 1814, and served the greater part of the time as a staff-officer—first as brigade-major, and afterwards as adjutant-general of the artillery. He died in London, May 8, 1847.
Captain Baynes, later Colonel Henry Baynes, K.H. Died 1846.

★★★★★★★★★★

Marshal Victor, the French commander, behaved, however, with the utmost humanity and kindness to the wounded British, and among others, Captain Taylor recovered, and was sent to France, where he remained a prisoner till the end of the war. Lieutenant Henry Wyatt was the only artillery officer killed.

★★★★★★★★★★

Captain (afterwards Major) Taylor was born at Carlanstown House, Westmeath, in March, 1779. He received a commission in the Royal

Irish Artillery in 1799, and in 1801 was incorporated into the Royal Artillery. He served three years in the West Indies, and afterwards accompanied Sir John Moore to Sweden and Spain, and took part in the Corunna campaign. He died suddenly, of apoplexy, as he was returning from the mess to his residence on Woolwich Common, and was found in a sitting position, life being quite extinct, on the morning of January 2, 1830.

★★★★★★★★★★

On the morning after the battle, a division under General Crawford reached the army, accompanied by Ross's troop of Horse Artillery, (afterwards General Sir Hew D. Ross), after a march of sixty-three miles, accomplished in twenty-six hours, in the hottest weather.

The French overran nearly the whole of Spain during; the autumn and winter of 1809, and in the spring of 1810 made preparations to invade Portugal and drive the English into the sea.

In June Massena laid siege to Ciudad Rodrigo (occupied by the Portuguese), and compelled it to surrender on the 10th July. He then advanced to Almeida, and in so doing came in contact with Crawford's division of the British Army on the banks of the Coa. An engagement took place, but Crawford was overpowered and compelled to retire. Captain Ross's troop was for some time engaged with the guns attached to the enemy's cavalry, which were of much larger calibre, and as the infantry retired, they were effectually covered by Ross's guns. (See *Hew Ross of the Chestnut Troop: With the Royal Horse Artillery During the Peninsular War and at Waterloo* by Hew Dalrymple Ross & Francis Duncan, Leonaur: 2020).

This was on the 24th July, and the French advanced to besiege Almeida, which they captured on the 27th August. There was now no further obstacle to their advance, and on the 16th September, Massena, having been considerably reinforced, commenced his march towards the British Army, which he found strongly posted on the heights of Busaco. The whole French Army halted in front of the British position on the 26th September, and on the following morning, at daybreak, they moved on to the attack. Brigadier-General Howarth commanded the artillery in this battle, during which the whole of the batteries maintained a heavy and incessant cannonade.

That portion of the corps was reinforced by two troops under Captains Bull and Lefebure (died at Madrid, October 23, 1812), which, with some additional brigades of field artillery, took part in this action.

★★★★★★★★★★

Captain (afterwards Lieut.-Colonel) Robert Bull was born at Stafford on March 3, 1778. He entered the Royal Artillery in 1794, and served as lieutenant in the West Indies in the campaigns of 1796-98, during which he was nine times engaged in the island of St. Domingo. He commanded the I troop of Horse Artillery in the Peninsula, until compelled, from the severity of his wounds, to return to England. He afterwards distinguished himself at the Battle of Waterloo. His death took place at Bath, April 17, 1836.

****

The battle was begun by two guns under Captain Lane, which were ordered up with the 88th regiment to meet the advancing enemy, while the Portuguese battery, under the German major, Arentschild, passed at a trot towards the St. Antonio pass, in front of the 74th regiment. (Captain Lane was compelled to leave the regiment on account of the effects produced upon him by a sunstroke).

The troops of Horse Artillery rendered great service, detachments moving about with the infantry to all the desirable points. A portion of Ross's troop, under Lieutenant Macdonald, played sharply upon Marchand's column in the pine wood, from which it was soon afterwards driven by the Guards. (Lieutenant Macdonald, afterwards Major-General Alexander Macdonald, junior, died at Aix-la-Chapelle, May 31, 1856).

After an hour's fruitless effort, the French withdrew, and the roar of battle ceased.

Wellington now withdrew his troops to the strongly fortified lines of Torres Vedras, and was followed by Massena, who no sooner witnessed the impregnable defences which sheltered the English, than he in turn retired towards the frontiers of Portugal, followed by portions of the British Army, who greatly harassed his troops, rendering their retreat a most difficult and unpleasant operation.

On the 11th March, 1811, the army having advanced, overtook the enemy at Pombal, when a smart skirmish ensued, and the French were driven out of the town. At Redinha, on the following day, they made a daring stand, but at last were obliged to retire.

Excepting a small skirmish at Casel Nova, the hostile armies did not again engage until the 15th March, when the French were vigorously driven from a strong position at Foz d'Arouce. In all these actions the troops of Horse Artillery rendered most important service.

Captain Ross was twice wounded—at Redinha on the 12th, and at Foz d'Arouce on the 15th.

On the 3rd April, the enemy being defeated at Sabugal, on the

Coa, were driven out of Portugal. Massena now retired on Salamanca, and after restoring order among his troops and receiving reinforcements from France, he again advanced towards Portugal. On the 3rd May he came up with and attacked our troops stationed in the village of Fuentes d'Onor, and on the 5th, both armies being fully drawn up, a severe battle took place in and about the same village.

It was on this day that an officer of the Royal Artillery attracted the attention of the whole army and elicited the admiration of the world. This was William Norman Ramsay, the second captain of Bull's troop, an officer alike distinguished for his kindly disposition and gentlemanly qualities as for his bravery and skill as a soldier.

The conduct of Bull's troop throughout the action was admirable. Nothing could exceed the skill and boldness with which it was manoeuvred; but while covering the infantry (temporarily thrown into confusion by the cavalry passing through the intervals) it was surrounded and cut off by the French cavalry.

Guns thus dealt with are almost always lost, and consequently the army ceased to think of Ramsay and his men, except as prisoners. Presently, however, a great commotion was observed among the French squadrons; men and officers closed in confusion towards one point, where a thick dust was rising, and where loud cries and the sparkling of blades and flashing of pistols indicated some extraordinary occurrence. The spectators gazed with intense interest.

Suddenly the multitude was violently agitated; an English shout arose, the mass was rent asunder, and Norman Ramsay burst forth at the head of his battery, his horses breathing fire and stretching like greyhounds across the plain, his guns bounding like things of no weight, and the mounted gunners, in close and compact order, covering the rear.

The escape of Ramsay's guns is wholly without a parallel in the annals of modern warfare. The French came on at a rapid pace, but in bad order, and were checked by different squadrons as they came up. Ramsay was still followed by the French, *chasseurs*, and the number of *chasseurs* and hussars of the French appeared to be much greater than that of anything opposing them. The British, however, formed whilst the French seemed to be galloping about in detached parties, and immediately charged and drove them back. Later in the day a squadron of French hussars charged and broke a picket of the guards, but Captain Thompson's battery immediately opened on them with grape, and forced them back. (Captain Thompson afterwards Major George

Norman Ramsay at Fuentes d'Onor

Thompson, died at Guernsey, November 26, 1814).

For a considerable time, the attention of the army was occupied in observing the practice of the French artillery and Captain Thompson's brigade, and it was admirable on both sides.

After this battle the French retired beyond the Agueda, and steps were taken by the British to secure a capture of Almeida.

While Wellington's army was thus engaged, another army, under General Beresford, was reducing the fortresses taken by the French in 1810. The artillery of this army was commanded by Major Dickson, who had under him Captain Lefebure's troop of Horse Artillery, six companies. of the Royal Artillery (under Major Hawker), three troops and twenty-eight batteries of foreign artillery. (Major Hawker afterwards Colonel James Hawker, C.B. Died at Woolwich, October 12, 1827.)

On the 17th March this army advanced towards the enemy, who occupied a position at Campo Mayor, and came up with him on the 25th. A slight skirmish ensued, and the enemy retreated and were pursued by our cavalry to Badajoz.

On the 11th April a portion of Beresford's army, under General Cole, sat down before Olivenca, and on the 15th the batteries opened and effected a breach, when the governor made an unconditional surrender of the town.

Beresford writes:

> I am free to say that it has been principally owing to the exertions of Captain Squire, R.E., and those of Major Dickson, that I am indebted for the speedy surrender of this place.

★★★★★★★★★★

> Captain Squire received his first commission in the Royal Artillery, and was promoted into the Royal Engineers in 1797. He died in Spain before the conclusion of the war.

★★★★★★★★★★

Active operations were immediately commenced against Badajoz. The place was completely invested on the 8th May, and a breaching battery opened against Fort St. Christoval on the 11th. This battery was manned by Portuguese artillerymen, who were raw and inexperienced and the guns, which were brass, were soon injured by the frequent firing. The fire of the fort was vigorous and well-directed; and the consequence was, that in the course of a few hours the whole of the guns in the battery rendered unserviceable.

Fresh guns were then ordered up, but Beresford hearing of the ad-

SIR ALEXANDER DICKSON

vance of Soult, relinquished the further prosecution of the siege, and advanced towards him.

The hostile armies met at Albuera on the 16th May. A furious battle ensued, which terminated in favour of the allies. The loss, however, was very severe on all sides. The artillery, which was most importantly posted and hotly engaged, was commanded by Major Hartmann, of the King's German Legion; the British batteries being directed by Major Hawker, and the Portuguese by Major Dickson.

The first artillery to come into action were Dickson's Portuguese guns, which, opening from a rising ground above the village, ploughed Goudinot's column. The fire of the troop of Horse Artillery, under Captain Lefebure enabled Lumley to check the advance of the enemy's cavalry at a most critical part of the battle; and the British batteries under Hartmann coming into action, they engaged those of the enemy at half-range, showers of grape being discharged on both sides, causing enormous losses. Five of our guns were at one time in the enemy's position, but they were recaptured by the Fusiliers under Cole.

The celebrated Polish Lancers made a furious charge on Cleeves's German battery. Cleeves gave the word "Fire" when they were within fifty yards of the guns. Many saddles were of course emptied, but the charge was not prevented; the enemy rushing right between the guns and sabring so many gunners and horses, that as they retired Cleeves could only man two guns with which to fire into them. This was the only occasion on which this *renowned* body of cavalry ever appeared before the British Army. (Major Cleeves died at Selby, June 8, 1830, being at the time on his way to Hanover, whence he had come to visit his friends in this country).

Lefebure's troop distinguished itself at Usagre a few days after the battle, it having been sent with the cavalry in pursuit of the enemy, who were retreating towards Seville. "*Cette position est rendue encore plus critique par l'artillerie Anglaise, tirant à mitraille sur nos regimens agglomérés en avnnt de ce defile*," said Latour Maubourg, who commanded the enemy on this occasion. There is no doubt that whatever bravery and skill could accomplish was done by Captain Lefebure's troop on this as on every other occasion, but as this troop was the whole amount of that arm which the British had at Usagre, we cannot believe but Latour must have had a larger artillery force, as he had three brigades of cavalry; he could not have left himself so unprovided with artillery as to be bullied by five light 6-pounders and a light howitzer.

A junction was now effected by the armies of Wellington and Beresford, and Badajoz was laid siege to for the second time on the 30th May.

Lieut.-Colonel Framingham commanded the artillery; the direction of the siege, however, was confided by Lord Wellington to Major Dickson.

The Horse Artillery, which formed part of the covering army, was commanded by Lieut.-Colonel Downman. (Later Sir Thomas Downman, K.CB. Died at Woolwich, August 10, 1852, aged seventy-nine).

The service of the batteries was performed by detachments of the Portuguese artillery, aided by Captain Raynsford's company of Royal Artillery, who were indefatigable, some of them never quitting the batteries. (Captain Raynsford resigned November 11, 1811). Lieutenant Edmund Hawker, a young man of much promise, who had distinguished himself by his zeal in the batteries, was killed on the morning of the 6th June.

On the 10th Lord Wellington received intelligence that Soult and Marmont were about to unite their forces and advance against him. He therefore promptly determined on converting the siege of Badajoz into a blockade, and on the night of the 12th the last of the guns and stores were withdrawn to Elvas, without molestation from the garrison.

The troops now went into cantonments in the villages of Aldea, El Boden, etc., but in September they were concentrated about Ciudad Rodrigo.

The troops of Horse Artillery having proved of such service, a fourth, under Captain Alexander Macdonald, was sent to the Peninsula, and joined the army about this time. (Later Major-General Alex. Macdonald, C.B. died at Leamington, May 21, 1840). Additional field batteries also arrived at Lisbon, some of which joined the army. These were commanded by Major Joseph Carncross, Captains Robert Macdonald (died at Inchkenneth, Argyleshire, November 10, 1856, aged eighty), Robert Douglas, and Stewart Maxwell (died at Paris, June 17, 1824, having been ten years on sick leave).

An action was fought at El Boden on the 25th September, and the village of Aldea de Ponte was attacked by the enemy on the 27th. The Portuguese artillery under Major Arentschild was severely handled by the French on the former occasion, but they behaved nobly, those who were not cut down at the guns returning to them as soon as the enemy retired. Detachments of the Royal Horse Artillery were in action at Aldea de Ponte. Lieutenant Dunn received a musket-ball in his groin during this engagement, and it remained unextracted till the day of his death, 24th July, 1863.

The campaign of 1811 closed with some smart affairs between Hill's division and the enemy, the former being victorious on all occasions. Major Hawker's battery was distinguished throughout these operations.

The campaign of 1812 opened with the siege of Ciudad Rodrigo, which was invested on the 6th January. Here the whole of the Royal Artillery were engaged, (*i.e.*, the whole of the artillery with the army, there were, of course, companies in garrison at Cadiz, Lisbon, etc.); the siege companies in the batteries and the troops and field brigades with the covering army.

The corps was commanded on this occasion by Major-General Borthwick (died at Margate, July 28, 1820), the direction of the siege being entrusted to Major Dickson. The companies which served in the batteries were commanded by Captains Holcombe, Power, Dynely, and Dundas. The field artillery was commanded by Lieut.-Colonel Downman.

★★★★★★★★★★

> Captain Holcombe, the life of this gallant officer, distinguished in after years for his attachment to and zeal for the service of his Great Captain the King of kings, was published a few years ago under the title of *The Change*. The son of a minister in the West of England; he was born in 1781, and died at Edinburgh, March 6, 1847.
>
> Captain Power, afterwards General Sir William G. Power, K.C.B., colonel-commandant of the 10th brigade. Died at Shanklin, Isle of Wight, January 23, 1863, aged eighty-one.
>
> Captain Dynely afterwards Lieut.-General Thomas Dynely, C. B. Died in June 21, 1860.
>
> Captain Dundas, afterwards Major-General William Dundas, an officer distinguished for his scientific attainments, and his inventions and improvements in gunnery, etc. Died at Edinburgh, August 8, 1858.

★★★★★★★★★★

The rapid execution produced by the well-directed fire kept up from our batteries afforded the best proof of the merits of the officers and men of the Royal Artillery, while their sufferings are a sufficient testimony to the manner they were exposed and the difficulties under which they had to perform their duties. Major-General Borthwick, Captains Power, Dynely, and Dundas were all severely wounded, and the loss in artillerymen was very severe. On the 19th January the fortress was assaulted and captured; and as soon as it was garrisoned and

FIELD ARTILLERY OF THE NAPOLEONIC PERIOD

supplied with stores and provisions, Wellington planned his arrangements for the reduction of Badajoz.

He had artillery sent out to sea from Lisbon, as for some distant expedition, and then secretly carried in small boats up the Setubal, to Alcacor de Sol, and thence by land to Badajoz. The infantry arrived before the place on the 16th March, and it was invested on the same day. Major Dickson conducted the details of the artillery service, as well as upon former occasions, under the general superintendence of Colonel Framingham, Major-General Borthwick having been obliged to quit the army through the suffering caused by his wounds.

The same companies served in the batteries, with the addition of Captain Gardiner's, and some Portuguese companies under Major Tulloh, Lieutenants C. C. Mitchell and T. Cox of the Royal Artillery.

****

> Lieutenant Cox served as captain of a Portuguese battery from this time till the end of the war, having previously served with the Royal Artillery during the Corunna campaign. He remained with the Portuguese Army till 1819, and returning home, became adjutant of the King's County Militia, retaining that appointment till December, 1854.

****

After extraordinary exertions several batteries were completed, which, on the 25th March, opened on Fort Picurina, the enemy's advance-work. The fort having been much injured by our fire, Wellington deemed it advisable to assault it the same evening; accordingly, after dark, 500 men of the third division moved forward to the attack. A short but violent contest ensued, and the work was in possession of the British. The reserve was led to the support of the assaulting party by Captain Power, R.A., to whom the commandant of the fort surrendered.

By the capture of Picurina the besiegers were enabled to establish their second parallel with little loss, and on the night of the 26th two breaching batteries opened fire within 300 yards of the place. Lieutenant John J. Connel, R.A., was killed on the 28th.

About six o'clock on the morning of the 31st March, as advanced battery (known as No. 7), armed with twelve 24-pounders, commenced its tremendous fire against the defences of Badajoz. The enemy answered with shot and shell so effectually as to explode the magazine three hours afterwards, and by noon a considerable part of the battery was in ruins. An officer who took an active part in this siege, and afterwards in the assault, in making mention of this battery, says—

> I was proceeding in the trenches and met two artillerymen carrying in a blanket a wounded gunner from No. 7 battery, the left side of whose head had been struck by a cannon-ball, and his brains, in the unbroken membrane (like a bag), hung on his shoulder. I remonstrated on the uselessness of dragging this poor expiring man to the camp, the half of his head having been shot away. They laid him down to rest, and at that moment he expired; and judging that the men had no objection to be employed out of the battery, I recommended them to bury their comrade on the spot and return immediately to the battery, where they were much required. Soon after I met some more artillerymen conveying (also in a blanket) from the same battery an artillery officer.
>
> Captain Dundas, very severely wounded: he was a heavy man, and his left arm dreadfully shattered, the shirt and coat torn to rags, his arm was bent over the side, and the weight of his body swagged to the ground. I stopped to assist in putting him into a better position and laid his left arm straight by his side (it was later amputated): his left thigh was also dislocated, and his hip-bone broken. I then passed to the battery as a spectator; it was indeed in ruins; the embrasures and buttresses, and nearly all the parapet, were demolished and open to the town. The embrasures were repaired, and the bombardment continued vehemently; the enemy also threw some shot and shells in rapid succession.

Under such circumstances as these did the artillery nobly perform their duty at Badajoz. By the 6th April there were three breaches open, and orders were given to storm. Captain William Latham was killed on this day, and the loss in artillery was very great.

After a desperate struggle, during which some 2,000 men were killed, our infantry obtained possession of Badajoz, which was at once put in a state of defence by Lord Wellington The commander-in-chief had on all occasions exhibited a predisposition in favour of Major Dickson, R.A., and at the conclusion of this siege he brought him prominently to the notice of the Government by the following passage in his despatch:—

> Adverting to the extent of the details of the ordnance department during this siege, to the difficulties of the weather, etc.,

with which Major Dickson had to contend, I must mention him most particularly to Your Lordship. (The Earl of Liverpool, prime-minister).

And in a letter to Colonel Torrens, the military secretary, he says:—

I likewise wish again to draw the notice of His Royal Highness (the Duke of York, commander-in-chief), to Major Dickson. I am certain that there is not an officer in this army who will not admit that he deserves any favour which can be conferred upon, him.

Lieutenant Daniel Bourchier, R.A., (retired a major on half-pay 1829; died at Dublin October 22, 1852), was also mentioned by Wellington, as well as the captains of companies.

An army under Sir R. Hill was now despatched to effect the destruction of the enemy's works at Almarez, which was accomplished after a sharp struggle on the 19th May. A brigade of 24-pounders, a company of the Royal Artillery, and a company of Portuguese artillery, under the command of Dickson (now lieut.-colonel), were attached to this force. Circumstances did not permit the guns to be brought into play, but the exertion of the corps daring the attack and destruction of the place was unwearied.

Wellington now advanced on Salamanca. The army crossed the Tormes on the 17th June by the fords above and below Salamanca, and preparations were immediately made for the reduction of the forts. On the 19th Sir S. Cotton ordered Ross to turn his battery of 6-pounders upon a group of French officers. At the first shot the enemy seemed surprised, and at the second their gunners ran to their pieces, and in a few minutes a reply from eight 12-pounders showed the folly of provoking a useless combat, later in the day the guns in battery, commanded by Lieut.-Colonel Hay, R.A., opened fire.

Unfortunately, the ammunition became exhausted before the breach was rendered practicable, and an attempt was made to escalade the forts, which, however, was unsuccessful. Captain S. P. Elige, R.A., was killed on this day, and Captain Dynely received a wound in the face.

A cavalry skirmish took place on the 20th, and Bull's troop was ably manoeuvred. A few days after, the deficiency in ammunition being supplied, a spirited cannonade was commenced.

On the 27th the largest fort, St. Vincente, was in flames, and preparations were at once made for an assault. The smaller forts were soon carried, and the governor of St. Vincente surrendered. About 700 men were made prisoners, the works were blown up, and the captured guns and stores given to the Spaniards.

Wellington and Marmont kept cautiously manoeuvring and watching each other's motions, with the hope of advantageously making an attack. Never upon any former occasion were, and scarcely ever since have been made such incessant movements of one army in the face of another for so long a period without a decided attack. It was not till the 22nd July that a general action took place, the Battle of Salamanca, the consequences of which were very great.

The whole of the troops and batteries, under Lieut.-Colonel Framingham, were engaged more or less during this eventful day; the battery under Captain Douglas, however, rendered most effective service, silencing the French guns, which were pouring a most destructive fire on our advancing columns.

A few days after the Battle of Salamanca the troop of Horse Artillery under Captains Lefebure and Whinyates (afterwards General Sir E. C. Whinyates, colonel-commandant of the B brigade of Horse Artillery), which was on the Tagus with Hill's force) distinguished itself in a brilliant affair, resulting in the total defeat of the French cavalry at Ribera. Major-General Long, who commanded, spoke in the highest terms of all the troops under his command, particularly the Horse Artillery, who displayed great activity in their movements and precision in their fire, by which the enemy suffered considerably. Our loss was only one man killed and seven wounded; whereas the enemy had thirty men and a great many horses killed, eleven men and above thirty horses taken.

Marmont having been wounded, the command of the French Army devolved on General Clausel, who, after the defeat at Salamanca, retreated to Burgos. Wellington, therefore, marched his troops against the army commanded by Joseph Buonaparte.

On the 10th August an engagement took place with a body of the enemy's cavalry, which had been sent forward to watch the motions of the allies. This force was driven in in the morning by Brigadier-General D'Urban, who moved on to Majalahonda, where he took post with his brigade of Portuguese cavalry, Captain Macdonald's troop of Horse Artillery, and the cavalry and light infantry of the German Legion,

The enemy's cavalry having again approached, Brigadier-General D'Urban ordered the Portuguese brigade to charge the leading squadrons of the enemy, which appeared too far in advance to be supported by the main body. The Portuguese cavalry advanced to the attack, but before they reached the enemy, turned about and fled, leaving behind them, unprotected and unsupported, the guns of Macdonald's troop, which had been moved forward to cooperate with them. By the activity of the officers and men of the troop, the guns were moved off; but owing to the unfavourable nature of the ground over which they were moved, the carriage of one was broken, and two others were overturned, and these three guns, with Captain Dynely and the detachments of the troop, which remained trying to get them off, fell into the enemy's hands. (Captain Dynely escaped from the enemy, and rejoined the army on August 23).

On the 12th August the allies entered the capital of Spain, from which Joseph had retreated with his army; and it is needless to say that the British were received by the whole population with the greatest enthusiasm.

On the 1st September Wellington quitted Madrid; on the morning of the 7th the army passed the Douro, and on the 19th, they entered Burgos, the French retiring into the castle. The investment of the place was at once commenced, though the whole of the siege artillery with the army consisted of but three 18-pounders and five 24-pounder howitzers, and the supply of ammunition was very deficient. The siege was allotted to the 1st and 6th divisions, while the main body of the army advanced to the neighbourhood of Quintanapala. The siege lasted from the 20th September to the 29th October, during which time the castle was assaulted four times, and at the end of the period our few guns were all either destroyed by the enemy or rendered useless by excessive firing. The siege was then raised, but it was acknowledged on all sides that the failure was owing to the want of artillery, as certainly there was neither want of skill or zeal in those present.

Wellington said:—

> The officers at the head of the artillery and engineer departments, Lieut.-Colonel Robe, Lieut.-Colonel Burgoyne, and Lieut.-Colonel Dickson, who commanded the reserve artillery, rendered me every assistance; and the failure of success is not to be attributed to them. By their activity we carried off everything in the course of one night, excepting three 18-pounders destroyed by the enemy's fire, and the eight pieces of cannon which were taken from the enemy on the night of the 19th.

The Royal Artillery had fifteen men killed during this siege, and forty wounded, including Lieut.-Colonel Robe, Captains Dansey died in London, July 21, 1853), and Power, Lieutenants Elgee (died 1850), and Johnstone.

The covering army was constantly harassed by the enemy during this siege, and their duties in covering the retreat were most dangerous and difficult. Major Downman with the Horse Artillery rendered himself most conspicuous throughout the whole of the operations. Bull's troop was especially distinguished; Captain Bull himself was twice wounded and compelled to quit the army, and during the retreat the troop was commanded by Captain Ramsay, who was reported by Wellington to have distinguished himself.

The sufferings of the army during the retreat from Burgos are matters well known. The weather was desperate, rain fell in torrents, the roads were rendered almost impassable, the men were knee-deep in the sloughs, and the transport of the guns and baggage had become a work of infinite difficulty. Added to this, the troops were almost destitute of provisions.

A writer in the *United Service Journal* for 1831 says:—

That on meeting the artillery who had served in the batteries before Burgos, we at first took them for prisoners, as they were mostly in French clothing, many of them riding on the carriages sick and wounded, drawn some by oxen and some by mules and horses. I never saw British soldiers in such a state.

On the 24th November the retreat closed, and the troops went into cantonments, the headquarters being established at Frenada, and the artillery at Malhada de Sourda, three miles distant.

During the winter considerable changes were effected in the artillery department. Colonel Robe (who, however, was suffering most severely from the wounds received at Burgos, succeeded Colonel Framingham in the chief command, and Lieut.-Colonel May was appointed adjutant-general. Major Frazer arrived from England and relieved Major Downman of the command of the Horse Artillery.

★★★★★★★★★★

Major, afterwards Colonel Sir Augustus Frazer, was born at Dunkirk on September 5, 1776; his father, who was a colonel in the Royal Engineers, being engaged in the demolition of the works of that fortress. He received his earliest education at Edinburgh, and in 1790 he was admitted into the Royal Military Academy. He was commissioned into the Royal Artillery on September 17, 1793, and in the following December he joined the army in Flanders. In January he was attached, with two field-pieces, to the 3rd regiment of Foot Guards, with whom he served until the return of the army in May, 1795; having, during that period, been present at the affair of Mouvaix, the Battle of Cateau, the affairs near Tournay, at Boxtel, and the recapture of Fort St. André.

In September, 1799, being in the Horse Artillery, he embarked for North Holland, and was present at the affairs of Bergen, Egmont, and Alkmaar. Captain Frazer commanded the artillery of the expedition against Buenos Ayres.). After the war he held various appointments at Woolwich, where he died, June 11, 1836. His son, Augustus Henry, who was born in 1810, served in the Royal Artillery from 1828, till compelled from the state of his health to retire from the service in 1843. He died at Sindia, in Persia, August 11, 1848.

★★★★★★★★★★

Captain Gardiner succeeded Macdonald (promoted), and Captain Beane succeeded Lefebure (deceased) in the command of troops. An additional troop under Captain Webber Smith also arrived in the Peninsula. (He died at Brighton, March 21, 1853, aged seventy-five. He was lieut.-general and colonel-commandant of the 4th battalion). An additional field brigade, temporarily commanded by Captain Cairnes, joined the army from Cadiz.

In May, 1812, Lieut.-Colonel Holcombe, with Major Williamson's, Captain Thomson's, and Major Campbell's companies, embarked at Lisbon and joined the army of Sir John Murray at Alicant. They were afterwards joined by two companies under Captains Lacy and Gilmour, which came from Italy with Lord W. Bentinck. These companies served at the siege of Tarragona, the Battle of Castalla, and all the operations on the east coast of Spain in 1813.

★★★★★★★★★★

Major Williamson died at Woolwich, April 26, 1836.
Captain Lacy died at Woolwich, March 9, 1852.
Captain Gilmour died at Hammersmith, August 31, 1859, aged seventy-eight.

★★★★★★★★★★

Captain Arabin, with four mountain guns, was attached to the advance of the army under Colonel Adam, which, on the 11th April, 1813, engaged the enemy on the pass of Biar. (Captain Arabin afterwards Colonel Frederick Arabin died while in command of the Royal Artillery in Bermuda in 1843). After a contest of several hours, during which two of these guns were disabled, our advance was obliged to retire on to the main body, leaving the disabled guns in the hands of the enemy. On the following day the French, under Suchet, advanced and attacked our army at Castalla. They were defeated, however, and compelled to retreat. The whole of the batteries were engaged in this action, including some guns under Lieutenant Patton. The Royal Artillery had four men killed.

The advance guard under Colonel Adam, including Captain Arabin and his battery of four guns, was again attacked and defeated by the French on the 12th September. On this occasion the whole of the guns were lost. Captain Arabin escaped by riding amongst the French cavalry who were in pursuit of the Spaniards, and most of the non-commissioned officers and gunners escaped into the mountains and rejoined the army. The whole of the operations in this quarter were miserably conducted.

About this time, however, news arrived of the retreat of Buonaparte from Russia, and the rising of Germany; Suchet was therefore compelled to break up his army, sending the best of his troops to reinforce Napoleon, disarming the German regiments, and sending them to France under guard, and despatching the remainder to resist the Austrians in Italy.

Under these circumstances the campaign closed in the south-east of Spain.

CHAPTER 9

The Campaigns in the Peninsula—Operations in Andalusia

Early in January, 1810, the French Army under Soult advanced into Andalusia, and on the last day of the month. Joseph Buonaparte entered Seville in triumph. Elated by their success, the French at once pushed on for Cadiz; and, though disappointed in their expectations of entering the place, they at once seized on Rota, Port Royal, Port St. Mary's, and Chiclana, where they established camps and batteries from whence shells were thrown into Cadiz. Reinforcements speedily arrived from the British camp at Torres Vedras, and also from Gibraltar, and the defensive operations were conducted, on the part of the British at last, in a most praiseworthy manner. There were five companies of the Royal Artillery in Cadiz, commanded by Captains Owen, Birch, Hughes, Shenley, and Roberta; the whole under the command of Major Alexander Duncan.

Fort Matagorda, which had been abandoned by the Spaniards on the approach of the French, was hastily occupied by a detachment under Captain Maclean (including twenty-five men of the Royal Artillery under Lieutenant Brereton) during the night of the 22nd February; and although the French cannonaded the work with field artillery all the next day, the garrison, supported by the fire of Fort Puntales (which was directed by a gallant young officer, Lieutenant Brett, R.A.), was immoveable.

In March General Graham arrived from England and assumed the chief command of the British. Additional reinforcements also reached Cadiz on the 31st.

The importance of Matagorda was now felt. It had been held fifty-five days, though frequently cannonaded, and now impeded the completion of the enemy's works. It was very small, however, and could only bring seven guns to bear, and on the 21st April a vigorous attack was made upon it. The fire of forty-eight guns and mortars, of the largest size, was concentrated upon the little fort, and the feeble parapet disappeared in a moment. The naked rampart and the undaunted hearts of the garrison remained, but the troops fell fast and the enemy shot quick and close; a staff bearing the Spanish flag was broken six times in an hour, and the colours were at last fastened to an angle of the work itself, while the men besought the officers to hoist the British ensign.

Thirty hours this tempest lasted, and sixty-four men out of one hundred and forty were down when General Graham sent boats to carry off the survivors. The bastion was then blown up under the direction of Major Lefebre, an engineer of great promise; but he also fell—the last man whose blood wetted the ruins thus abandoned. Lieutenant Brereton was severely wounded, and his place was taken by Lieutenant Wright. Captain Maclean, in his despatch, says:—

> I beg in a most particular manner to mention the services of that most excellent officer Lieutenant Brereton of the Royal Artillery, for his unremitted attention to his duty, and the masterly style in which he kept up his fire on the enemy.

In May the French prisoners, about 1,500 men, cutting the cables of two hulks, drifted, in a heavy gale, to the French side of the bay, and made their escape. These poor creatures had been treated by the Spaniards with horrible cruelty; and so incensed were the Spaniards at losing their prey that they continued to fire on the vessels after they had run aground. Lieutenant Brett, who commanded the artillery at Puntales and the upper battery, refused to fire on them, knowing that they had been cruelly and unjustly confined since the battle at Baylen. This refusal on the part of Lieutenant Brett was commended by General Graham, the British commandant.

Captain Cowley and Lieutenant Mitchell, of the Royal Artillery, had been sent from Gibraltar to excite the inhabitants of the Ronda to take up arms against the common enemy, and to direct their operations. They were very successful; and in June General Lacy, with 3,000 infantry and 200 cavalry, was sent from Cadiz to aid them. This expedition was badly conducted; Lacy was defeated by the French general Rey, and obliged to re-embark his force and make his way quickly back to Cadiz.

It was in this garrison that Gunner Wellington, the father of the heroine of the Rev. Mr. Cobbold's stirring narrative, received his death-wound. He was employed on the 9th September, 1810, in extricating a ship from the fire of the French batteries, when he was struck by a shot from one of the guns on the heights. He was a worthy old soldier, and had served with distinction in the defence of Gibraltar. Among the wounded during this siege was Lieut. Cozens, R.A., in connexion with whose misfortune an amusing story is told by Benson Hill.

> When a cadet, Cozens had a happy knack of imitating the noise of a stump, thereby greatly irritating the French master, the Chevalier Warren, who had a wooden leg; at the same time causing great fun among his companions. One day Warren caught him in the fact, and said—'Meestair Cozen, saar! for why you ensoolt my *malheur?* Young gentilman, I did not get my wooden leg by jompeeng out of a bad-'ous vindow. No, by Gar! I lose my leem in de sairveece of my keeng, fighting for my contre in de field of *honneur, ma foi.* Saum day, *monsieur,* you shall be soree and weesh you had nevare afironte de brave man in de strange lan' by de joke on his vooden leg—eet is bad mannaire.'
>
> After his return from Cadiz, Cozens one day met the *chevalier* on the barrack field, and on making himself known to him, Warren cried out—'Ah, by Gar! Monsieur Cozens, saar, now we are queets.' In a moment more he threw his arms about the wounded man, exclaiming through his tears and kisses—'Ah, my poor, dear, fonny boy! I am so sorre for him! I have had my joke—forgive me, and be prode dad you get de vooden leg in de glorious *battaile—la fortune de la guerre*—not by jompine out of bad-'ous vindow, eh!'

In October, 1810, a malignant and pestilential fever, known by the name of the "black vomit," burst forth in the garrison of Cadiz. One of the first victims was Lieutenant Godby, R.A., who died on the 26th October. It subsided for a time, but again broke out with increased virulence in 1812, carrying off hundreds of the inhabitants as well as many of the defenders of the garrison.

Lieutenant John Maxwell and Captain Jonathan Mallett were the first officers of the Royal Artillery who fell victims to this fatal disease in 1812. Captain Shenley's company were dreadful sufferers; and when, at last, he himself was carried off, there was perhaps more sympathy shown on his behalf than for any other officer who had preceded him. Poor Shenley was a right joyous fellow, but his qualities of good comradeship are best given by the epitaph he selected for himself:—

Here lies a jolly dog
Who lived every day of his life.

The circumstances of his death were very affecting. The delirium of fever was upon him when his wife and children arrived from Woolwich, and although he survived two days, no lucid interval granted them the consolation of knowing that he was conscious of their presence.

On the 2nd February, 1811, an army, including three batteries of the Royal Artillery under Major Duncan (having under him Captains Hughes and Roberts), was embarked at Cadiz for Tarifa, to attack the rear of the besieging French Army at Chiclana. After much delay, occasioned by tempestuous weather, the English troops and artillery were assembled at Tarifa on the 27th, and the following morning they moved through the passes of the Ronda hills, and halted within four leagues of the French outposts. Movements were continued on both sides till the morning of the 6th of March, when the combatants met at Barossa. In this action the British artillery covered themselves with glory.

The field batteries galloped up and unlimbered within 250 yards of the enemy, annihilating their advance. In coming into action one of the guns got entangled with a pine tree; there was no time to disengage it, and setting to with the whip, they pushed the horses forward, and tore up the tree completely by the roots, although one of considerable size. This appeared a good omen, and showed that a trifling obstacle would not be allowed to impede their career. Never were guns better served; and the gaps in the enemy's ranks showed the precision with which the spherical shells were thrown.

Towards the close of the action, when the French divisions fell back on each other for mutual support, and endeavoured to rally, the guns were again moved forward, and opened a close and murderous fire that prevented a possibility of reforming. Nothing could save the shattered battalions from that exterminating cannonade but an instant retreat. The French acknowledge to have lost more men by artillery in this battle than in any other during the war; the near approach to their infantry, however, was fatal to the British artillery, whose loss was very great. Lieutenants Woolcombe and Maitland were mortally wounded, and Captains Hughes and Cator, Lieutenants Pester, E. Mitchell, Brereton, and C. Manners, received wounds more or less severe.

****

Lieutenant Woolcombe's wound was of a remarkable nature. The bullet entered the stomach, never breaking his shirt, but driving it into the wound. He died the following day.

Captain Hughes died at Bristol while in command of the artillery in the western district, in 1830, aged fifty-three years.

Captain Cator, afterwards General Cator.

Lieutenant Pester, afterwards Major-General Pester.

Lieutenant Manners retired in 1816.

****

The preservation of Tarifa from the hands of the French was at this time of great importance, the object being to prevent the supplies that the Campina could afford from reaching the blockading army. For the accomplishment of this purpose two regiments, with a detachment of the Royal Artillery under Captain Mitchell, commanded by Colonel Skerrett, sailed from Cadiz for Tarifa, accompanied by some Spanish regiments and artillery.

The place was assaulted by the French on the 31st December, 1811, when, after an obstinate struggle, they were repulsed with great loss. The Royal Artillery on this occasion displayed their usual courage and science. The fire from the guns under Captain Mitchell is particularly to be noticed, as connected with the 87th regiment in defending the assault.

Had it not been for the steady conduct of the garrison, and the never-to-be-surpassed or forgotten exertions of Captain C. F. Smith of the Royal Engineers, and Captain Mitchell of the Royal Artillery, death or Verdun, (the place in France where the English prisoners were confined), must have been the fate of the garrison. In later years, when Sir Charles Smith was compelled from the severity of his wounds to relinquish the command of the Syrian Army, he was succeeded by his old comrade Mitchell.

During the war in the Peninsula there were parties of the Royal Artillery stationed at most important points, and subjected to dangers of all descriptions, both from the attacks of the enemy and the still more deadly attacks of fever which broke out in the various garrisons in the south of Spain.

Yet these were not only prohibited from sharing the honours earned by their comrades, but their very existence was barely thought of.

Lieutenant Grantham, Royal Artillery, (died a major-general, June

18, 1860), was town major at Carthagena, which contained a very mutinous garrison of foreign levies, and it was often his painful duty to sit as president of courts-martial, and sentence his fellow-creatures to death. On one occasion, after the execution of a murderer, he was obliged to draw his sword and defend himself and the hangman from the fury of the Spanish populace.

The news of Wellington's defeat of Marmont, and his occupation of Madrid, caused Victor to relinquish the blockade of Cadiz and retire into Grenada. The French after destroying their works—the creation of so much toil and expenditure—retreated with such precipitation from before Cadiz, that they left behind a vast quantity of their stores and several hundred pieces of ordnance, some of which, of extraordinary length, had been cast for this very siege, and thirty gun-boats.

A force consisting of 1,600 British and Portuguese troops, and about 3,000 Spaniards, was instantly despatched to Seville, the only place in Andalusia now held by the enemy. Three field pieces, with the requisite number of men of the Royal Artillery, under Captain William Roberts, accompanied this expedition. (Captain Roberts died at Southampton, July 9, 1851). They left Cadiz on the 8th August, and were before Seville on the 27th. The outworks of the suburb of Triana were surrendered by the enemy, and the British at once marched into the main street. At first it was thought the city was abandoned, but on passing a side street they were saluted with case-shot, which struck some of the horses of the howitzer as they passed the opening.

Captain Roberts immediately halted his two rear guns, unlimbered to the left, and engaged the enemy. It was here that the gallant Lieutenant Brett was slain; he received a grape-shot between the eyes. The death of this officer, who was alike distinguished for knowledge of his profession, for gallantry, and the most urbane manners, was the greatest loss the force sustained.

He had commanded for more than two years the dangerous post of Fort Puntales, at Cadiz, where he had escaped unscathed, and he volunteered to accompany Captain Roberts on this expedition, and thus lost his life, and the service a most promising young officer.

The next day Captain Roberts and Lieutenant Raynes visited the Cartusa, for the purpose of taking account of any stores that might have been left there, and on entering they observed powder loosely scattered about the beautiful marble pavement which leads up to the high altar, and at a short distance from them were some Spaniards, one of whom was smoking. The captain suddenly called out, "Run,

Raynes, run!" and they had scarcely fled out at the gate when the whole building appeared one sheet of flame, accompanied with a low rumbling noise.

★★★★★★★★★★

Captain W. A. Raynes served at Copenhagen, 1807, the Corunna campaign, at Cadiz, and the subsequent campaigns in the Peninsula. He died at the Isle of Man, October 29,1850.

★★★★★★★★★★

Fortunately, no one was injured by this explosion; but we have now to recount a more serious occurrence, the trap laid by a treacherous enemy being this time successful!

A division from Cadiz, under the command of Major-General Cooke, including Lieut.-Colonel Duncan and Major Hughes's battery of the Royal Artillery, arrived at Seville shortly after its capture.

On the 20th September, Colonel Duncan, accompanied by Hughes, Roberts, and Second Captains Cairnes and Bedingfield, went to examine a powder-mill which the French had made use of. On the party entering the building some loose powder was observed scattered carelessly about, but this excited no suspicious of treachery; in fact, such a thing was not for a moment thought of. Upon one of the Spaniards who accompanied the party, however, setting some part of the machinery in motion, an almost instant explosion took place, followed by several others, and the entire building was shaken to the ground.

Colonel Duncan, who happened to be near the door, rushed out, and his body was found lying on a heap of rubbish, without any appearance of injury from the fire, but with two deep wounds on the head, caused by the falling stones and materials of the building.

Thus, perished ignobly the gallant Alexander Duncan, who as a subaltern had highly distinguished himself at Toulon and Corsica, and who by his conduct at the Battle of Barossa had proved himself second to none as a commanding officer of artillery.

He was a remarkably fine, handsome man; and, as a commanding officer, he possessed not only the love and respect of all who served under him, but their confidence in the highest degree. Every man knew he was safe so long as he did his duty to the best of his ability; for Duncan was a straightforward, honest soldier, and as such despised all underhand or vindictive proceedings.

His reports were open and manly, not "secret and confidential."

Captains Bedingfield (died at Northallerton, Yorkshire, December 26, 1864, aged eighty), and Cairnes were very severely injured by this explosion; both of whom ultimately recovered, but the latter—the kind, generous, and amiable Robert Cairnes—perished afterwards at Waterloo.

Captain Birch (died at Dublin, June 29, 1851), succeeded Duncan in command of the artillery at Cadiz, the companies being kept in the garrison until the end of the war.

Major-General Cooke, who succeeded Graham in the command of the garrison, appointed Lieutenant F. Warde (afterwards major-general), Royal Artillery, divisional brigade-major; and such was the confidence felt in him as a staff-officer that he was afterwards appointed by General Capel to the responsible post of deputy assistant adjutant-general. This appointment he held till the end of the war, when he resumed his duty as a *lieutenant in the Royal Artillery*.

CHAPTER 10

The Campaigns in the Peninsula, 1813-1814

Winter passed away, the army recovered from its hardships, and Lord Wellington was indefatigable in perfections the equipment of every department, to enable him to take the field efficiently when the season should come round and active operations be again renewed. Nothing could surpass the splendid state of discipline produced by this period of inactivity while the army was reposing in winter quarters. Its *matériel* was now truly magnificent, powerful reinforcements having arrived from England; *the artillery was complete in every requisite for the field.*

Colonel Robe arrived at Lisbon, carried on the shoulders of his men, on the 13th December, and as soon as he could be moved, was conveyed on board ship for England.

★★★★★★★★★★

Colonel, afterwards Sir William Robe, was the son of a sergeant in the Royal Artillery, who, by virtue of his long service and exemplary conduct, was promoted to a second-lieutenancy in the Invalid Battalion, and afterwards appointed proof-master of the regiment, and who was rewarded by living to see his son a knight, and his grandson mentioned by the Duke of Wellington as having distinguished himself in the Peninsula. He died at Woolwich, July 1, 1814. Sir William Robe received his commission as second-lieutenant, May 21, 1781, a year after his father's elevation to the same rank. He served in various parts of the world, including the expedition to Copenhagen and the early campaigns in the Peninsula, until, disabled by wounds, he was totally unfit for active service, and obliged to return to England. He never recovered the proper use of his leg, but suffered great pain until his death, which took place at Woolwich, November 5, 1820, his age being fifty-five years. Sir William Robe was the father of four distinguished officers; the eldest, William Livingstone, was killed at Waterloo; the second, Alexander Watt, served in the Royal Engineers, and was present in most of the actions of the Peninsula in 1813-14, afterwards went on the New Orleans expedition, and returned to England for the purpose of proceeding to the Netherlands in 1815; he died in 1849. The third son was the late Colonel Thomas Congreve Robe, Royal Artillery, who died at Bermuda, September 21, 1853. George Mountain, the fifth son of Sir William Robe, belonged to the Bengal Native Infantry; he died in 1825.

★★★★★★★★★★

Robe's place was supplied by Colonel Fisher, the next senior officer, but shortly before the commencement of active operations in May, 1813, Lord Wellington persuaded that officer to relinquish the command of the artillery, which he at once bestowed on Lieut.-Colonel Dickson. By so doing Lord Wellington not only wounded the private interests and feelings of many, but violated military usages by giving him command of several officers senior to him in the corps.

Colonel Fisher was a kind gentleman, accomplished, and with all the spirit of a soldier; but there is an immense difference between the elderly officer who respectably adheres to the line of duty laid down for him with the same methodical precision that he would use in the barrack field at Woolwich, and one who possesses energy of mind and vigour of body to set difficulties at defiance, defeat stratagem by stratagem, grapple with adverse circumstances, and even turn them to good account. Such an officer Colonel Fisher was not—such an officer Colonel Dickson was.

★★★★★★★★★★

Colonel, afterwards Sir George Bulteel Fisher was a son of the Rev. John Fisher, of Calbourn, Isle of Wight, and brother to the Bishop of Salisbury. He was commandant of Woolwich garrison from February 1827 until his death, and is remembered as a most kind and amiable gentleman. He died in the Arsenal, March 8, 1834, aged sixty-nine years.

★★★★★★★★★★

Fortunately for the service, Colonel Dickson was a man so generally beloved, that his appointment over the heads of his seniors did not produce those effects of jealousy and sullen obedience which might, perhaps, be expected on such an occasion. When he assumed the command, he appeared in an old and very shabby Portuguese uniform, and from considerate motives he never changed it during the whole of the campaign, thus escaping the feelings of jealous envy which he feared might at times arise in the breasts of his seniors if he arrayed himself as a brigadier-general of the British Army.

Major Frazer, who arrived in the Peninsula during the winter, and who, on the return of Lieut.-Colonel Downman to England, was appointed to the command of the Horse Artillery, was one before whom Dickson was preferred. His feelings, which are expressed in the following extract from one of his letters, will give a tolerable idea of the general feeling of the corps on this occasion:—

> I shall get on very well with Dickson; he was second to me in the South-American expedition, and then obeyed my orders with the implicit readiness which I shall now transfer to his. He is a man of great abilities and quickness, and without fear of anyone.

★★★★★★★★★★

Sir Alexander Dickson, the son of Admiral Dickson, of Sydenham, near Kelso, was born June 3, 1777, and received his first commission as second lieutenant November 6, 1794. He served at the attack on Minorca in 1798, and the siege of Malta in 1800. In 1807 he was on the South-American expedition, and served in the Peninsula with the Portuguese artillery until he was selected by the Duke of Wellington to the command of the Royal Artillery. He served subsequently in America and the Waterloo campaign. On the death of Sir John Macleod, he was appointed adjutant-general of artillery, and he held that appointment till his death, which took place in London, April 22, 1840. Sir Alexander Dickson had three sons, who followed in his footsteps. The eldest, William, was a lieutenant in the Bengal Artillery; he died in India in 1827. The second, Alexander Stephen, entered the Royal Artillery in 1833; in 1840 he was sent with a party of non-commissioned officers to instruct the Turks in the practice of artillery; and he died at Constantinople, January 27, 1845. Sir Alexander Dickson's third son is the present (1865) Colonel Collingwood Dickson. In 1847 a handsome monument was erected to the memory of Sir Alexander Dickson by the officers of the corps, upon which is given the names of all the battles and sieges in which he took part. It is in the grounds of the Royal Military Repository at Woolwich.

★★★★★★★★★★

The headquarters of the army left Frenada on the 22nd May, and the artillery bade *adieu* to Malhada de Sourda on the same day, arriving at Ciudad Rodrigo in the evening.

Most of the troops and batteries had already started, the different divisions and brigades having marched so as to reach the Douro by the

23rd May. Major Ross's troop was attached to the light division under the immediate command of Lord Wellington, and moved forward on Salamanca by the direct route. Captain Beane's troop was with the second division under Lord Hill, and advanced on the same point by Alba de Tormes. The other divisions and cavalry brigades marched under General Graham, with instructions to effect a junction with the remainder of the army at Valladolid.

The artillery of this force was composed of three troops of Horse Artillery, under Captains Gardiner, Ramsay, and Webber Smith, and six batteries (or brigades) of Royal Artillery, under Captains Douglas, Lawson, Maxwell, Brandreth, Dubourdieu, and Cairnes. Hill's cavalry engaged the rear-guard of the enemy near Salamanca on the 26th May. On this occasion Beane's troop played effectively, causing them to retreat, leaving upwards of 200 prisoners, seven tumbrils of ammunition, and a quantity of baggage on the field.

There is no occasion to dwell upon all the skirmishes which took place at Morales, Osma, San Millan, etc., in which Ross's and Gardiner's troops played important parts, nor upon the retreat of the French from Burgos; suffice it to say that no movements daring the whole war exceeded in brilliant effect the rapid advance of the army from the Douro to the Bayos, from the left bank of which stream the enemy's rear-guard was driven on to the main body at Vittoria.

The moment had at length come when the enemy, whose whole movements since the commencement of the campaign had been those of retreat, was compelled to make a final and decisive stand on the Spanish territory, or suffer himself ingloriously to be driven headlong on the Pyrenees. Joseph Buonaparte, who commanded (having Marshal Jourdan as his general), decided on the former, and on the 19th June concentrated his forces in position in front of Vittoria. During the 20th the English Army was collected together, and on the following morning began the attack.

The right column, under Sir Rowland Hill, drove the enemy's left from the mountains of Puebla at the point of the bayonet, then crossed the Zadora and attacked the heights of Subijana de Alava. The first shot from our side sent a wheel off one of the enemy's gun-carriages on the other side of the river, spinning it into the air; others of the guns opposed to Mill's advancing column were similarly served by those of Beane's troop before the heights were gained.

The enemy's front was now attacked by the 3rd, 4th, and 7th divisions, but his artillery poured so destructive a fire upon these columns as to check the advance. Fifteen of their guns, well served, presented a battery somewhat formidable. It was to this fire, supported by their infantry, that we had to oppose our guns; and for the space of more than half an hour this brilliant battle of artillery continued on both sides; the enemy's fire being weakened, however, our infantry, supported by two troops of Horse Artillery, resumed the advance, and bearing down all opposition, carried the heights, captured twenty-eight pieces of artillery, and drove the enemy back on Vittoria. Captain Cairnes was thanked in general orders by General Dalhousie for his services on this occasion.

Major Frazer, observing some squadrons of cavalry near our guns, rode forward to ascertain who they were, and was surprised to find himself alone among the enemy. Fortunately, no one heeded him, and he at once rode back and brought up Gardiner's troop, who quickly caused them to shift their quarters. As Major Frazer was bringing up this troop along a narrow road, with the guns almost at a gallop, he saw a wounded French officer lying in the centre of the road.

Another minute, and the ponderous weight of the guns would have crushed the sufferer into the earth as they passed over him; but with the rapidity of thought Frazer threw himself from his horse, dragged the Frenchman to the bank that skirted the road, and remounting with the same rapidity, had barely time to escape the fearful death from which he had saved an enemy. Providing him with some brandy, and leaving him in charge of Bombardier Smith, Major Frazer afterwards sent a surgeon to attend the wounded officer, who turned out to be General Sarrut. He said he was grateful, but dying, being dreadfully wounded with case-shot.

★★★★★★★★★★

Major Frazer, in a letter dated June 22, writes:—"General Sarrut is dead. Poor man! I wish now I had taken his decoration of the Legion of Honour; but though I saw it, the general thanked me so warmly, and squeezed my hand with such earnestness, that I felt it would have been ungenerous to have taken the prize."

★★★★★★★★★★

Aa soon as the heights were in our possession the village of Gamarra Mayor was most gallantly stormed by a brigade of the 5th division, assisted by two guns of Major Lawson's battery. The enemy suffered severely and lost three pieces of cannon. Lieut.-General Graham then proceeded to attack the village of Abechuco with the 1st division, by forming a strong battery against it, consisting of Captain

Dubourdieu's brigade, and Captain Ramsay's troop of Horse Artillery, and under cover of this fire the German Legion advanced to the attack of the village, which was carried, and three guns and a howitzer were taken.

Two powerful attempts to regain the village having been repulsed, the result of the day was no longer doubtful, and the last stroke, to the total discomfiture of the French, being given by driving from the heights of Zadora two divisions of reserve infantry that commanded the passage of the river, our victorious army joined in one general pursuit of the fugitive foe.

Captain Webber Smith's guns now arrived, and as soon as he could clear away our men he opened with canister upon the retiring dragoons, who abandoned the whole of the baggage of the French Army—waggons, carriages, and packages of every description. Another division of infantry now came up, preceded by Norman Ramsay with some guns. He was pressing forward with as much anxiety as if the success of the day depended on his personal exertions, as soon as he saw the column of French dragoons he unlimbered, and dismounting, laid one of the guns himself, and marked the effects of his fire, heedless of the friendly cheer of the infantry, so completely was he engrossed in his own occupation.

The victory was now complete; the enemy had left on the field 160 pieces of cannon, 400 caissons, 12,000 rounds of ammunition, 2,000,000 musket cartridges, and 1,000 prisoners, and were now flying, a helpless and disorganised mob, along the road to Pampeluna.

Immediate orders were now sent for horse artillery, those on the ground having expended all their ammunition, and in a few minutes Ross's troop, regardless of roads, had crowned the heights, from whence it showered down balls and howitzer-shells upon the terrified masses, now urged into efforts of accelerated flight by the slaughter around.

Though the artillery played so important a part in this battle, their losses were not very severe. Colonel May and Lieutenant Woodyear, both on the staff, were struck with spent balls; and Lieutenant Swabey, of Gardiner's troop, received a severe wound in the knee. (Lieutenant Lumley Woodyear's wounds appeared slight at first, but he succumbed to the effects of them, and died September 1, 1813).

These were the only casualties among the officers; there were nine gunners killed, and one sergeant and fifty-two rank and file wounded.

By Lord Wellington's mention of the artillery, he was evidently satisfied with the conduct of the corps in this action; and the Prince Regent was graciously pleased, in consideration of the very striking and unexampled circumstance of the whole of the British artillery having been brought into action at the Battle of Vittoria, and the whole of the enemy's artillery having been captured in that glorious victory, to grant to all the officers commanding divisions of artillery ten shillings *per diem*, to the officers commanding brigades five shillings *per diem,* and to Colonel Dickson, as commanding officer of the whole, twenty shillings *per diem.* ("The artillery was most judiciously placed by Lieut.-Colonel Dickson, and was well served; and the army is particularly indebted to that corps."—*Wellington's Despatch*).

As night threw its shadows over the scenes just described all further pursuit of the enemy was abandoned, and Vittoria became the rendezvous of Lord Wellington and his staff. On the following morning the army resumed its march in two grand divisions—one, under Wellington, following up the enemy to Pampeluna; the other, under Sir T. Graham, proceeding by the great road from Vittoria to Bayonne.

It was on this day that Norman Ramsay, the idol of the corps, committed an error through which he lost the good opinion of Wellington and his share in the honours bestowed on his brother officers. Passing him on the road. Lord Wellington ordered Ramsay to take his troop to a village then near, adding that if there were orders for the troop in the course of the night, he would send them. Early the following morning Ramsay received orders from a staff officer to rejoin his brigade. He at once proceeded to do so, when he was met by Wellington, who angrily ordered him to be put under arrest, and his troop handed over to Captain Cator, for having disobeyed his orders in not remaining at the village until he received further directions from himself. This measure nearly broke the soldier's heart, to be thus separated from those he had led through so many a bloody field, and the parting was as keenly felt by the officers and men.

Lord Fitzroy Somerset and the whole of Wellington's staff, as well as Colonel Dickson and the officers of the artillery, made every effort to move his lordship in Ramsay's favour, but to no purpose. Sir T. Graham addressed a letter to him on the subject which made him angry with that officer, and it was not till three weeks afterwards that Ramsay was restored to the command of his troop. His name was omitted, however, in the brevet that came out after the battle of Vittoria, and he did not receive his majority until the conclusion of the war, though none had earned it so faithfully and so well. (This incident is introduced by Lover in his novel of *Handy Andy*.)

****

"At the Battle of Vittoria," says Sir Augustus Frazer, "Bull's troop (which I have no hesitation in saying is much the best in the country) had, under Ramsay's command, been of unusual and unquestionable service."

****

About six o clock on the morning of the 25th June our advance-guard came upon the retreating French. A cry was at once raised for artillery, when a gun of Ross's troop, commanded by Lieutenant Macdonald, galloped up the road and plied round-shot with such effect that it succeeded in dismounting one of the only two cannon which the enemy had extricated from Vittoria's bloody field. One shot struck down seven of the enemy, some of whom were dead; others, still alive, had either their legs or arms off, or were otherwise horribly mutilated.

Two hours afterwards our troops came in sight of the enemy labouring with all possible energy to get off with their remaining gun. Lieutenant Belson's (afterwards Major-General G. J. Belson), detachment of Ross's troop now prepared for action; but the French, seeing their case was hopeless, fled furiously, throwing their gun over a precipice, when it was immediately taken possession of by a body of infantry in the vale below. Wellington at this moment rode up to Lieutenant Belson and congratulated him on having taken their last gun.

On reaching Pampeluna, Wellington found that King Joseph, with the main body of the French Army, had retreated into France, leaving a garrison in the fort. He accordingly blockaded the place with a force under Sir R. Hill, and proceeded with the main body to drive the enemy from the positions they had occupied in the Pyrenees, the greater part of the artillery, however, being sent to besiege San Sebastian.

The force under Sir T. Graham came up on the 25th with the enemy under General Foy, at Tolosa, he having barricaded the gates of the town and occupied the convents and buildings around. A general attack began between six and seven in the evening. Two guns of Ramsay's troop, and two 9-pounders of Dubourdieu's battery, quickly dispersed a body of the enemy on the plain, and one of the 9-pounders was afterwards brought up to burst open the Vittoria gate. The troops then entered, but the enemy made their escape in the dark through the Pampeluna gate. Sir T. Graham continued to push them along the road to Bayonne, dislodging them from every position in which they attempted to make a stand. They were at last driven across the Bidassoa by a brigade of the Gallician Army, and the garrison of Passages having surrendered to a Spanish force, Graham proceeded at once to the attack of San Sebastian.

This fortress was invested on the 1st July, and the necessary preparations were at once made to besiege it. The artillery was commanded by Colonel Dickson, Lieut.-Colonels May and Frazer having charge of the batteries. The men who worked in the batteries were under the control of Major Smith, Captains Lawson (died at Bath, April 23, 1819), Dubourdieu, Power, Morrison, and Parker. A naval brigade under Lieutenant O'Reilly also assisted in the batteries.

On the 15th July a battery of four guns was established for the purpose of demolishing the convent of San Bartolomeo and an adjoining redoubt which the enemy had occupied. Not having had the anticipated effect, on the 16th some howitzers were placed so as to take the redoubt in reverse, and the enemy was compelled to abandon it. An attack was accordingly made on the convent by the infantry, but without success.

On the morning of the 17th a number of field guns were brought up, and at ten o'clock the convent was assaulted and carried.

****

I cannot conclude this report without expressing my perfect satisfaction with all the officers and men of the Royal Artillery, both in the four-gun battery, employed for three days against the convent, and on the opposite bank of the river, whence several field pieces were served with great effect."—*Graham's Despatch.*

****

The way being thus cleared, operations were pushed forward against the town, and the siege began on the 20th July. The artillerymen were at their posts, and everything in readiness, and at ten o'clock, by preconcerted signal, fifty-nine pieces of heavy ordnance commenced a rapid and terrific fire. Standing in the battery, close in rear of the 24-pounders, from whose months issued an incessant and deafening sound, the noise of the other batteries was inaudible; but on looking round, columns of smoke ascended in all directions, while dust and fragments of stone flying from the masonry of the Mirador indicated the perfect direction and overpowering effect of the British artillery.

On the 21st Captain Dubourdieu was killed by a splinter of shell which struck him on the head. (Saumarez Dubourdieu was one of the officers of the Royal Irish Artillery, incorporated with the English in 1800).

On the 25th the town was assaulted, but our troops were repulsed with a loss of 500 men. As soon as the troops regained the trenches the batteries reopened a tremendous fire, which was kept up the whole of the night.

During this night Captain Alexander Macdonald made a reconnaissance, by fording the River Urumea and getting under the Mirador battery. By this daring act it became known that the river was fordable—this knowledge being of the greatest service to the besiegers.

At daylight on the morning of the 26th, Colonel Frazer, then in the 24-pounder battery, noticed a French officer standing in the breach, and making signals with his sword to our batteries. Colonel Frazer instantly caused the firing to cease; this was responded to by the French, whose batteries were quiet at the same instant, and upon an officer being despatched for an explanation, it appeared that numbers of our own wounded officers and soldiers lay strewed about under the walls of the fortress, and the shells from our batteries were bursting over these defenceless men, killing and wounding the already wounded, the shots also rebounding from the walls among them. This suffering could not be calmly witnessed by their enemies, hence the nobleness of this young French officer, who, upon the breach of San Sebastian, risked a thousand times his life in the cause of humanity.

The siege was now converted into a blockade, and was not resumed until the 28th August. During this month the belligerent armies were in constant motion, and fought no fewer than ten actions in and about the Pyrenees. The only artillery engaged in these affairs were the troops of Horse Artillery; Ross's troop being conspicuous on nearly every occasion.

When the siege of San Sebastian recommenced, two additional field officers, Major Dyer and Buckner (both volunteers), assisted in the working of the batteries. An increased fire of artillery, from batteries erected on the isthmus, opened on the breaches and defences, enlarging the former and silencing the guns in the latter.

★★★★★★★★★★

Major afterwards Lieut.-Colonel Sir John Dyer, K.C.B. On July 4, 1816, Sir John Dyer was field officer of the day at Woolwich, and observing the horses of Colonel Fyers' carriage take fright and run away, he made endeavours to stop them. In so doing he was struck on the breast by the pole of the carriage and knocked down, the wheels passing over his body. He survived only a few hours, leaving a widow

and four children to lament his untimely end.
Major afterwards Colonel Buckner, C.B., died at Chichester, March 12, 1837, aged sixty-four.

****

Lieutenant Jones, of the Engineers, who was a prisoner in San Sebastian during this bombardment—having been taken during the assault of the 25th July—speaks of the artillery as follows:—

> The excellence of the British artillery is well known; nothing could surpass the precision with which the shells were thrown, and the accuracy with which the fuses were cut. It is only those who have had the opportunity of witnessing their fire, and comparing it with that of the French, that can speak of its superiority.

A little before noon on the 31st August the columns advanced to the assault. Many desperate efforts were made to carry the breach, but each time on attaining the summit, a heavy and close fire from the entrenched mine within destroyed all who attempted to remain, and those at the foot fell in great numbers from the blank fire.

Then, in that desperate moment, when hope might have been supposed to be over, an expedient unparalleled in the records of war was resorted to. The British batteries opened on the curtain, and the storming parties heard with surprise the roar of cannon in the rear, while but a few feet above their heads the iron shower hissed horribly and swept away the enemy and their defences.

The conduct of the batteries during the assault of San Sebastian offers an example of precision of aim and absolute coolness on the part of the gunners never surpassed. When the column of attack stood upon the breach, checked, but not dismayed, by the extent of the obstacles opposed to it, six guns from a battery about 300 yards in rear of the sap opened their fire, throwing shot and shell with such accuracy over the heads of the troops, that large gaps were cut in the ranks of the defenders, and a mine was fired before its time, through which the assailants entered. (The firing of these guns was proposed to Sir T. Graham by Colonel Dickson).

A long and obstinate resistance was continued in the streets, but by five in the evening opposition had ceased, and San Sebastian was in possession of the British. Many valuable soldiers fell in this assault, but none more regretted than Lieut.-Colonel Sir Richard Fletcher, the commanding engineer, an officer who had served in the Royal Artillery, and who was greatly esteemed by the whole army for his gallantry and professional talent.

Lieutenant Hugh Morgan (died at Cheltenham, June 28, 1860), and two gunners were wounded during the bombardment of the castle, which surrendered on the 8th September, the garrison marching out and laying down their arms. Colonel Frazer recognised among the prisoners the officer who had so gallantly come down the breach after the first assault to assist our wounded. He ran up to him and offered his services, and discovered his name to be Loysel de Hametiere, captain of the grenadiers of the 22nd regiment. "There, said he, "are the remains of the brave 22nd; we were the other day 250, not more than fifty now remain."

Colonel Frazer introduced him to the Duke of Wellington, by whom he was restored to liberty unconditionally.

The high character sustained by the Royal Artillery during this laborious siege cannot be given in better language than that of Sir T. Graham in his different reports. In that of the 27th July, after the unsuccessful attack, he says:—

> The conduct throughout the whole of the operations of the siege hitherto of the officers and men of the Royal Artillery and Engineers never was exceeded in indefatigable zeal, activity, and gallantry; and I beg to mention particularly to Your Lordship Lieut.-Colonels Dickson, Frazer, and May, and Major Webber Smith.

At the capture Sir T. Graham reports:—

> I have now only to repeat the expression of my highest satisfaction with the conduct of the officers of the Royal Artillery and Engineers as formerly particularised in the report of the first attack. Every branch of the artillery service has been conducted by Colonel Dickson with the greatest ability.

And after the surrender of the castle:—

> Besides the officers of artillery formerly mentioned, who have continued to serve with equal distinction, I should not omit the names of Captains Morrison, Power, and Parker, who have been constantly in the breaching batteries and in the command of companies."

After the fall of San Sebastian nearly a month elapsed unmarked by any hostile movements on the part of either army. During the interval both were employed in strengthening their respective positions by the construction of field-works, and in preparing for the further prosecution of the campaign.

On the morning of the 7th October the Allied Army moved against the French, and after a hard day's fighting effected the passage of the Bidassoa, causing the enemy to retreat. Ross's, Ramsay's, and Smith's troops and Michell's battery (late Dubourdieu's) were engaged at the commencement of the action, in different parts of the position; but on crossing the river the enemy retired, and there was no further need of their services. (Michell afterwards Lieut.-General Sir J. Michell, K.C.B., colonel-commandant of the 5th brigade).

The artillery encountered many difficulties in crossing the Pyrenees. The rugged mountains, the bad roads, and above all, the intricate windings they were compelled to take to avoid the enemy, occasioned many disasters, such as the upsetting of carriages, etc.; the snow on the tops and sides of the mountains, and the heavy rain in the valleys, increased the difficulties tenfold.

On the 27th October Ross's troop, with Douglas's and Sympher's (German) batteries, received orders to advance. The former, which was particularly active during the whole of the campaign, reached Vera on the morning of the 28th, after struggling nearly twenty hours among the mountains; the batteries did not arrive at Salines (an adjoining village) until the afternoon of the 29th. Three guns of Maxwell's battery were so firmly imbedded in the mud and snow, that all attempts to withdraw them were fruitless; they were therefore buried and abandoned.

On the 10th November the Battle of the Nivelle was fought, and the allies entered France.

Though the whole of the Allied Army conducted itself in a manner impossible to be surpassed, no small portion of the success of this action must be attributed to the artillery under Colonel Dickson. By the indefatigable exertions of that officer, and those under him in command of batteries, artillery was brought to bear on the enemy's works from situations which appeared utterly inaccessible to that arm. A mountain battery under Lieutenant Robe, consisting of guns harnessed on mules trained for the service, ascended the most difficult ridges, and showered down destruction on the entrenchments below.

****

The artillery which was in the field was of the greatest use to us; and I cannot sufficiently acknowledge the intelligence and activity with which it was brought to the point of attack, under the directions of Colonel Dickson, over the bad roads through the mountains in this season of the year."—*Wellington's Despatch.*

****

The attack was begun at daybreak by eighteen guns, which opened on the enemy's advanced redoubt near Sarre. After a severe pounding from these guns, the infantry of the 4th division stormed and carried the redoubt. Ross's troop then galloped to a rising ground in rear of another redoubt (Grenada), drove the enemy from it, when the British infantry carried it and the village of Sarre, and advanced to the attack of Clausel's main position. Part of it was carried, but Clausel stood firm, covered by another redoubt and a powerful battery. These were speedily silenced by Ross's guns, the only battery that had been able to surmount the difficulties of the ground after passing Sarre. The British infantry then carried the redoubt, drove Clausel from his position, forced the French to retire, and the rout was complete.

Sir Howard Douglas, when in committee on the Ordnance Estimates in 1845, said—

That operation was worth all the money the Horse Artillery ever cost the country.

Other troops and batteries, though they did not play so important a part, rendered effective service at different parts of the position. Ramsay's troop, Brandreth's, Michell's, Douglas's, Sympher's batteries, and Tulloh's Portuguese artillery, all contributed to the success of the day, and great consternation was created among the enemy by the shot from Robe's mountain guns, which came tumbling down among them when they thought themselves secure. (Brandreth served at Malta, 1800; coast of France, 1803; Corunna campaign and Walcheren, 1809. Died at Chudley, Devon, September 24, 1851).

The artillery had six men killed in the action, and thirty-five wounded, including Lieutenant J. Day, of Ross's troop.

The achievements of the 10th November were followed by an interval of repose. The Allied Army went into cantonments between the Nivelle and the sea, while Marshal Soult withdrew his army within an intrenched camp in front of Bayonne.

Wellington now determined, in order to extend his line of supply, to seize the strong ground between the Nive and the Adour. The Allied Army accordingly advanced on the 9th December, and after five days' severe fighting, the enemy was compelled to retreat to the Adour.

On the first day, the only guns engaged were those of Ramsay's troop and a Portuguese battery. Ross was on the ground, but was not called upon to engage. Ramsay behaved with his usual gallantry; he was twice struck with musket-shot—first on the chin, and afterwards in the breast, a ball having flattened a button of his waistcoat He never left the field, but remained with his troop until the 14th, when the enemy retreated; he was then compelled to report himself wounded, being unable to move from his quarters. On the 10th, Ramsay's troop did considerable execution among the enemy, as did Captain Mosse's battery (late Lawson's), which arrived on the field most opportunely. (Captain Mosse died at Devonport, February 9, 1831). Captain Cairnes, who was present as a spectator, his battery being at Fuenterabia (a few miles in the rear), received a severe wound in the head.

The artillery were not in action on the 11th, and on the 12th there were but two guns of Mosse's battery engaged.

Most of the batteries which could be brought up, especially those of Hill's division, were warmly engaged in the final struggle on the 13th; Ross's troop was particularly engaged, and, with a battery of Portuguese guns, kept the enemy from advancing by the main road. One of Ross's guns was dismounted by a shot which broke the axletree; but a spare carriage being at hand, the gun was soon replaced and in action.

The following extracts from the despatches speak for the services of the artillery in the Battles of the Nive:—

> Captain Ramsay's troop of Horse Artillery moved with the left and centre columns, and I had much reason to be pleased with the active and judicious manner in which he and his officers conducted themselves, and with the effect of the fire of the troop.—*Sir John Hope, 10th December.*
>
> In my former reports I ought to have mentioned that the troop of Horse Artillery commanded by Captain Ramsay. and the brigades of artillery commanded by Captains Carmichael and Mosse, have been employed with the advanced troops on the 10th and 11th, and that they conducted themselves to my satisfaction.—*Sir John Hope, 13th December,*
>
> The two brigades of artillery under Lieut.-Colonel Ross and Lieut.-Colonel Tulloh were most judiciously posted to command the road, and caused considerable loss to the enemy in his advance, and during the contest upon, our centre; the zeal

and activity of these officers were most conspicuous throughout the day.

I feel myself particularly indebted to Major Carncross of the Royal Artillery, with the officers of his department.—*Sir R. Hill, 16th December.*

The winter had now set in with severity, and ended all military movements for a season. Towards the middle of February, the weather having then become more favourable, the army prepared to take the field.

On the 17th the enemy were driven across the Gave de Mauleon by a corps under Sir Rowland Hill; the 92nd regiment, supported by the fire of Captain Beane's troop, crossed the ford, and made a most gallant attack upon the French infantry, forcing them to retire with considerable loss,

On this occasion Lieutenant G. A, Moore was killed by a musket-ball.

On the night of the 22nd February the first division got under arms and marched upon the Adour. The advanced guard consisted of three light companies of the 1st brigade, Captain Morrison's battery, and a rocket troop under Captain Lane. Their route lay through a deep, gloomy pine forest, over a bad country road. By daylight the next morning a battery of 18-pounders was established on the left bank of the river, which was very shortly engaged with a corvette—the *Sappho*—and a few gunboats. A number of rockets were fired, and one of them stuck in the bow of one of the boats and sank her. The French soldiers were so frightened that they jumped overboard with all their accoutrements, and were drowned.

The practice of the battery was not good at first, from want of platforms; but this was soon rectified, and a corvette got a most handsome pommelling, and was glad at last to sheer off, with the loss of her captain, and more than half her crew killed and wounded. One of our shots cut her flagstaff in two, and the tricolour flag was seen floating down the stream. An artillery man, stripping off his clothes, swam in and brought it out, and it was soon seen waving on our own battery as a trophy. Captain Morrison had the skirts of his coat shaved off by a shot, and being rather Dutch-built, his comrades were rather amused at the circumstance, and at the curious appearance he presented.

A bridge which had been constructed by Colonel Sturgeon, and completed by the staff corps, was now to be thrown over the Adour; to effect which a number of *chasse-marées* were sent round the coast from Passages, laden with anchors and other essentials for the foundation.

The entrance to the Adour was at all times attended with peril to craft of every description, owing to a bar of sand, over which the waves rolled with fearful violence.

The enemy had removed the buoys which mark this dangerous spot, and consequently when the little flotilla bearing the materials appeared at the mouth of the river, it was necessary, before they proceeded any further, the bar should be discovered. A boat commanded by Lieutenant O'Reilly and Captain Faddy of the artillery (who had volunteered to accompany him), led the way.

★★★★★★★★★★

Captain Faddy afterwards Colonel Peter Faddy. Prior to entering the Royal Artillery, Colonel Faddy served as a midshipman on board the *Asia*, at the capture of the Dutch fleet in Saldanha Bay, in 1795. As a lieutenant in the Royal Artillery, he served in the West Indies in 1808-9.

★★★★★★★★★★

A high wind was at this moment dashing the waves over the bar; and defying the approach of the invaders. They paused for a moment, during which O'Reilly whispered to Captain Faddy to unbuckle his sword, then shouted—"Give way, my lads!" and through the surf the cutter dashed; but was presently driven on the shore, overwhelmed by the waters.

O'Reilly was thrown senseless on the sands; but, being quickly borne away by the soldiers, soon recovered. Faddy managed to swim to shore, as did also some of the crew: the rest were drowned.

Two boats swamped, and Captain Elliott and all hands perished. It was not until the wind had gone down that the attempt was renewed, and even then, our boat's crew were all drowned. Five gunboats, having ten artillerymen in each, escaped with difficulty.

In the meantime, 500 men of the Guards and 60th Rifles, with Captain Lane's rocket brigade, had crossed the river by means of a raft, and the enemy, becoming alarmed, advanced to attack them. The Guards awaited the approach of the French columns till within a short distance of their front, and then commenced a well-directed fire; the guns of Ramsay's troop and Carmichael's battery, which were stationed on the left bank, began to cannonade them and the rockets were discharged with terrific effect piercing the enemy's column, killing several men, and blazing through it with the greatest violence.

(Carmichael died at Elgin, September 21, 1823).

The result was the almost immediate rout of the French, who, terror-struck at the unusual appearance, and at the effect of this novel and destructive projectile, made the best of their retreat towards the citadel of Bayonne, which was invested on the night of the 26th. The bridge across the Adour was completed on the same day, by means of which a direct communication was opened between Spain and Bordeaux, and was of the utmost importance till the end of the war. Three companies of the Royal Artillery remained with Sir John Hope for the siege of Bayonne, Ramsay's and other troops of Horse Artillery forming part of the covering army. Sir John Hope, deeming it expedient to invest the city more closely, on the night of the 27th attacked the village of St. Etienne, drove the French out of it, and captured some prisoners.

Part of Cairnes' battery was engaged, but there was not much call for artillery, the principal work being done by General Himiber and his German brigade. General Himiber applied for some of our artillerymen to bring off a French field piece which was standing behind a traverse in the road between the enemy and his own troops, but they could not be spared, and Colonel Frazer volunteered to lead a party of the Germans for that purpose. Frazer ran forward, turned the gun round, and the Germans brought it in. Several of them lost their lives, however, and Frazer received a musket-ball in his shoulder.

The opposite sides were about 100 yards asunder, and they remained so, firing away at each other for some time. Two or three attempts were made by the French to charge a howitzer of Cairnes' which was stationed in the road, but they never came up to it, and were eventually obliged to retire into the citadel.

On the same day Wellington, with the main army, attacked Soult at Orthes. Boss's and Gardiner's troops particularly distinguished themselves on this occasion, but not more so than Sympher's German battery, which suffered great losses, including that of its commander, who was justly esteemed in private and highly valued in public life by his comrades of the British artillery.

Maxwell's, Turner's, and Michell's batteries were engaged in this action; twice they had eighteen guns in line, and made splendid practice. (Turner, afterwards General Sir G. Turner, K.C.B., colonel-commandant of the 12th brigade. Died at Menie, near Aberdeen, December 9, 1864, aged eighty-four years).

"The conduct of the artillery throughout the day deserved my highest approbation," is the only notice of the corps in Wellington's despatch.

The battle was followed by skirmishes at Aire, Etauliers, Vic Bigorre, etc., and the Battle of Toulouse.

Captain Beane's troop was engaged at Aire on the 2nd March, and Captain Macdonald greatly distinguished himself in attempting to rally the Portuguese troops.

Four guns under Captain Jenkinson were engaged aft Etauliers on the 5th.

****

At Kingston-on-Thames is a monument erected to the memory of this officer, on which appears the following inscription:—"Near this place lie the remains of Lieut.-Colonel George Jenkinson, C.B., third son of John Jenkinson, Esq., brother of Charles first Earl of Liverpool: born 24th February, 1783: died 21st March, 1823. Early in life he entered into the Royal Artillery, and was immediately employed on active service in Holland. He served five years in Spain under the Duke of Wellington, at whose recommendation he was promoted to the rank of lieut.-colonel. Brave, open, and generous, he gained the love of his friends and the esteem of the army. Amidst the temptations and vicissitudes of the military profession, he maintained a steady and uniform course of Christian conduct, and during a long and painful illness, which terminated his life, he derived from religion that support and comfort which religion alone can impart, and met the awful summons with resignation to the will of God, and humble confidence in His mercy through the merits of the Redeemer. This tablet is erected to his memory by his surviving brothers as a token of their affection and esteem"

****

Lieutenant-Colonel Sturgeon, an officer of superior merit, who was attached to Lord Wellington's staff, was killed at Vic Bigorre on the 18th. He began his services in the Royal Artillery, and served seven years in the corps, during which he took part in the Egyptian campaign of 1801; he was promoted into the staff corps in June, 1803.

The batteries of Marshal Beresford's division, under Major Dyer, were constantly in action during the Battle of Toulouse. Gardiner's troop (with the hussar brigade) was brought up to silence the enemy's artillery at important points, and the German and Portuguese artillery under Colonel Arentschild were most warmly engaged. Lieutenant Blumenbach, of the German artillery, was the only officer killed.

Lieutenant Charles Cornwallis Mitchell, R.A., who, as captain of a Portuguese battery, had rendered great service throughout the campaigns, especially at Badajoz and Vittoria, was brought most prominently forward during this battle. The Spaniards, having been ordered to attack a fortified chapel, in their advance entered a hollow road leading to Toulouse, and finding themselves under cover from the guns of the fort, distant about eighty yards, they could not be induced to quit that position of safety. But the French infantry came out of the fort, and from the brow of the ravine poured down a destructive fire. At this moment Mitchell's guns were ordered up to cover the Spanish division and drive back the French infantry. In their advance the driver of the leaders of his first gun was killed.

Mitchell instantly sprang from his horse, and, vaulting into the driver's vacant saddle, dashed forward with his brigade, placed his guns in position, and quickly drove the enemy back into their stronghold. He was at this time about one-and-twenty, and one of the tallest and handsomest men in the Peninsular Army. His cap had fallen off, and his appearance, as at full speed he led onward the foremost gun, excited as much interest as admiration. Towards the close of the battle Mitchell received a severe contusion from a spent ball, which kept him some weeks on crutches; and he had previously been saved from the shot of a French rifleman by a gunner named Vaz, who, pushing his captain over the gun he was pointing, received himself the ball.

Don Josef de Espileta, the commander of the division to which Mitchell was attached, and who had not been on good terms with him, on witnessing his gallant conduct at Toulouse suddenly embraced him, and asked to be forgiven the ill-will he had evinced towards him. Soon afterwards the following letter was sent to Sir Alexander Dickson:—

> Sir,—I have sensibly felt the omission in the reports of the name of Captain Charles Mitchell, who, with two guns, was placed under my orders on the 10th *ult.*, and who followed afterwards with the remainder of the Portuguese artillery. My wounds, and other circumstances it concerns me not now to state, have prevented me from making any report, and hence many Spanish officers have been deprived of their merited commendation. Nevertheless, I trust that justice will be done to them; and I beg to assure you that Captain Mitchell was unsurpassed for his great serenity in the action on the 10th, notwithstanding that the guns opposed to him were triple his own force. I am, one of the most obedient and faithful of your servants,
>
> Josef de Espileta, etc. etc.

****

On the return of the Portuguese Army to Lisbon, Mitchell was attached to the staff of Marshal Beresford, whom in 1820 he accompanied to the Brazils, and thence to France. In 1825 he was appointed Professor of Fortification at the Royal Military Academy, and a few years afterwards was sent to the Cape of Good Hope as Surveyor-General, Civil Engineer, and Superintendent of Works. His attention to the important duties of his triple department for nearly twenty years, during which he constructed many important roads, lighthouses, etc., won for him the esteem and admiration of the colonists, who, on his retirement in 1848, pronounced him "An old and valued friend, an efficient public servant, an elegant and accomplished gentleman and officer." During the Kaffir war of 1834 Mitchell served as assistant quartermaster-general on the of Sir Harry Smith. He returned to England in 1848, and at Eltham, March 28, 1851.

****

On the occasion of the sortie from Bayonne (14th April), the last event of the war, Lieutenant Henry Blachley (afterwards Major-General), received a wound, his head being grazed and part of his ear carried away by a musket-ball. He was the last artilleryman whose blood was shed in this memorable war.

Napoleon having abdicated, peace was proclaimed, and the army prepared to embark at Bordeaux; the cavalry and artillery, however, marched through the country.

CHAPTER 11

The War with America, 1812-1814

The American people, goaded by Buonaparte, had, though not actually at war, been on the most unfriendly terms with Great Britain for some years, and in 1812 (having previously made extensive preparations) they declared war. Canada being at this time very deficient of troops, and the defences having been greatly neglected, on account of the great struggle going on in Europe, the Americans no doubt conceived that this vast colony would fall an easy prey.

In one of the first movements on the part of the British, the capture of Detroit, thirty of the Royal Artillery, under Lieutenant Felix Troughton, an active and intelligent officer, rendered most effective service. (He died on passage from America, June 24, 1815). At the Battle of Queenstown, where the Americans were so signally defeated, and where the brave General Brock lost his life, a small detachment of the Royal Artillery under Captain Holcroft assisted by the Militia artillery under Captains Powell and Cameron, acquitted themselves with great bravery, their fire contributing materially to the fortunate result of the day. (Captain Holcroft received his majority for this action. He retired, and emigrated to Canada in 1835).

At the defence of Fort Erie, in November, 1812, the only artillery employed were the militia under Captain Kirby, who, however, was assisted by Lieutenant King and some non-commissioned officers of the Royal Artillery. Lieutenant King was in command of two field-pieces attached to Lieutenant Lamont's detachment, which, unfortunately, was surprised and routed, Lieutenant King being dangerously wounded and taken prisoner. He died while in the hands of the Americans, on the 22nd February, 1813. Bombardier Jackson, of the Royal Artillery, distinguished himself by firing a 6-pounder rapidly against the enemy, who were retreating across the river in boats.

At the unsuccessful defence of Frenchtown (18th January, 1813), which was only provided with one gun. Bombardier Kitson, of the Royal Artillery, and three of the Essex Militia, whom he had trained as gunners, distinguished themselves by firing it with success upon the enemy, and carrying it off with them in the retreat.

During the night of the 21st a force under Colonel Proctor advanced towards Frenchtown, and on the morning of the 22nd captured or destroyed the whole of the Americans under General Winchester, except about thirty who escaped into the woods. In this affair Lieutenant Troughton, R.A., was wounded.

Proctor, in his despatch says:—

> I have fortunately not been deprived of the services of Lieutenant Troughton, although he was wounded; to whose zealous and unwearied exertions I am greatly indebted, as well as to the whole of the Royal Artillery for their conduct in this affair.

On the 19th April two brigs, with three tenders, 150 marines, and five artillerymen, under Lieutenant Robertson, destroyed the boats and stores at Frenchtown, and returned without molestation. A similar undertaking took place against Havre-de-Grace on the 22nd May, and met with success.

The Americans having surprised and captured the post of York on Lake Ontario, advanced towards Fort George, which was occupied by a small garrison under Brigadier-General Vincent, including thirty of the Royal Artillery under Major Holcroft. These, with the exception of one gunner, were in the plain with field guns awaiting the enemy's advance. Vincent soon perceived that the Americans numbered more than four times his little force, and consequently gave orders for them to withdraw. The 9-pounder battery in the fort, although worked by militiamen, assisted by one gunner of the Royal Artillery, was most ably served during the whole period of the enemy's first attempt to land; nor was the gun abandoned till nearly all the men stationed at it had been, killed or wounded.

On the other hand, the 24-pounder, manned also by the militia, and which ought to have sunk one or two of the enemy's schooners, was spiked and totally abandoned almost at the commencement of the attack. After some gallant fighting, Vincent, with his troops, retired to Burlington, about fifty miles from Fort George, and collecting the little garrisons from Fort Erie and other points, found himself at the head of 1,600 men, and resolved to make a stand. The American general, Dearborn, marched after him, and on the 4th June was seen approaching the English position.

He encamped at Stoney Creek, about five miles from Vincent, with 3,500 men and nine pieces of artillery. He intended to attack the nest morning, but in this he was forestalled, for Colonel Harvey, with 700 men, assaulted his camp at midnight, and the Americans fled in all directions, leaving two generals, one hundred prisoners, and four guns in the hands of the English.

A detachment of the Royal Artillery accompanied the assaulting party for the purpose of taking any advantage that might occur in the working of the enemy's guns. Owing to the darkness of the night, however, and the precipitate flight of the Americans, the guns could not be used, but having captured nine horses, with harness, they took a 6-pounder and a 5½-inch howitzer to the British camp, spiking and dismounting the remaining two pieces.

At the Miami (5th May), and in all the subsequent operations, "the Royal Artillery, in the laborious duties they performed, displayed their usual unwearied zeal."

On the 3rd June three gunboats, assisted by a small body of troops on the Isle aux Noir, after a spirited action, captured the United States armed vessels *Growler* and *Eagle*, manned with fifty men in each and twenty-two guns. There were three gunners of the Royal Artillery in each boat, and a detachment on shore under Captain F. Gordon, who materially contributed to the surrender of the enemy.

On the morning of the 11th July a small force under Colonel Bisshopp, including twenty of the Royal Artillery under Lieutenant R. S. Armstrong, crossed the Niagara, and attacked the enemy's batteries at Black Rock. (Lieutenant afterwards Major-General Armstrong. He was slightly wounded during the enemy's attack on Fort George, May 27, 1813).

Having landed, they moved with rapidity up to the post, when the enemy fled, leaving a considerable quantity of guns, clothing, and stores behind them. Our force being insufficient to maintain the post, they instantly set to work to destroy the captured ordnance, bringing away, however, 4 guns, 177 muskets, 6 ammunition kegs, and a quantity of shot. They also brought away 181 barrels of provisions, about 270 blankets, and a considerable quantity of clothing, iron, leather, etc.

The Americans, seeing the British retire, returned and poured a destructive fire upon them, as they crossed the river, by which the commander (Colonel Bisshopp) and about thirteen men were mortally wounded.

Towards the end of the year three American Armies, under Generals Harrison, Wilkinson, and Hampton, were marching towards Kingston and Montreal. The three generals were routed, their forces having been defeated by the troops under Generals Rottenburg and Vincent, and the Americans were completely driven out of both Upper and Lower Canada before winter.

In one of the principal actions during these movements, which took place at Christler's Farm on the 11th November, the artillery were commanded by Captain H. G. Jackson. (Died at Warley, September 4, 1849).

In their retreat the Americans committed savage empties, burning down villages, and driving the defenceless population out into the snow. This ferocity excited the British and Canadians to retaliation. They crossed the water, and pursued them in their own territories.

Fort Niagara was attacked on the 19th December, and the whole garrison captured or killed. An army of 2,000 men, under General Hull, then came up to check the onward course of the British, but it was met by General Riall and his little force on the 30th December, and repulsed with great slaughter, followed through the villages of Buffalo and Black Rock, which were set fire to by the Canadian militia, whose homes had been so ruthlessly destroyed by the Americans.

The artillery of this column was commanded by Captain Bridge, who was in consequence allowed the honour of bearing the word "Niagara" on his appointments. (He died at Cheltenham, December 31, 1843.) In General Drummond's despatch relating to the operations of this period, he says—

> Of the conduct of the officers and troops too much cannot be said. The patience and fortitude with which they have borne the privation of almost every comfort and the severity of a most rigorous climate at this advanced season of the year, reflects the highest credit upon all. To Captain Bridge, Lieutenants Armstrong and Charlton of the Royal Artillery, and Captain Cameron of the Militia Artillery, whose zeal and exertions in transporting the heavy ordnance were very conspicuous, great praise is due.
>
> (Lieutenant Charlton died in Newfoundland, May 31, 1822).

During this campaign (on the 16th November, 1813), Lieutenant Henry Kesterman, of the Royal Artillery, met with his death under most painful circumstances. One of the soldiers was lighting his pipe by a flash from the flint of his musket; unknown, to the man, the piece was loaded, and on striking the flint the ammunition exploded, the ball entering the body of the officer.

In the spring of 1814, the Americans made a fresh attempt to invade Canada. Wilkinson was the first to cross the frontier, but he was repulsed and followed to Sackett's Harbour, where he took refuge.

Early in May General Drummond, having among his troops a detachment of the Royal Artillery under Captain Edwin Cruttenden, crossed Lake Ontario, stormed Fort Oswego, destroyed it, and burnt the barracks.

At the beginning of July, the American general, Brown, crossed the Niagara with a strong force, attacked and took Fort Erie, and advanced into Canada. General Riall attempted to stop him at Street's Creek, near Chippewa, with an insufficient force, and was compelled to retreat to near Fort Niagara.

★★★★★★★★★★

"In this action the artillery, under the command of Captain Mackonockie, was ably served, and directed with good effect."—*Riall's Despatch*. A staff-officer who was present says: "We had great superiority in the fire of our artillery, which was admirably served under an energetic officer, Captain Mackonockie, and we should have made it our principal arm, firing obliquely on the American line until it was shaken, when we might have charged with proper effect."—*U. S. Mag.* 1855.

★★★★★★★★★★

There he was reinforced by Drummond with a detachment of the troops recently landed from the Army of the Peninsula. The Americans were met, and a severe battle was fought on the 25th of July, at Lundy's Lane, almost close to the cataract of Niagara. In this action the artillery were most warmly engaged. At one time, being nearly dark, the enemy got among our guns, and for a short time had Lieutenant Tomkyns in their possession, but he made his escape. Our artillerymen were bayoneted by the enemy in the act of loading, and the muzzles of the enemy's guns were advanced within a few yards of ours.

The darkness of the night daring this extraordinary conflict occasioned several uncommon incidents: our troops having for a moment been pushed back, some of our guns remained for a few minutes in the enemy's hands; they were, however, not only quickly recovered, but the two pieces brought up by the enemy were captured by us, together with several tumbrils; and in limbering up our guns at one period, one of the enemy's 6-pounders was put by mistake upon a limber of ours, and one of our 6-pounders limbered on one of his, by which means the pieces were exchanged. Captain Maclachlane (died at Woolwich, November 12, 1835), who had charge of the batteries at Fort Mississaga, volunteered his services in the field on this occasion, and he was severely wounded. Captain Mackonockie (died at Plymouth, October 25, 1815), and Lieutenant Tomkyns received great praise for the manner in which the guns under their direction were served; as did also Sergeant Austin, who directed the Congreve rockets, which did much execution.

The Americans, being totally defeated, retreated to Chippewa, and thence to Erie, closely followed by our troops. Drummond then rashly undertook the siege of Fort Erie, and after bombarding it for two days, gave orders for an assault. Unfortunately, after our infantry had obtained a footing in the enemy's works, an explosion took place which caused a panic and almost instant retreat to the batteries. The skill and exertions of Major Phillot (died March 12, 1839), who commanded, Captain Sabine, and all the officers and men of the Royal Artillery, received their commander's entire approbation. Lieutenant Charlton entered the fort with the assaulting column and fired several rounds upon the enemy from his own guns; he was wounded by the explosion.

In September the garrison of Fort Erie, being strongly reinforced and elated by their repulse of General Drummond, marched out and made an attack on the British lines. They were received with such effect that they rapidly fell back on Fort Erie, and no longer feeling themselves safe even there, they evacuated the fort, demolished its works, and retreated altogether from the shore of Upper Canada. Many attacks on smaller forts, etc., were made by our troops in the summer of 1814; among these may be mentioned the capture of Moose Island (Captain W. Dunn commanding R.A.), 11th July; the affair of Hamden, 3rd September (R.A. Lieutenant Garstin); Castine (R.A. Major G. Crawford, died at Nice, April 1, 1847, aged seventy-one); Machias, 11th September (R.A. Lieutenant J. Daniel); and the capture of the little post of Prairie du Chien.

****

"A detachment of thirty seamen from H.M.S. *Bacchante*, under Mr. Bruce, were attached to the Royal Artillery under the command of Lieutenant Daniel of that corps for the purpose of dragging the howitzer, as no other means could be procured to bring it forward. To their unwearied exertions and the judicious arrangement of Lieutenant Daniel I am indebted for having a 5½-inch howitzer conveyed through a country the most difficult of access I ever witnessed."—*Pilkington's Despatch.*

★★★★★★★★★★

This post, or fort, situated on the Mississippi, about 450 miles from Michilimacinac, and garrisoned by between sixty and seventy men with six pieces of ordnance, was also defended by a gunboat mounting fourteen guns and manned with seventy or eighty men with muskets. The force destined for the attack of this fort consisted of 150 militiamen, 500 Indians, and one sergeant of artillery, with a 3-pounder field piece, which was served by the Michigan Fencibles. They arrived before the fort on the 17th July, and the garrison having refused to surrender, the 3-pounder was directed against the formidable gunboat, and it was so well directed and so ably served, that in three hours the crew of the *Governor Clark* (the gunboat) cut her cable and dropped down the current. The fort had now to be reduced with six round-shot (including three of the enemy's which had been picked up), all the ammunition having been expended against the gunboat.

The first ball was about to be put into the 3-pounder, when a flag was hung out from the fort, and the American garrison, numbering sixty-one combatants, each possessed of a stand of arms, surrendered as prisoners of war. The commander of the expedition, Colonel M'Kay, says:

> As to the sergeant of artillery, too much cannot be said of him; for the fate of the day and our success were to be attributed in a great measure to his courage and well-managed firing.

England having her hands freed by the general European peace of 1814, determined to act on the offensive with her unruly son, and by the end of May a descent on the American capital was decided on. Before leaving France Major-General Ross, with some regiments and two companies of the Royal Artillery under Captains Mitchell and Carmichael, received orders to proceed to America, and by the end of July the transports with these troops on board were anchored in St. George's Harbour, Bermuda.

Soon after a fresh arrival of troops from Genoa, including Captain Crawford's (afterwards Major-General A. F. Crawford), company of artillery, completed this army, with which, on the 2nd of August, Major-General Ross sailed from Bermuda, arriving on the 17th off the mouth of the Potomac, and proceeding at once to the Paxtuxent, about twenty miles further up the bay.

No sooner had they cast anchor in the Paxtuxent than Lieutenant Speer, (later died insane), Assistant-Surgeon Nelson, and Mr. Chesterton, R.A., (afterwards governor of Coldbath-fields Prison), attended by a few armed artillerymen, signalised their arrival in the country by the timely capture of some sheep, foraging parties being allowed by the commander-in-chief, with the understanding that they were to pay for what they seized.

When landed the guns and waggons were dragged by the men; but as they proceeded, the roads, hilly and capriciously stony and sandy, offered such obstructions to their progress, that all but one 6-pounder were sent afloat at Marlborough; and that one gun, under Captain Crawford, was destined to fire away at Bladensburgh against heavy ordnance landed from the American ships.

The army was destitute of cavalry, but a small detachment of artillery drivers, under the prompt leadership of Captain Lempriere, acted as cavalry, rendering most effective service. (Captain Lempriere died at Ewell, Surrey, January 19, 1858, aged sixty-nine).

The guns were brought up by Captain Mitchell for the action at Bladensburgh (26th August). The enemy's first line giving way, it was driven to the second, which yielding to the irresistible attack of the bayonet and the well-directed discharge of rockets from Captain Deacon's brigade, got into confusion and fled, leaving the British masters of the field. During this action the artillery had six men wounded. (This officer commanded the artillery on board the *Volcano* bomb during an engagement with the *Saucy Jack*, American, privateer. Died at Clapham, Octobers, 1850).

The army marched at once upon Washington, and arriving in that city at eight o'clock the same evening, commenced directly the destruction of all public property, Lieutenant Speer and a portion of his company were particularly conspicuous in the work of devastation, setting fire to the Capitol, the Arsenal, Dockyard, Treasury, and other Government buildings.

The guns taken, in all 194 pieces, were parted by Lieutenant T. G. Williams, acting quartermaster of Royal Artillery.

On the 30th the army re-embarked, and proceeded to descend the Paxtuxent.

At the Battle of Baltimore, on the 12th September (where General Ross was killed), the British artillery, especially the guns under Captain Carmichael, did great execution, and created a panic, of which the infantry promptly availed themselves, and the rout of the enemy became inevitable. The Americans fled, leaving their position strewed with dead and dying.

During the night of the 12th a very heavy rain fell, and the troops were greatly in want of shelter. Captain Mitchell, the commanding officer of the artillery, found a *comfortable* night's lodging in a pigsty.

On the 15th the force took to the ships, and standing out at sea, awaited the arrival of reinforcements from England.

In miserable inactivity the troops remained on board the fleet until the 25th November, when they were joined by General Keane and a small reinforcement.

With this arrival was Major Munro's company of artillery; this officer being the senior, at once assumed the command of the corps. The troops destined for the advance were embarked in small boats on the evening of the 22nd December, and pushing their way up a narrow creek, landed a few miles from New Orleans on the morning of the 23rd.

A brigade of 3-pounders under Captain Deacon, and the rocket brigade under Captain Lane, were with the advance. One of the vessels which conveyed the artillery, and which was laden almost to the water's edge with ammunition, took fire, but after two hours' hard work (during which Captain Lempriere set a gallant example to his men) the danger was got under.

On the night of the 23rd, just after our troops had encamped, as Captain Deacon and his brother officers were enjoying some fowls that had once been the property of General Villeré (whose house was now the British headquarters), they were startled by a cannonade. Well assured that it must be on the enemy's side, the brigade was instantly manned, and, with the aid of drag-ropes, advanced at a rapid rate along a road running parallel with the Mississippi. The night was very dark and foggy, but it was soon discovered that the firing came from a large armed schooner and two gunboats which had dropped down the river for the purpose of harassing our camp.

The guns upon the road were prevented from being brought into action by the certainty that they would destroy both friend and foe, who were jumbled together before them. Two men of the Royal Artillery were killed and eight wounded, including Lieutenant James Christie. The latter received a severe wound in the spine, it is supposed from the musket of a soldier of the 95th regiment, as his back was never towards the enemy till he fell. He suffered intolerable agony, and lingered on until the 1st March, when he died at New Orleans, having been left in the hands of the Americans.

The 24th passed quietly over, excepting that a stray shot was now and then pitched into the British camp from the American schooner.

On the 25th (Christmas Day) Sir Edward Pakenham arrived to take command of the army, and with him Sir Alexander Dickson, who at once assumed the command of the Royal Artillery.

A few guns having been got up to the front, they were placed in battery, and a temporary furnace constructed to heat the shot; and at daybreak on the 27th the guns (two 9-pounders, four 6-pounders, and two howitzers), loaded with red-hot shot, commenced a rapid fire upon the schooner.

The second shot drove her crew to their boats, and the third set fire to her; and after blazing away for some time, the magazine was reached and the vessel blew up with a loud explosion. A large vessel had come up the river to the assistance of the schooner, but, warned oy the fate of the latter, her commander had her towed out of the reach of our guns.

The British commander determined to make a demonstration on the enemy's fortified line on the left bank of the Mississippi. Accordingly, at daylight on the morning of the 28th, the troops moved forward in two columns, driving in the whole of the enemy's line of outposts. A strong picket posted at a house the property of Monsieur la Ronde was speedily destroyed by the rocket troop and 3-pounder brigade. Our 9-pounders, under Captains Mitchell and Carmichael, were brought into action, but they were overmatched by the ordnance in the American lines, and by the guns of the ship which had escaped the day previously but which was now brought up against our forces.

Our guns were withdrawn from the enemy's fire, and the troops retired.

During these operations, the artillery had four men killed; Lieutenant B. L. Poynter and five men wounded. Lieutenant F. G. Williams died in the camp on the 28th. (Lieutenant B. L. Poynter died at Leamington, September 11, 1837).

On Sunday, 1st January, 1815, a terrific cannonade commenced against the city of New Orleans, which was as hotly replied to. Rockets, shot, shell, and other missiles filled the air, and at the close of the day our batteries were nearly destroyed, while New Orleans remained intact.

Many artillerymen were killed on this day, and among them was

Lieutenant Alexander Ramsay, who fell under most distressing circumstances.

> He was the youngest brother of Norman Ramsay, but, unlike the 'bravest of the brave,' when brought into actual conflict his nerve failed him (most probably a presentiment of his approaching end troubled him), for when at his post in the foremost battery, terror so completely paralysed his faculties that he retreated from the guns and vowed to resign his commission.
> On the urgent remonstrance of Major Munro, the commanding officer in the battery, he once more approached his proper post, only to be fearfully shattered by a cannonball and hurried into eternity."

An affecting story is also told by Chesterton of Ramsay's servant, Gunner John Walker, who sat for hours at the foot of his deceased master, weeping over his remains. They were buried in the evening near a group of beautiful trees in the garden attached to the house of Mr. Bieuvenu, the last sad offices being performed by Captain Crawford, Lieutenant Hill, and Walker. Captain Crawford was so affected at the fidelity of this gunner that he took him into his own service, and the man remained with him until discharged with a pension.

On the 8th a detachment under Colonel Thornton, including a brigade of artillery under Captain Mitchell, crossed the Mississippi and attacked the enemy's redoubts on the right bank or the river, while the main body of the army assaulted New Orleans. The death of Sir Edward Pakenham and General Gibbs, the two senior officers, the severe wound received by General Keane, the third in command, and the total repulse of our troops on this occasion, are matters well known to every military reader. Colonel Thornton's detachment, however, was more successful. They drove the enemy out of their intrenchments, and captured all their guns. Colonel Dickson having been sent over the river by General Lambert, immediately after the repulse from New Orleans, reported that, under the circumstances, the newly-captured redoubts could not be held, and consequently the troops recrossed the river.

On the 19th the British retreated, but in perfect order, unmolested, from before New Orleans, and haying been embarked on board the fleet, arrived off Fort Bowyer, on Mobile Point, on the 7th February. This fort capitulated on the 11th, and the troops were landed.

Two days afterwards news arrived from England that a treaty of peace had been concluded between Great Britain and the United States. It was signed on the 24th December, a week before the disastrous attack upon New Orleans began.

Though the last great event of this campaign was disastrous to the British, the issue of the war was in their favour, and the enemy's grand design on Canada was a total failure.

We had invaded Washington and destroyed the public property, and at the end of the war we were in possession of their fortresses of Niagara, Fort Bowyer, and of Michilimakinac, the key of the Michigan territory; and they had nothing to give in exchange for them but the defenceless shore of the Detroit.

Chapter 12

The Waterloo Campaign

As soon as the landing and reception of Napoleon in France became known, the Duke of Wellington wrote from Vienna to Lord Castlereagh, urging him to reinforce the army in the Netherlands as much as he could, *particularly in cavalry and artillery*. This could not at once be attended to, the war in America having taken most of the veteran Peninsular troops; and such was the demand for artillerymen, that at Woolwich there was scarcely a sufficient number left to mount guard.

By the beginning of the month of June, however, no fewer than eight troops and seventeen companies of the Royal Artillery were stationed in and about Brussels, or in the Belgic fortresses; three of the companies had no sooner landed in England from America than they were despatched to the scene of the impending struggle.

The commander of the artillery in the Netherlands was Sir George Adam Wood, an officer in high favour with the Prince Regent, who had distinguished himself in recent campaign in Holland.

★★★★★★★★★★

Sir T. Graham made frequent mention of Sir G. Wood and the artillery under his command in the despatches from Holland. At the unsuccessful assault on Bergen-op-Zoom (March 8, 1814) Wood Volunteered to lead one of the attacking columns, and behaved with the most astounding bravery. Sir George Wood became *aide-de-camp* to the king, and governor of Carlisle; he died in London, April 22, 1831, aged sixty-four years.

★★★★★★★★★★

Sir Augustus Frazer appointed to the command of the Horse Artillery, and the troops and batteries were equipped and disposed follows:—

HORSE ARTILLERY.

WITH THE CAVALRY.

Lieutenant-Colonel Alexander Macdonald commanding.

Lieut.-Colonel Sir R. Gardiner's troop	6-pounders
Lieut.-Colonel Webber Smith's troop	6-pounders
Lieut.-Colonel Sir A. Dickson's troop (commanded by Captain Mercer)	9-pounders
Major W. N. Ramsay's troop	9-pounders
Major R. Bull's troop	5½-inch howitzers
Captain T. Whinyates' troop	Rockets and 6-pounders

WITH THE RESERVE.

Lieut.-Colonel Sir H. D. Ross's troop	9-pounders
Major Beane's troop	6-pounders

ROYAL ARTILLERY.

Lieut.-Colonel S. G. Adye*	Captain Sandham's 9-pounder battery	1st division (Cooke's)
Lieut.-Colonel C. Gold	Captain Alms' 9-pounder battery (commanded by Capt. Bolton)	2nd division (Clinton's)
Lieut.-Colonel J. S. Williamson	Major Lloyd's 9-pounder battery	3rd division (Alten's)
Lieutenant-Colonel Hawker	Major Brome's 9-pounder battery	4th division (Colville's)
	Major Rogers's 9-pounder battery	5th division (Picton's)
	Major Unett's 9-pounder battery	6th division (Cole's)
Major P. Drummond	Captain Gordon's 9-pounder battery (commanded by Captain Sinclair)	Reserve
	Major Morrison's 18-pounder battery	

* Colonel Stephen G. Adye, C.B.: died at Woolwich, September 13, 1838.

IN GARRISON.

At Antwerp	Major Marsh's* company (commanded by Captain Maitland)
	Captain Tyler's company
At Tournay	Captain Hunt's company
At Brussels	Captain Ilbert's company
At Ostend	Major Younghusband's company
	Major Munro's company
	Major Mitchell's company
	Major Carmichael's company
	Captain Hutchesson's company

* Major Henry Marsh went with his company into France; whilst there he was thrown from his gig, and received injuries which caused his death, July 12, 1816.

Captain Dewell was attached to the Dutch artillery, and served at Mons, Conde, etc. (He died at Brighton, August 29, 1853, aged sixty-seven).

Brussels at this time was the scene of great and untiring festivity: dinners, *soirées*, balls, theatrical amusements, concerts—in which Catalani, then in her prime, played a prominent part—caused the streets of that beautiful and picturesque city to echo with sounds of gladness; while the fields and meadows around were alive all day long with military parades and reviews. There was not a grove or a wood within six miles of the place but afforded shelter, as the summer advanced, to frequent encampments.

The officers of the Royal Artillery appear to have had their full share in this revelling, those on the staff being foremost in mischief, for on the night of the 29th May a brilliant party were being driven home from a supper, when one of the carriage horses fell; in picking him up the driver got a blow on the chest which stunned him; Percy Drummond ran to the nearest village for water; Sir George Wood held the horses, and Sir Augustus Frazer lugged the body of the said driver to the side of the road to get off his neckcloth. After a decent time, the man revived, and the party arrived home in safety. Sir Augustus Frazer, in one of his letters from Brussels, says:

> Another such a day as yesterday and we shall be ruined as soldiers-ruined with burgundy and champagne, and with all that, as the Duchess of Gordon says, carries a man off his legs.

But there was to be an end to all this. Sir Alexander Dickson arrived at Brussels on the night of the 14th June he having only been a few hours in Woolwich after his arrival from America before he embarked for the Continent), and was appointed to the command of the siege companies, or battering train, and attached to the Duke of Wellington's staff.

On the following day it was evident that serious work was about to begin, and shortly after midnight the mustering of the troops began, and before the sun of the 16th June arose, "all were marching to the field of honour, and many to an early grave."

At about 2.30 p.m. Picton's division, with Major Roger's battery, came up to Quatre Bras, and were instantly engaged.

The enemy's batteries opened on them directly they appeared, making good practice, and Picton at once directed Major Rogers to answer them. (Afterwards Colonel Thomas Rogers: died at Woolwich,

August, 1839). A bombardier, laying one of the guns, had his head taken off by a round-shot, and Captain Scott's horse was shot under him before they could engage.

This battery suffered greatly. Two of the guns were dismounted, and for a time lost, during the repeated charges of the enemy's cavalry, when our artillerymen took shelter in the infantry squares. It was for a moment feared the whole battery was taken, but when the enemy withdrew, there stood the uninjured guns untouched. Lloyd ran out from the square towards them, and seizing a rammer tried one of the pieces, which, to his great surprise, was still loaded. This he discharged with effect, the enemy being scarcely 150 yards distant.

A second gun was also found charged, with the contents of which Lloyd favoured the *cuirassiers*. This was the work of about a couple of minutes, and now the gunners resumed their post.

Major Lloyd was slightly wounded, and the total casualties in the two batteries engaged that day were nine men killed, two officers and seventeen men wounded. Among the wounded in the Battle of Quatre Bras was Captain Harry G. Macleod, who was attached to the staff of the army. This officer was the fourth son of Sir John Macleod, and had served six years in the Royal Artillery, during which time he was at the Battle of Talavera and the defence of Dantzic. After his removal to the infantry, he served with the 35th regiment during the campaign in Holland (1813-14), and on the staff in Belgium in 1815 until the 16th June, when he received several stabs from the enemy's lancers. He was at once attended to by his cousin, Captain H. Baynes, brigade-major to the Royal Artillery. (Captain Baynes was himself wounded on the 18th).

In a short time, he recovered, and afterwards served for many years in the West Indies. He was eventually knighted, and died governor of Trinidad in 1847. The disabled guns of Lloyd's battery were soon remounted, and assisted in covering the retreat of the Prussians on the following day. On this day (17th), at the Battle of Ligny, a fine young officer of the British artillery, Lieut. R. Manners, who was attached to Cleeves' German battery, received his mortal wound.

On the ever-memorable morning of the 18th June the artillery were placed in the most important positions. In the words of a popular writer, "Wherever a gun could see, there it stood."

On the extreme left were Sir R. Gardiner's six guns, which had been seriously engaged in covering the retreat of the army from Quatre Bras. Going at a gallop through fields and country roads, the French

Artillery in the Battle of Waterloo

cavalry frequently ahead of him, Sir R. Gardiner had great difficulty in getting his troop up to join the army. "Fortunately," says Sir Robert, "we had not received the 9-pounders (as had the other troops), or we should have been all cut to pieces." Major Rogers's battery was stationed in front of Kempt's brigade, near La Haye Sainte; Lloyd's with Alton's division, a little to the left of the wood of Hougomont; and Sandham's with Cooke's, near the centre of the line.

Sir Hew Ross's troop took post on the height immediately in rear of La Haye Sainte, with two pieces on the Charleroi road. These, with four foreign batteries, were the artillery of the first line. Bolton's battery was with Clinton's division, and Major Beane's troop and Captain Sinclair's battery formed a reserve at Mont St. Jean. The other troops of Horse Artillery remained with the cavalry. In the course of the day every one of these batteries was brought into action, and not even the records of that noble corps can point to an occasion in which they better did their work.

It was verging towards twelve o'clock when the opening thunder of the battle pealed through the air from Cleeves' (German) battery: the leading column of the enemy was seen to lose its firmness and hurry onwards, when a second roar of artillery from Captain Sandham's battery stopped its progress by laying low the front ranks. (Afterwards Colonel B. F. Sandham).

Before the rear could fill up the gaps, Cleeves' guns were again at work, and as the two batteries threw their showers of shot and shell with deadly aim, the columns whirled round and retired in precipitate disorder. The French advanced again, however, and succeeded forcing their way into the wood of Hougomont. The duke saw at once the necessity of dislodging them from this point, and spoke to Sir Augustus Frazer on the subject. The latter, however, with a foresight for which he was ever remarkable, had seen the importance position, and sent his adjutant, Lieutenant Bell, to order up Major Bull's howitzers.

> The troop came up handsomely; their very appearance encouraged the remainder of the division, then lying down to be sheltered from the fire. The duke said, 'Colonel Frazer, you are about to do a deliberate thing; can you depend upon the force of your howitzers? Part of the wood is held by our troops, part by the enemy;' His Grace calmly explained the nature of the position. Sir Augustus answered, that he could perfectly depend upon the troop; and, after speaking to Major Bull and his offic-

ers, and seeing that they, too, perfectly understood their orders, the troop commenced its fire, and in ten minutes the enemy was driven from the wood.

This service, which, considering the proximity of the allied troops in the wood, was of a very delicate was executed with admirable skill, and attended with the desired effect.

This troop effected the greatest possible service throughout the early part of the battle, but owing to the loss sustained both in men and horses, together with the disabled condition of the guns (through excessive firing), it was obliged to retire before the close. Major Bull himself was wounded in the left elbow; Captain Cairnes, the second in command, was killed by a cannon-ball striking his head; and Lieutenant W. Smith was wounded thereby leaving the troop with only two subalterns command it.

Major Robert Macpherson Cairnes was the second son of Major W. Cairnes of the 39th regiment, who, after serving all through the defence of Gibraltar, died in India.

His mother was married to General Cuppage Royal Artillery, by whom she had three sons and one daughter, the eldest son, who was a lieutenant in Captain Bolton's company, but who was attached to the Horse Artillery for the day, being near his lamented brother at the time of his fall.

Robert Cairnes was marked as nature's favourite. Endued with a strength and activity of mind rarely surpassed, he carried them into his profession with the happiest results to himself and to the service. An undaunted bravery, an exquisite sense of honour, a cool and discriminating though quiet judgment, and a steady perseverance were his peculiar characteristics as a soldier; a noble and generous temper, and undeviating sweetness of disposition, a most engaging person, and manners highly polished, and universally amiable, were his qualifications as a member of society; a heart the most affectionate, and an urbanity the most conciliating, completed his character in the different relations of son, brother, and friend.

Adored by his friends, beloved by his brother officers, and respected by the world, this gallant man met the death his noble spirit ever panted for, in the thirtieth year of his age, and left behind him unutterable regrets for his fate—to his friends, indeed, untimely, but to himself matured.

During his short life he saw much service, having been present in the Copenhagen campaigns, at the Battle of Barrosa, defence of Cadiz, battles of Vittoria and the Pyrenees, and the siege of Bayonne; and was twice severely wounded. A monument is erected to his memory in Canterbury Cathedral.

Lieutenant William Smith died at Dublin on the 3rd of April, 1835, from the effects of injuries received by being thrown out of a car. His son, a cadet in the Academy at Woolwich, met with a violent death in May of the following year. Whilst bathing in the Repository, he fell off a piece of timber, and pitching on his head in the mud, could not be extricated from it until life was extinct.

Meanwhile the fire of cannon gradually extended from one extremity of the hostile lines to another.

A body of the French infantry at one time crept on amid the concealment which some tall rye afforded, till they got within pistol-shot of Lieutenant-Colonel Webber Smith's troop, which was stationed on the Nivelles road. Now artillery, however effective it may be at a distance, has no chance with infantry in a close fight. Men and horses dropped beneath the fire of these skirmishers so fast, that Smith was obliged to withdraw his guns into a hollow beyond, and the consequences might have been even more serious had not timely aid been afforded.

Two officers of this troop were wounded—Lieutenants D. Crawford and H. Foster.

★★★★★★★★★★

Lieutenant Donald Crawford died in Perthshire, October 21, 1819.
Lieutenant Henry Forster, who was severely wounded in the foot by a grape-shot, served with the expedition to Copenhagen in 1807, and in the Corunna campaign. He died at Aix-la-Chapelle, October 24, 1855, aged sixty-six years.

★★★★★★★★★★

An immense column, supported on either flank by artillery, approached that part of the position where Major Rogers's battery was stationed. Picton posted himself on the right of the battery, ordered them to load with grape, and reserve their fire until he himself gave the word. It was an anxious moment. The gunners stood with, their port-fires ready lit. A dead silence prevailed. Suddenly, "*Vive l'Empereur!*" with other cries became audible.

"Point blank!—Aim low!" was passed from gun to gun. "Fire!" shouted Picton, and after a few rounds the French were seen hurrying down the hill as fast as their legs could carry them, pursued not only by the Highlanders, who bayoneted them by dozens, but by our gunners, who, brandishing their sponges and portfire amid the excitement, could not be persuaded to remain at their guns. (*Picton* by H. B. Robinson John William Cole, the life of Wellington's hard swearing and fighting subordinate is also available from Leonaur).

Sir Hew Ross's troop being found inadequate for the defence of La Haye Sainte, which was alternately held by friend and foe (the troop retiring to the right or rear of the farm as circumstances required). Major Beane's was ordered up from the reserve.

Both these troops were most hotly engaged, as is evident by the casualties among the officers. Major Beane was struck by a cannonball, which completely ploughed him up the middle; Captain Webber; the second in command, was wounded, and Lieutenant Cromie had both his legs taken off by one shot. The latter lingered in great agony for two days, when he died while undergoing amputation.

★★★★★★★★★★

> Captain William Webber was employed on the expedition to, and at the capture of the colony of Surinam, in 1804. On this occasion he was wounded by the falling of a building, in consequence of the explosion of a magazine. He served in the Corunna campaign and the subsequent campaigns in the Peninsula to the end of the war. Between that time and the Waterloo campaign he was engaged with the Americans in Canada. Died March 1, 1847.

★★★★★★★★★★

Of Ross's troop, Captain Parker and Lieutenant J. Day were wounded. A party of Whinyates' rocket troop proceeded under Captain Dansey to the front of the line, on the left of La Haye Sainte, and came into action with rockets, leaving its two guns in the rear under Lieutenant Wright. Captain Dansey very soon received a severe wound which obliged him to retire, and the party, after firing a few rockets, fell back a little to where its horses were standing. It was then commanded by Sergeant Daniel Dunnett, who on perceiving the advance of the nearest French column, dismounted his men as coolly and deliberately an if exercising on Woolwich Common, though without any support whatever, laid rockets on the ground, and discharged them in succession into the mass, every one of them appearing to take effect.

★★★★★★★★★★

> Captain afterwards Major John Boteler Parker, lost his leg on this occasion, served at Walcheren in 1809, and in the Peninsula from February, 1812, to the end of the war. He was governor of the Royal Military Academy, Died in March, 1851.

Lieutenant James Day served in the Peninsula, and was wounded at the Pyrenees; he was only slightly wounded at Waterloo. Died 1843.

Sergeant Dunnett was promoted to staff-sergeant, April 1, 1822, and pensioned at 2s. 2d. *per diem*, May 1, 1826

****

The advance of the column was checked, and was not resumed until Sergeant Dunnett, having expended all his rockets, retired with his party to rejoin the guns in rear. The other half of this troop was engaged in the rear of La Haye Sainte during the deadly assaults of the French on that position. Major Whinyates was here wounded, as was also his lieutenant, Strangways. The latter was struck in the hip and spine as he was pointing his gun. He was at once removed to the rear. The surgeon gave an opinion that the wounds were mortal, and such had been the sufferer's idea from the moment he was disabled, and which caused him to request to be "allowed to die near his gun." He was conveyed to the village of Waterloo, and here he remained in the greatest torture for several days, the carnage of the 18th having left more cases than the surgeons could attend to. He was at length sent with a many others to Brussels, where the ball was extracted. He lay there for some months in a state or danger, but unexpectedly recovered and returned home with the army.

The next movement was that which so seriously affected our artillery, calling forth all their courage and devotedness—the advance of the French cavalry. Our infantry were all formed in squares, and the artillerymen at their guns a short distance in front of them. Lloyd's battery was foremost, with Sandham's and Bolton's to the right.

Ramsay's and Mercer's troops being disengaged, were at once ordered up to the support of these batteries. (Mercer afterwards General Mercer, colonel-commandant of the 9th brigade).

The duke observing six guns abandoned by the Belgians, desired Colonel Sir G. Wood to have them withdrawn to the rear, a duty which was immediately executed by Lieutenant W. C. Anderson (afterwards Major-General Anderson), and a party of Captain Bolton's battery. One gun, however, was unavoidably left, in consequence of its more advanced position and the rapid approach of the French columns. The duke's order was "to withdraw the men from their guns, if charged home, into the adjacent squares of infantry." In a few minutes the *cuirassiers* of the Imperial Guard were but a short distance from the guns. To pour the contents of grape and canister into the advancing foe, and to seek shelter within or along the faces of the squares, occupied our gunners but a very few minutes.

Captain Mercer's troop was posted in front of two squares of the Brunswick infantry, which were very unsteady, they having been previously dislocated by a heavy cannonade. The *cuirassiers* made a furious dash towards this portion of the line, but Captain Mercer took upon himself to contradict the duke's order by commanding his men to remain firm, and reserving his fire until they were within ten yards of the muzzles, opened upon them, causing them to wheel about and retire in precipitation and disorder. They advanced in a like manner three times, and each time were similarly repulsed. Major Lloyd and his men took refuge in a square of the guards, which was charged five or six times by the enemy, running out and firing into them each time as they advanced, retiring again as soon as the gun was fired.

At last, an officer of the Imperial Guard rushed at one of the guns, and would not suffer our artillerymen to approach until he was killed by a Brunswick rifleman. By this noble act of self-devotion, he prevented the guns from being fired at least once, thereby saving a great number of his comrades.

Lloyd's battery maintained a tremendous fire throughout the whole of the day. Shortly after the charges made by the French cavalry, as Lloyd was giving orders to Lieutenants Wells and Phelps, who commanded two of his guns, he received a severe wound in his thigh; his men were so exposed to the enemy, and so warmly engaged in the contest, that he was only moved a short distance to the rear, without being able to obtain proper assistance. He was afterwards moved to Brussels; but his wound turned to a gangrene, and he died in a very short time.

★★★★★★★★★★

Lieutenant later Captain Fortescue Wells: died at Slade, September 29, 1861, aged seventy-one.
Lieutenant Samuel Phelps died in Pembrokeshire, December 13, 1827.
Major William J. Lloyd, as brave an officer as the army possessed, died at Brussels, June 29, from the effect of wounds received at the battle. It was this noble officer's fortune to be placed in a low, bad situation and ground, where he could obtain little or no assistance, and exposed most severely to the enemy; but no one could behave better or obtain more honour than he did in his accidentally perilous situation.

★★★★★★★★★

Lieutenant Harvey, who had just been married in England, leaving his bride at the church door, joined his battery just in time to accompany it into the field, where he had not been five minutes before he lost his right arm. (He received 70*l. per annum* for the loss of his right arm, and was appointed to the Invalid Battalion in 1817. He retired on full pay in 1819, and died at Eltham, August 18, 1826).

During these advances of the French cavalry the British artillery had to lament the loss of the brave and universally beloved Norman Ramsay. He fell, covered with wounds, at the moment when three other officers of his troop were hit by mounted riflemen who advanced behind the *cuirassiers*. In a momentary lull of the fire the men of his troop dug a grave, and buried his warm body in the spot where it fell, and, before their tears were dried, were called to a renewal of the struggle.

★★★★★★★★★★

Captain A. Macdonald, Lieutenants Brereton and Robe (mortally). Lieutenant William Livingstone Robe was the eldest son of Sir William Robe; he died at Waterloo, June 19, through the wounds received on the previous day. During eight years of service this gallant officer was thirty-three times in the presence of the enemy, frequently at the side of his father. He had the singular honour, as a subaltern officer, to be distinguished for his conduct by the Duke of Wellington, and in consequence a medal and clasp for the battles of the Nivelle and the Nive were forwarded to his family after his death. With his latest breath he sent a message to his father to assure him he died like a soldier. A monument was erected to his memory in the church at Waterloo, and an epitaph placed on his grave in the forest of Soignes.

Ramsay fell and was buried close by a stone 800 yards to the left of Hougomont. The news of his death produced a most painful effect upon his father, an old retired officer of the Royal Navy, at that time living in Edinburgh. Bowed down as he was by the loss of his youngest son), the fall of Norman, his darling boy, the pride of his old age, affected his intellect; he became almost imbecile, and would wander from room to room, asking if any news had arrived of his son, and when Norman would return. A friend of the family, conceiving that the recovery of the son's body might have the effect of restoring the father to sanity, wrote to Sir Augustus Frazer on the subject.

Fortunately, that officer, having assisted at his funeral, did not consider it impossible to find the grave; and speaking to Sergeant Livesay, of Ramsay's troop, the latter said he felt certain he should know the place; he had himself dug the grave, and should know its situation as long as he lived. Accordingly, he was sent from Paris to Waterloo, for the purpose of seeking his late commander's grave, and, with as extraordinary precision, decided on the spot the moment he reached it. This disinterment was attended with very little difficulty—the corpse being almost unchanged, though three weeks had elapsed since the day of the great battle. From Ostend the body conveyed by sea to Scotland.

The afflicted father was led by friend to the side of the coffin; he gazed wildly upon it for moments; a change came over his spirit; he burst into tears, and sobbed forth. "Norman is come home," and from that moment reason resumed her empire. The poor old gentleman was left childless by the death of his only surviving son, David, a captain in the Royal Navy, which took place at Jamaica, July 31, 1816, six weeks after the death of his elder, and six months after that of his younger brother.

★★★★★★★★★★

Sir Augustus Frazer assisted at the interment of his friend Ramsay, and took from his corpse what relics he could find. Among them was the portrait of his wife, which he always carried in his breast; and two snuffboxes, one of which he had received as a present from Sir G. Wood; through the other a ball had passed ere it reached his noble heart.

The last scene of this eventful drama was about to commence. The Old Guard, Napoleon's last resource, were seen to advance. As soon as they descended the declivity above which the French guns were posted, the latter opened with a rapidity, weight, and precision such as they had not exhibited during any portion of the day. Vainly did the English artillery, overmatched both in numbers and weight of metal, strive to keep down this storm. Gun after gun was struck and upset, horses were killed, men destroyed; yet the gallant Blue-Jackets kept their ground, as they always have done, and reserved their strength for an occasion which drew rapidly towards them.

Down the slope went the leading column of the Guard—now they were in the hollow—now they began to ascend the lower wave of ground which intervenes between the positions of the two armies— now they crown this height, and while their own guns cease firing for a space, those on the external slope of the English position open with terrible effect. But the Old Guard, thinned as they were by this iron hail, never paused for a moment. The survivors closed up the spaces which the dead and wounded had left, and in due time the entire mass was again under cover of a valley. By-and-bye the leading sections began to breast the English hill. Rapidly, but at a fearful cost of life, the column passed the line of fire along which the English guns told, and then they became silent.

Captain Bolton's battery was most importantly posted during these trying moments–; the Guards were just behind, lying down, sheltered by the brow of the hill. Ere the Old Guard had reached the foot of the hill upon which the guns were posted, Captain Bolton received a musket-ball through his heart. The duke, seeing the importance of this position, rode up and inquired for Captain Bolton. He was answered by Lieutenant Sharpin, that the captain was killed, and the battery was now commanded by Captain Napier.

"Look out, load with canister," was the order given by His Grace to Captain Napier. The bearskin caps of the veteran guard now appeared on the summit of the hill, and seemed astounded at seeing nothing but a few field pieces, with the gunners and officers attached, and instantly opened upon them a storm of musketry. It was answered by a salvo of grape and canister pouring into the head of the column, which was already within fifty yards of the muzzles. The artillerymen, under these close fires, could not long stand to their guns, but either lay beneath them, or retired beyond the abrupt dip of the hill; two or three brave fellows now and then springing up to hastily load, fire, and drop again behind cover. In a few seconds the headmost companies of the Imperial Guard, with rattling drums and deafening shouts of "*Vive l'Empereur!*" crowned the very summit of the position.

Their dead bodies, the next day, bore unanswerable evidence to the fact. It was at this moment the duke gave his signal, when instantly a column seemed to rise from the ground on the left of this apparently unprotected battery. The Old Guard wavered, and after receiving a few more hurried rounds from the battery, their left gave way, and were then met by the Guards, who broke the column and compelled them to fly in disorder. It was now that a German battery poured a fire on the retreating column, not knowing that our own brave infantry were mixed with it, and Captain Napier, leaving his own battery to stop them, received eight wounds from the bursting of a shrapnel shell.

The battle was now at an end, so far as the artillery were concerned, and, in less than an hour, the splendid army of Napoleon was a mere wreck, having been broken and dispersed in all directions, leaving on the field 122 guns, and upwards of 200 waggons, etc.

After the Battle of Waterloo, while the main army marched to Paris, Sir Alexander Dickson and six companies of the Royal Artillery served at the reduction of the frontier fortresses still held by the soldiers of Napoleon. They were attached to the Prussian Army under Prince Augustus, and their services, though not very arduous, were exceedingly valuable.

Each fortress was taken in succession; Maubeuge in five days, Landrecy in two days, Phillippeville in four days, Marienburg in three days, and Rocroy in five days. (Phillippeville having made an obstinate resistance, suffered severely; the houses being burnt, as well as the fortifications destroyed).

TOTAL CASUALTIES IN THE ROYAL ARTILLERY AT THE BATTLE OF WATERLOO.

Officers . .	5 killed.	16 wounded.	(4 died of wounds.)
Sergeants .	2 ,,	13 ,,	
Rank and file	60 ,,	215 ,,	10 missing (7 recovered).
Horses . .	356 ,,	137 ,,	36 ,,

CHAPTER 13

Syria—Kaffraria

By terms of a treaty dated 15th July, 1840, Mehemet Ali was required to accept certain conditions within a limited time, and if he declined, the forfeiture of the *pachalic* of Acre and the loss of Egypt were to follow.

Having allowed the time to elapse, offensive operations commenced to compel him to evacuate Syria. England being greatly involved in the treaty, a, fleet under Admiral Sir Robert Stopford was at once sent to the coast, accompanied by detachments of the ordnance corps, to assist the troops of the *Sultan* in this service. Colonel Sir Charles Smith, R.E., had command of this party, which sailed from Gibraltar in H.M.S. *Pique* on the 8th August, 1810; the artillery—Lieut. Rowan, one sergeant, one corporal, and thirty men—being under Major Gordon Higgins. They served at the capture of Beyrout and the bombardment and capture of Acre. During the winter the artillery were stationed at Beyrout, being quartered in a very good barrack near the harbour, the officers taking up their quarters in the Seraglio with Sir C. Smith.

A rumour having reached Beyrout that the enemy had broken up his cantonments and retired across the Antilibanus, a party of three officers (of whom Lieutenant Rowan, R.A., was one) was despatched by Sir C. Smith on the 22nd November to watch his movements. It having been ascertained that Ibrahim Pacha had retreated. Lieutenant Rowan was sent back with the intelligence, while the other officers proceeded in different directions, endeavouring to gain information as to the whereabouts of the enemy. It having been discovered that he had retired on Damascus, the party returned to Beyrout.

On the 13th December the *Hecate* arrived from Woolwich, having on board Brigadier-General Michell (who was to replace Sir Charles Smith in the chief command), Lieut.-Colonel Colquhoun, Major

Robe, and Lieutenant Ross of the Royal Artillery, besides other officers.

****

Colonel Colquhoun was "one of the best officers in the corps; of that class the most useful, practical, and devoted to the service; a sincere friend, a safe companion, an honourable and upright man." Though he was forty-five years in the regiment, his war services were not very numerous: he served as commander of the artillery under Lord John Hay in the Spanish Civil War, and in Syria. But as a practical man, both in the invention and perfecting of ordnance, and in the more humane inventions and improvements in connexion with the lifeboat, etc., he was most conspicuous. At the time of his death, which took place at Woolwich, September 17, 1853, he was inspector of the carriage department in the Royal Arsenal, and it was truly said "Her Majesty had lost one of her best servants."

Major Robe was the third son of the late Sir William Robe. Died while in command of the artillery in Bermuda, September 21, 1853. Lieutenant Ross was the eldest son of Sir Hew Ross. Killed by being thrown from his horse at Newcastle-on-Tyne, November 26, 1848.

****

Edward Michell was one whose gallantry and skill, kindness and affability, were equally conspicuous. As a lieutenant, in the Peninsula, he was entrusted with important commands, and earned especial distinction at Tarifa.

As a captain, during the campaign in Holland (1814), he rendered himself most conspicuous. On one occasion a shell struck into the centre of a waggon of ammunition, when Captain Michell by a rapid movement succeeded in extinguishing the fire of the fuse before it could reach the powder.

At the attack on Bergen-op-Zoom (8th March, 1814), he volunteered to take part in the assault. As all military readers are aware, this attack was a failure, but Michell persevered to the last, and while in the act of escalading the scarp wall of the place he was covered with wounds.

He afterwards, as lieutenant-colonel, served in Spain during the Carlist war.

At the time he assumed the command in Syria he is spoken of as an open-hearted, frank old soldier—in person small, and with a stoop from the effects of a severe wound received in former days; yet there was that in his clear penetrating eye which marked the known attributes belonging to the man—that firmness, activity, and energy of mind, which, had he been spared, might have rendered him a leading character in the service, of which, even then, he was one of the brightest ornaments.

One of the first movements after the arrival of General Michell was the advance of the Turkish Army (under General Jochmus) on Gaza. This army was accompanied by the English officers (who, however, with one voice disapproved of the movement), and on the 15th January, 1841, came up with the Egyptians at Medjdel, and after a smart engagement compelled them to retreat. General Michell, who at first disapproved of the advance, now urged Jochmus to seize the opportunity and march upon Gaza, distant only about six miles. This commander, however, though he had marched from Jaffa in torrents of rain and bivouacked each night in mud, pleaded the badness of the roads, and at once retired into Jaffa.

Two days afterwards the news arrived that a convention had been signed at Alexandria, and the war ended.

It is needless to say how much the British officers were mortified. Colonel Anderson, R.E., writing on the subject, says:—

> If we had disapproved of the expedition in the first instance, how much greater was our mortification at having to abandon it after having come in contact with the enemy!

To General Michell the affair proved fatal.

> The cold caught by him that wretched night of incessant rain that followed the affair of Medjdel, under single canvas, acting on a delicate frame arising from repeated wounds, together with the mortification he felt at the result of the movement on Gaza, brought on a fever, under which poor Michell sank in a few days.

He died at Jaffa, at noon on the 24th January, 1841.

The similarity between this and the expedition under Koehler in 1799 has more than once been noticed.

Each mission was composed of about a dozen staff officers, with a few artillerymen and sappers, designed to co-operate with the Turks against their enemies. Each ended in the death (at Jaffa) of the English general (an artillery officer) commanding, and of many of our officers and men; and both served to prove how utterly useless and unavailing was any attempt at co-operation with such people as the Turks without an adequate British military force to follow up whatever active measures might have been considered advisable.

General Michell's remains were deposited in a vault hastily constructed by the British sappers, in what is called the English or southeastern bastion at Jaffa. (Also called the "bastion of Sir Sydney Smith.") It is in the left flank of the bastion, overshadowed by a fig-tree, and opposite, on the interior face of the parapet in front of it, is placed a tablet of white marble of large dimensions, bearing the following inscription, headed by two lines of Arabic poetry:—

(Translation).
This narrow grave contains the remains of one whose fame during life was widely extended. Let all respect it, for he was one of those who have rendered their period illustrious.'
Sacred to the memory of
Brigadier-General Edward Thomas Michell,
of the Royal Artillery; Commanding the Forces of Her Britannic Majesty in Syria; Companion of the Bath, and Knight of the Orders of Isabella the Catholic, St. Ferdinand, and Charles III. of Spain, who died at Jaffa on the
24th January, 1841, aet. 54.
He was distinguished by high and noble qualities, by long and brilliant services, and by the affectionate regards
of all who knew him.
The officers of Her Britannic Majesty's Forces serving in Syria, in testimony of their esteem and regret, and to render sacred the spot where his remains repose, have erected this stone to his memory.

★★★★★★★★★★★★

The Kaffirs had long been accustomed to levy blackmail on the settlers whose farms were near the borders of Cape Colony; but in the year 1834 their depredations assumed so formidable a character, that not only the property, but the very existence of all the inhabitants was in danger; many, indeed, having been murdered by the savages, against whom it was therefore necessary to tend a force of regular troops.

Detachments of the Royal Artillery were stationed about the different forts and block-houses erected along the frontier, and others marched with the various bodies of troops; but nothing of any importance or interest in connexion with the corps occurred till 1838, when Major Charters and Lieutenant Levinge, accompanied by two other officers and an interpreter, went on a mission of peace to Faku, the

Kaffir chief. They travelled six hundred miles in thirty-five days, being received most hospitably by the Kaffir, and experiencing much kindness from the missionaries whom they fell in with during their return journey. Indeed, had it not been for them, the party would have had to destroy their oxen, their only means of conveyance, for subsistence.

In January, 1842, a small force under the command of Captain Smith, 27th regiment, with which was a detachment of the Royal Artillery under Lieutenant Wyatt, was sent to watch the movements of the Boers, who had attacked a native chief in alliance with the English.

The troops remained near the Umgazi for about two months, when they broke up their camp and started for Natal, a distance of 600 miles.

Great difficulties were encountered during this march in the way of steep and rugged hills, bushes, rivers, &c, but they were all surmounted in six weeks, the force reaching Natal on the 3rd May.

On the 23rd the Boers showed themselves in force, when they were attacked, and obliged by our guns to retire.

On the 24th the force attacked the Boers at Congella, when a severe action took place on the beach during a spring-tide, the troops being at times up to their waists in water.

The artillery had two field pieces and a howitzer, which were served under the greatest difficulties. Of eighteen gunners twelve were killed or wounded. Lieutenant Wyatt himself worked at the guns, and was in the act of firing when he fell pierced by seven bullets— three in his head and four in his body. The oxen having been all shot away, the enemy advanced to take the guns, which he succeeded in doing, as, in addition to our loss in men and oxen, the tide was rising so rapidly that it was found impossible for the few men remaining to remove them.

The artillery then took up a position with two 1mpounders, guarded by fifteen men of the 27th regiment. On the 25th the Boers attacked this position, which, after a desperate fight, they succeeded in capturing, together with one of the guns. The party of artillery—one sergeant, two corporals, and four gunners—fought well, but they were soon overpowered. The two corporals were wounded, two gunners were killed, and the remaining two wounded.

The wounded men spiked the guns; and when the enemy discovered it, they ripped them up from the bottom of the stomach to the throat. The sergeant and most of the infantry men were taken prisoners.

On the 31st the Boers, having about 1,200 men and nine guns, began to besiege the camp. We had but one 18-pounder and one howitzer. As the siege progressed provisions became scarce, and the troops were put on the smallest possible allowance. Horses were killed, and with ground oats their flesh formed the daily repast of the camp. Upon this fare it was impossible to hold out more than fourteen days, but on the 26th June a strong reinforcement arrived, under Colonel Cleote, when the Boers made a hasty retreat.

The artillery of the relieving force consisted of Lieutenant P. Maclean, two bombardiers, and six gunners. Other detachments of the corps, under Captain Wood and Lieutenant Turner, were employed against the enemy; twelve gunners (of whom one was sick) being the only artillery left in Cape Town.

Early in 1846 war broke out again at the Cape. The first notification of an irruption of the Kaffirs was received at Fort Beaufort on Sunday, 25th January, when the troops were at once ordered to be in readiness, the artillery being marched out of church during divine service.

One of the first to meet the enemy was a gunner who, with a corporal of the Sappers, was ordered to Post Victoria in charge of a waggon with twelve oxen and two natives. In crossing a drift, after marching seven miles, the oxen were knocked up, and the corporal sent the driver back for more cattle. At night the sapper corporal and the artilleryman took turn as sentry over the waggon.

Next morning at daylight the Kaffirs fired at and wounded the native leader; and though bravely attacked by the corporal, they succeeded in capturing the cattle. The artilleryman, having only a short sword, remained in charge of the waggon. A patrol of the 7th Dragoon Guards came up, however, and hearing what had happened, they pursued the Kaffirs and retook the oxen. The waggon and escort now resumed the route, and reached Post Victoria in safety.

The Royal Artillery engaged in the operations under Colonel Somerset and Lieut.-Colonel Richardson was commanded by Captains Burnaby and Browne (he died at Pembroke, May 19, 1861). The latter had lately arrived in the colony to assume the command rendered vacant by the death of Captain Sheppard, who was shot at Post Victoria on the 29th November, 1845, by Wheeler Long, R.A. Owing to want of evidence on the part of the prosecution (the witnesses being all in the field, from whence they could not be spared), it was nearly a year before the murderer was brought to trial and executed.

(It is rather a curious coincidence that a sergeant-major named Sheppard was shot in a similar manner by one of the men on the parade-ground at Woolwich).

The artillery was occasionally divided into very small detachments; but in the action during the retreat from Burn's Hill to Block Drift, on the 17th April, they had four guns in the field. Lieutenant Hill, R.A. (later of the Military Train), got a gun into position, and made excellent practice into the dense bush along the banks of a river, the enemy pressing on, and opening a severe fire on our advance. Captain Browne's guns took up an admirable position, doing great execution under a heavy fire.

These guns were engaged during a perfect hail of bullets—though, strange to say, none of our men were killed. Several shots went through the clothes of the gunners, others grazed their skin, etc.; but no serious injury was sustained. The party of dragoons by whom the guns were covered, thinking they were uselessly exposed to so tremendous a fire, galloped, off to where they could find shelter. Captain Browne, however, took no offence at this movement, but encouraged his men, who were firing canister into the bush as fast as they could load and reload, saying, "Bravo! my brave boys, we'll have the day to ourselves."

A poor Hottentot passing by Lieutenant Hill's gun just as the word "fire" was given had his head taken clean off.

Two field-pieces, under Captain Browne and Lieutenant Gregory (died at Fiddon, 1859), were with Colonel Somerset's division in Lower Albany on the 1st May, and on the same day Lieutenant Hill's detachment was brought into action at Fort Peddie. The latter was hotly engaged for three hours on the morning of the 8th May at Trumpeter's Bush, though the only casualty was a gunner (George Smith) wounded.

A detachment under Lieutenant W. M. King was stationed in Fort Peddie (he died at Malta, May 8, 1860). This post was attacked by the Kaffirs on the 28th May, but they were speedily repulsed. Colonel Lindsay, the commandant, spoke highly of the practice made by the artillery, and said, "When they came within range, I directed Lieutenant King to send a round shot at one of the masses, which killed three men."

The Kaffirs now extended themselves in a line six miles in length. These advancing at the same time, so filled the valley that it seemed a mass of moving Kaffirs; rockets and shells were poured rapidly on them, however, which prevented them nearing the fort. While they were rifling a store, a few shots from the howitzer sent them flying, carrying off their booty, blankets, etc.; a rocket was then sent after them, causing them to drop their plunder.

The difficulties of Kaffir warfare, or the difficulty of giving anything like a detailed account of the movements of the troops in such warfare, need not be repeated here. Wherever a body could be met with they were engaged and defeated by our troops; but they, knowing their superiority in bush-fighting, hardly ever appeared but in small parties, posted in and about the woods and bushes, and completely hid from their adversaries. Having been well punished for their outrages on life and property, in 1847 the Kaffirs were glad to sue for peace, which was as gladly granted by the British, who were satisfied with having taught them that their ravages could not be carried on with impunity.

During a hurricane which took place in 1846 the bark *Francis Spaight* was wrecked in Table Bay; when, by perseverance, and at the imminent risk of his own life, Lieutenant Disney Russel, R.A., an officer who had distinguished himself during the war, saved the lives of two of the crew. (The son of the late Major-General Russel, R.A. Died at Woolwich, January 16, 1852). His conduct was noticed by the governor, and he was thanked in general orders.

In 1848 the Boers showed signs of disaffection, laying claim to the sovereignty of the Orange River. On the 2nd August a small force left King William's Town to chastise these rebels, with whom it came up on the 28th.

It was not long before they were beaten, and two days afterwards a great peace demonstration was held at Wynberg, the Boers bringing 800 horsemen and 1,500 foot warriors into the field to be reviewed by Sir Harry Smith.

The Royal Artillery in this affair was commanded by Lieutenant Dynely. (Son of the late Lieut.-General Dynely, R.A. Died in India, 1863). Peace was maintained till 1850, when the incursions of the Kaffirs became more frequent, and the cruelties exercised by them towards the settlers on the frontiers more dreadful than at any former period.

On the 18th December Sir Harry Smith marched all the troops in Albany and British Kaffraria to the Amatola Mountains, his object being to make such a demonstration as might overawe the Kaffirs without resorting to force.

A few days later, however, and it was evident the enemy was determined for war. The Royal Artillery at this time in the colony was commanded by Major Barnaby, who was appointed commandant of Graham's Town and the Lower Albany district. Major Wilmot, R.A. was also present at Sir H. Smith's headquarters, and he was entrusted with many important commands.

In March, 1831, with a patrol of 900 men, Wilmot encountered and defeated the tribe of Seyolo, and laid waste their country, destroying their *kraals* and stores. In April another patrol under Wilmot, including a detachment of artillery under Lieutenant Pasley (he died at Ticehurst, September 27, 1863), was despatched into the country about the Keiskama, when 100 huts were destroyed, several large granaries of corn captured, and the enemy kept at bay.

In May Major Wilmot's patrol was employed in the Amatola Mountains, and again in the country about Fort Peddie.

Detachments of the Royal Artillery under Lieutenants Field, Pasley, and Campbell were in the field with Sir H. Smith and Colonel Somerset in all the principal engagements.

A 6-pounder howitzer, with the usual detachment, accompanied a party which, on the 14th July, 1851, was sent out against Macomo. After two days' hard work, during which they had to drag the gun by hand up the steep and narrow Waterkloof Pass, and lift it bodily over large felled trees placed across the path by the enemy, they came in sight of the Kaffirs.

The gun was brought to bear upon them, but owing to the nature of the cover in which they took refuge, the effect could not be ascertained, though from the precision with which the shells were dropped their loss must have been considerable.

In September a force under Lieut.-Colonel Mitchell, 6th regiment, received orders to carry on operations against the Kaffirs and rebel Hottentots on the eastern side of the Fish River Bush. Lieutenant Campbell, with a detachment of the Royal Artillery and two 6-pounders, accompanied this force—Lieutenant Pasley, R.A., being attached as *aide-de-camp* and brigade-major to Colonel Mitchell.

In the engagement near the Blinkwater and Waterkloof (14th October), the practice of the Royal Artillery under Lieutenants Campbell and Field was most effective.

It was the shells from Lieutenant Field's guns which, falling among the enemy with wonderful precision, drove them from the rocks where they had taken shelter. On New Year's Day the artillery had to deplore the loss of Major Wilmot, who was killed while leading a patrol in the villages near the Fish River, where Sandilli had taken shelter.

He had left Fort Peddie on the morning of the 31st December, and proceeded to Committee's Post, where he burnt some huts, captured some cattle, and took a Kaffir prisoner. On the morning of the 1st January the patrol proceeded about a mile in the direction of Foonah's Kloof, when they came upon a nest of Kaffirs and Hottentots. Major Wilmot went into one of the huts, when three shots were fired; the third, striking him in the left side, passed out at the other. He lived about half an hour.

Major Henry Robert Eardley Wilmot was the fifth son of Sir John Eardley Wilmot, and brother of the present Colonel Wilmot, R.A. He was an officer greatly admired and highly respected in the colonies, he having served in Australia, New Zealand, etc., and as the *Graham's Town Journal* observed, "on every occasion when hard and gallant service was demanded he distinguished himself."

In the early part of 1852, many reinforcements were sent to the Cape, including fresh batteries of artillery, which, under Captains Faddy, Devereux, Robinson, Lieutenant Singer, etc., were usefully employed in various parts against the enemy.

In February Sir H. Smith made a grand attack upon the difficult and dangerous positions of Waterkloof, Blinkwater, and Fuller's Hock, completely clearing the spot known as "Macomo's Den."

Shortly afterwards he was recalled to England, and the command taken by Sir G. Cathcart. On the 30th June Major Burnaby left the colony, when the following general order appeared:—

> Major Burnaby was appointed commandant of Graham's Town by Major-General Somerset when hostilities first commenced, at the most critical period of the war, involving duties of the most vital importance and the greatest responsibility. In addition to the duties of equipping and completing the field battery, whose efficiency in the division has been so conspicuous, the duties of escorts for protecting the general supplies of the army had to be detached from the irregular levies hastily raised and called together, and other most important duties provided for, requiring great consideration. Major-General Somerset has the greatest satisfaction in expressing his opinion that Major Burnaby has conducted the whole of the important and numerous duties entrusted to him in the most efficient manner, with an energy and promptness that has been of the utmost advantage

to the public service and the frontier generally.

The war was continued till December, when the Kaffirs asked for peace, with many protestations of allegiance to Queen Victoria. General Cathcart, having so far humbled them, at once granted their petitions, assuring them, however, that a repetition, of their fiendish conduct towards the settlers would bring on them a repetition of the chastisement which in their appeal for peace they allow was merited.

CHAPTER 14

The War in the Crimea—Field Operations

During the latter part of the year 1853 the peaceful horizon of Europe became over-clouded, and the minds of many were uneasy at the aspect presented in the aggressive policy pursued by Russia towards her weak neighbour, the Ottoman Empire.

Diplomacy was resorted to for the purpose of inducing Russia to abandon her projects, but in vain, and in March, 1854, war was declared by England and France against the Emperor of all the Russias. Troops were at once sent to the East, but passing over the encampments at Gallipoli and Scutari, the reviews at Devna (where the Horse Artillery astonished Omar Pasha by the rapidity of their movements), and the inaction at Varna, we come to the invasion of the Crimea, which took place in September, 1854.

****

In July a reconnaissance of the Dobrudscha was effected by twelve artillerymen, mounted on pack-saddles and baggages, under Colonel Gordon. Captain Gage, R.A., had command of a party which marched to the Danube, a distance of 120 miles, and remained with the Turkish Army under Omar Pasha during the operations at Rudchuck and Giurgevo.

****

The disposition of the British artillery at this time was as follows:—
Brigadier T. Fox Strangways, commanding; Captain J. M. Adye, Assistant Adjutant-General; Captain Hon. E. T. Gage. Brigade Major; Captain G. T. Field, Deputy assistant Quartermaster-General; Captain E. B. Hamley, Staff Officer. Colonel J. E. Dupuis, commanding Horse Artillery.

Troops . . . . { Captain G. A. Maude.
                     „   H. J. Thomas.*

FIRST DIVISION.

Colonel R. J. Dacres commanding.
Batteries . . . { Captain E. Wodehouse.
                     „   D. W. Paynter.

SECOND DIVISION.

Colonel J. W. Fitzmayer commanding.
Batteries . . . { Captain J. Turner.
                     „   C. T. Franklin (Yates).

THIRD DIVISION.

Colonel W. R. Nedham commanding.
Batteries . . . { Captain W. Swinton.
                     „   G. R. Barker.

FOURTH DIVISION.

Colonel D. E. Wood commanding.
Battery . . . . Major S. P. Townsend.

LIGHT DIVISION.

Colonel N. T. Lake commanding.
Batteries . . . { Captain Anderson.
                     „   Morris.

* This troop, lately commanded by Major Levinge, who, in Turkey, fell a victim to an overdose of opium, taken as an antidote against cholera, was led into action by Captain Brandling, R.A., Captain Thomas not having arrived from England.

The allies landed at Old Fort on the 14th September, Captain Anderson's battery being the first of the British artillery to more inland. By the 16th nearly all the guns were landed, and a reconnaissance was made by the cavalry under Lord Cardigan, accompanied by Maude's troop of Horse Artillery. They started at one p.m., and went about fourteen miles in a north-easterly direction, over a very flat country.

They did not meet one Cossack, but the Tartars in the village supplied them with provisions at a very cheap rate. Lieutenant Taddy, R.H.A., bought fourteen pigs for twopence, and other officers of the troop obtained a turkey, a chicken, and four ducks for two shillings, while the men indulged in eggs, which they purchased at fourteen a penny. (Lieutenant Taddy died at Edinburgh, October 19, 1862).

After remaining an hour in the farthest village, the party returned to Old Fort by the same road.

Early on the morning of the 19th the armies began their march towards Sebastopol, the batteries of artillery maintaining a position on the right of the respective divisions of infantry, and Maude's troop advancing with the cavalry. In the afternoon they arrived at the River

Bulganac, from whence the Russians were visible, their cavalry (with guns) having taken up a position on the opposite hills.

One of the first to meet the enemy was Major Collingwood Dickson, R.A., the son of the great artilleryman of the Peninsula, who, with Dr. Elliott and some dragoon officers, was riding between the cavalry and the skirmishers, when the Russians descended the hill towards them.

After some thirty rounds from the enemy's guns, Maude's troop galloped up and opened fire. Their round-shot ploughed up the columns of the cavalry, who speedily dispersed into broken lines, wheeling round and round with great adroitness to escape the 6 and 9-pound balls. Our shells were not so successful, but one, better directed than the rest, burst right in the centre of a column of light infantry whom the Russians had advanced to support their cavalry. Our fire was so hot, and the service of the guns so quick, that the enemy retired in about fifteen minutes after we opened on them.

Morning dawned on the 20th of September, the day of the Battle of the Alma, amid a busy camp, for all expected that that day would become a memorable one in history. Nor were they disappointed. Before sunset the Allied Armies of England and France had driven the Russians from a position formidable by nature, and rendered doubly so by art, and the Army of England, by far the greater part of whom had never seen a shot fired in anger, proved to the world that they had in no way degenerated, but were worthy followers of the men of Creçy, of Blenheim, and of Waterloo. The remembrance of these actions however, was obliterated by the glories of this day; the soldiers of France, whom we had ever occasion to respect as enemies, we now learned to trust as firm and faithful friends. May they ever remain as such, and the world will have cause to remember with thankfulness the events of 1854.

It was noon when the allies arrived at the River Alma, on the southern side of which the Russians, in position on the heights, were waiting to receive them. The French commenced the battle by turning the enemy's left flank; the 2nd and light divisions of the British then dashed through the river and up the face of the heights, to attack the Russian batteries. The British artillery had been throwing shot into the Russian redoubts since the commencement of the French attack, and had lost one officer, Captain Dew, who was struck in the head by a round-shot; now they were ordered to advance.

Turner's battery was the first to cross the river. A wheel was knocked off one of the guns by a round-shot while in the middle of the stream, and officers and men vied with each other in their exertions to get the gun ready for action, they being all the time up to their middles in water and exposed to a most destructive fire.

Two guns of the battery quickly arrived at the spot to which they were ordered by Lord Raglan, but they had advanced so rapidly and the difficulties in crossing the river were so great that there was but one bombardier besides the drivers who came up with the guns. The officers of the battery instantly dismounted, and assisted by Major Dickson, Captain Gordon, and the officers of General Strangways' staff, served the guns until the gunners came up. The first shot fell too short, it was aimed at the Russian 18-gun battery, which was causing our second division, in its immediate front, and the light division and the brigade of Guards in its right front, great loss.

The guns were only 9-pounders, and the distance was considerable. The second shot, however, went through a Russian tumbril and killed two horses. These two shots were sufficient: the Russian general seeing that he was taken completely in flank, gave orders for them to limber up their guns. This they did admirably, but during the time our two guns kept playing on their retiring artillery, causing them great loss; and the gunners and two more guns of Turner's battery having now arrived, the firing went on rapidly.

This battery sustained many losses, and such was the scarcity of men at one of the guns that Lieutenant Walsham took a gunner's place, and was in the act of sponging the gun when he received a bullet in the right breast which instantly deprived him of life.

This young officer, the third son of Sir John Walsham, Bart., was one of that daring class of adventurers whose name became public by ascending Mont Blanc, and the feat, as performed by him, was duly mentioned in the papers of the day. At the Alma he ascended a more glorious height, and his devotion in acting as a common gunner, which brought his uniform to the enemy's mark, entitles him to the grateful remembrance of his country. He had just entered his twentieth year when he fell in the first battle in the Crimea. The only other casualty among the officers of Royal Artillery was Lieutenant Cockrell whose leg was carried away by a cannon-shot. He died after amputation.

As soon as the Russian guns ceased firing, Wodehouse's battery, which had been limbered up and led across the river by Colonel Dacres, came up on the right of the 30th regiment. The slopes in front were still covered with the enemy's skirmishers, obstinately contesting the ground with our own, and giving way, if at all, very slowly.

Over the heights beyond the contested battery, the helmets of a Russian column might be seen, and presently the solid mass, apparently about 2,000 strong, marched over the hill and began to descend towards the British line. A shell from a gun, laid by Colonel Dacres himself before the gun detachment could come up, dropped among the Russian skirmishers; the other guns coming up in succession, opened their fire on the column and struck it every time. Franklin's and Anderson's batteries, crossing the river, came up and opened on the left, and Paynter's followed; and the column, after marching about fifty yards down the hill, halted, turned about, and disappearing over the crest, was seen no more.

Maude's troop went up the hill and into action in the most gallant style, on the extreme left of the English position, and did great execution, as there were upwards of 200 dead Russians on the spot his shot had reached, and where no other battery had directed its fire.

The British infantry now crowned the heights, and the position was ours. While ascending the hill, some men of Wodehouse's battery discovered a Russian general (Shokanoff) and his servant lying on the ground as though they were wounded. Gunner M'Anasby and Trumpeter M'Laren, to whom I believe the credit is due for having discovered these impostors, at once delivered them up to their officer, Lieutenant Richards, by whom the general was received in a manner befitting his position. He was sent to Scutari, where he afterwards died of cholera.

At the summit of the hill a brief stand was made by the enemy, and it seemed as if the contest was about to be renewed, but the infantry, levelling their bayonets, advanced at a rapid pace, and the Russians, dashing down their accoutrements and arms, fled like frightened sheep down the declivity. The victory was complete—a great army in a position of immense strength had been ignominiously defeated in less than three hours by the sheer valour of English and French soldiers.

For two days the armies remained upon the field, and at early morn on the 23rd September commenced their southward march. They bivouacked that night on the banks of the Katcha, and on the following morning advanced towards the Belbek. This day the northern forts of Sebastopol were distinctly visible—indeed, at one time the allies were within range of the guns of the great Star Fort. They

ARTILLERY AT THE SOUTH COAST MID 19TH CENTURY

therefore turned somewhat to the left, and rested for the night on some hills around the little village of Belbek.

The 25th was a day to be remembered by all in the army, for it was a day of much difficulty and fatigue. The distance from the Belbek to Balaklava is but fourteen miles, but the troops had to pass through a thick forest or jungle, each man threading a path as he best could.

Lord Raglan and his staff were the first to emerge from the wood, and on so doing they came right upon the rear-guard of the Russian Army. Maude's troop was quickly got out of the wood and fired a few rounds; a volley from the Rifles and a charge of the cavalry followed, and the Russians rushed pell-mell along the road to Simpheropol, leaving everything behind that might have impeded their flight, and strewing the road for two or three miles with waggons, carts, tumbrils, provisions, ammunition, baggage, officers' uniforms, personal ornaments, and a countless array of miscellaneous articles.

Our gunners got hold of the baggage of some general officer and his staff, for they were soon laden with embroidered hussar jackets, *pelisses*, and garments of various kinds; they also got a quantity of jewellery and watches, and some, more lucky than the rest, got hold of the general's luncheon basket, and feasted on wild boar washed down with champagne.

An officer of the Royal Artillery, who was fortunate enough to become possessed of a whole side of a wild boar, politely sent Lord Raglan a leg. A quantity of ammunition was found among these spoils, six waggonsful being blown up by a party under Captain Fortescue, R.A.

A halt was made for an hour or two on the heights near Mackenzie's Farm, after which the army resumed its march towards Balaklava, reaching the River Tchernaya in the evening, and remaining there for the night.

Before the army commenced its march on this day Driver Robert Smeaton, of Major Maude's troop, gallantly jumped into the river Belbek, and succeeded in saving the life of a French soldier, who would have been drowned but for his timely assistance. This man served throughout the whole of the campaign, and at its close he received the medal for "*Valeur et discipline*" from the Emperor of the French.

On the morrow the armies approached Balaklava. A few shells fired from an old Genoese fort was the only resistance offered to our troops, who speedily occupied the town and established a communication with the fleet, which had already entered the small but peculiarly useful harbour of Balaklava.

Preparations were now made for the siege of Sebastopol. The details of the many occasions on which "British artillerymen" distinguished themselves during this glorious siege will be found in the next chapter. We have now to do only with the field artillery who were stationed in and about Balaklava.

By the 30th all the heavy guns were parked on the heights above Balaklava, and then it was that both men and horses of the field batteries experienced the hardest work they had during the whole of the campaign. These guns had to be dragged over hilly and rocky ground a distance of seven miles before they could be placed in position against Sebastopol. The horses fell under the heavy loads, never to rise again; the men also were worn out with the continual and harassing fatigue duties, and ere winter commenced reinforcements were sadly wanted to complete the efficiency of the field batteries.

On the 6th October Maude's troop was engaged in a little skirmish with a body of Cossacks who had come down for the purpose of annoying our working parties.

On the morning of the 25th October a Russian Army of about 30,000 appeared openly on the plain before Balaklava, ready to meet the allies in fair fight. At early dawn large masses of Russian cavalry, supported by artillery and infantry, advanced against the redoubts which had been thrown up for the defence of Balaklava, and which were manned by the Turks, having one English artilleryman in each. Gunners David Jenkins, Jacob M'Garry, and John Barrett were the men to whom the conduct of the Moslem gunners was entrusted, and nobly they performed their duty, and sustained for their corps that high character which it has ever had the good fortune to possess.

After a few rounds from the Russian batteries the Turks in No. 1 redoubt quitted their guns, and fled precipitately towards No. 3. They were followed by the English gunner, but not until he had spiked the guns. The Turks in Nos. 2 and 3, finding that their comrades on the right had fled, took the alarm, and the whole of them were in a few minutes running out of the redoubts, abandoning our guns and artillerymen to their fate. The latter were, of course, obliged to follow, but they took care first to render the ordnance in the redoubts unserviceable.

There was another Englishman in No. 4 redoubt, a sapper named Lankaster, with whom the artilleryman, sharing the kin of country, behaved as became their national character.

When No. 3 redoubt was evacuated the Russian battery increased its fire on No. 4, which, answering with an energy probably emboldened by the nearness of supports, checked the enemy in his career of success. It is due to the gallantry of the Turks in No. 4 to acknowledge, that while many of the infantry vaulted in alarm over the parapet at the first blush of the fight, and ran from the opportunity to cover themselves with honour, there were not wanting staunch artillerists, firm and courageous, to stand to the guns, and, as instructed by the British gunner, to work them manfully.

Regarding, however, any display of courage on their part as useless, and their position as untenable, the little garrison of this redoubt, after spiking the guns and breaking the wheels of the carriages, quitted the battery and took up a position under cover of the Highlanders. The names of Jenkins, M'Garry, and Barrett were recorded by order of Her Majesty; the former also received the French war medal, and the two latter were decorated with the Sardinian medal.

Maude's troop and Barker's battery, supported by the Scots Greys, were ordered up from Balaklava to the slopes between the outposts, and found themselves opposed to the fire of several field batteries and some guns of position, which covered an advance of infantry. As the troop was armed only with 6-pounders, it and the field battery were quite overmatched, both in metal and in numbers; nevertheless, our artillery maintained the contest till its ammunition was exhausted, when it retired, having lost a good many horses and a few men. Captain Maude himself was dangerously wounded; he was struck in the arm by a shell which burst at his saddle-bow and killed his horse.

Thomas's troop (under Captain Brandling), was stationed near the heavy brigade, under cover of a vineyard, ready to come into action at a moment's notice. After the heavy cavalry charge, Maude's troop (under Captain Shakespear) formed upon their left flank, and afterwards manoeuvred about, but never came again into action. After the repulse of the Russian cavalry by the Highlanders, Barker's battery fired into the retreating columns.

The Royal Artillery took no further part in the events of this memorable day, though all the batteries were drawn up in readiness for action.

The Russians remained satisfied with the redoubts they had captured from the Turks, and did not advance any further towards Balaklava.

On the following day (26th October) the enemy came out in force and attacked the camp of the second division. They had thirty-two guns, to oppose which the batteries of the second division, under Captains Turner and Yates, were quickly brought into the field. Presently Colonel Dacres, with Captain Wodehouse's battery, came up to their assistance, and in half an hour these eighteen guns forced the enemy's artillery to abandon the field.

Our batteries were then directed, with equal accuracy and vigour, upon the enemy's columns, which soon fell into complete disorder and flight. They were then literally chased by the infantry almost to the walls of Sebastopol.

On the 5th November the Battle of Inkerman took place. In this, the most memorable achievement of modern times—when the Allied Army of 14,000 men defeated the Russians, numbering 60,000, causing them to leave a greater number of killed and wounded on the field than the entire force of English and French who were engaged—the Royal Artillery nobly sustained their fame, both as good gunners and as brave men.

Two hours before daybreak the horses of Turner's and Yates's batteries, of the second division, were hooked in the guns, and the first line of waggons, as was their usual custom. As the men turned out, they could plainly bear the bells tolling in Sebastopol, and as it was the 5th November some of them jocosely remarked that "it was in commemoration of Guy Faux." However, just at the break of day, the Russians opened a deadly fire on the second division camp with several heavy guns which they had placed in position with muffled wheels during the night. The two pieces on picquet, a 9-pounder and a 24-pounder howitzer, under Lieutenant Broughton, were the first engaged. Turner's and Yates's batteries, however, being already horsed, quickly advanced to the front, and came into action. Wodehouse's battery soon followed, and before an hour had elapsed all the batteries were up and hotly engaged.

The 41st and 49th regiments were pushed on to check the advance of the enemy, and Wodehouse's battery was at once ordered up to the support of these regiments. Three guns of this battery were placed under the command of Captain Hamley, and were so advantageously placed by him that they continued to fire with deadly effect on the enemy's columns. "It must be remarked, says General Todleben, in his recent work on the defence of Sebastopol, "that the English artillery sustained its infantry perfectly. It followed them everywhere, and opened fire at sufficiently close distances against the assailing columns of the Russians."

Townsend's battery was taken up to the assistance Codrington's division by Colonel Wood, by whom it was most advantageously placed. The first few rounds must have told with murderous effect upon the Russians, who, however, favoured by the mist of the morning, crept up among the brushwood, picked off our artillerymen, and caused severe loss.

Major Townsend fell at this moment, and the Russians charging, captured four of our guns.

****

Major S. P. Townsend was the eldest son of the Rev. W. R. Townsend, rector of Agheda (Ireland), and a grandson of the late Major-General Brooke Young, R. A. He received his first commission in 1831, and in 1337 he served on the staff of the Royal Artillery during the suppression of the rebellion in Canada. Distinguished as he was in his military capacity, he was still more so in his manifold Christian qualities, which earned for him the love of his brother officers and the respect and affection of his soldiers. His excellent life has been borne testimony to on many occasions.

****

Hardly had hostile hands touched English iron, before our 77th and 88th, headed by Lieutenant Miller, R.A., were in the midst of the Russians. (This gallant officer received the Victoria Cross for his exertions in the recapture of his own guns). A second or so and the guns were our own again.

By this time, notwithstanding the tremendous struggle in which the infantry were engaged in the redoubt known as the two-gun battery, all our guns were in position, opposed to pieces three times their weight (so placed on the crest of the opposite hill that only their muzzles were visible), and exposed to their deadly fire, which caused great loss both in men and horses.

The incidents which occurred during this tremendous duel of artillery would fill a volume. A few, however deserve especial mention.

The batteries of the first division, under Colonel Dacres, suffered great loss. Dacres' horse was shot under him, when he immediately took that of Trumpeter M'Laren, of Wodehouse's battery, telling the boy to go home (that was to the camp) out of danger. The brave little fellow, seeing the loss his battery had sustained, requested to be allowed to remain, and he served as a gunner during the remainder of the action.

****

M'Laren received the French war-medal for his gallant conduct. After

A QUIET DAY IN THE DIAMOND BATTERY
Lancaster 68-Pounder, 15th December, 1854

the war he was transferred into the Royal Artillery band, in which he remained till his death, which took place March 15, 1859. He was interred in Charlton Cemetery, a stone being erected to his memory by his old companions with whom he had served in the Crimea.

★★★★★★★★★★

Sergeant Fairfax, Gunner Maloney, and Driver Hay were all noticed on the field by Colonel Dacres as having displayed extraordinary courage and zeal during this trying time. Captain Hamley's horse was killed by a round-shot, and fell heavily, crushing his rider under him. Sergeant M'Kown ran to extricate his officer. He had just lifted him from under the horse, and was assisting him to steady himself, when a shot carried off his thigh, and he fell back on Hamley, uttering cries as if of amazement at the suddenness of his misfortune. Captain Hamley laid him gently down, and called two men to carry him to the rear. He afterwards died at Scutari.

★★★★★★★★★★

Sergeant John M'Kown was the second son of the late Quartermaster M'Kown, R.A., a distinguished veteran of the Peninsular and American wars, who had received severe wounds in each. Sergeant James M'Kown his younger brother, also served throughout the campaign in the Crimea, and at its close received the French war-medal for his distinguished conduct.

★★★★★★★★★★

At one time the Russian infantry made a dashing charge at the guns of Turner's battery, which for a time remained in their hands. Sergeant Henry, who commanded one of the guns, called out to the gunners not to leave their posts, but defend the gun to the last. Setting an example, which was immediately followed by a brave gunner named James Taylor, he drew his sword and prepared for the worst. In a minute they were surrounded, and Taylor received his death-wound. Henry, seizing one of the enemy's bayonets with his left hand, and throwing the man off, cut away at the others with his sword. He was soon overpowered, however, and was struck in the breast with, a bayonet and lifted off the ground, and when he fell, he received no fewer than twelve wounds.

The French and one of our infantry regiments soon recaptured the guns, and then turned their attention to the wounded. A French soldier gave Henry a drink, which revived him, and he was then carried to the rear by two infantry soldiers. Suffering so much from loss of blood, he begged of the men to put him down and leave him, and he was afterwards rescued by Corporal Conway and Gunner M'Grath, of his own battery. (Sergeant Henry afterwards received a commission in the Land Transport Corps, and was decorated with the Victoria Cross. He is now (1865), a captain in the Coast Brigade, Royal Artillery).

Farrier Mark Sutton, who was taken prisoner with his guns, contrived to effect his escape.

Turner's battery suffered fearfully, having twenty men killed and wounded, and thirty horses killed, besides having their limber-boxes broken, etc.

Lord Raglan—seeing the difficulties under which the artillery were engaged, and wishing, if possible, in however small a degree, to equalise the contending ordnance—bethought himself of bringing into action any guns of position that we might have unemployed in the siege-train. He inquired what guns there were in the right siege-train, and was told there were two iron 18-pounder guns of position.

Lord Raglan immediately despatched an order for them to be brought up. The officer to whom it was delivered sent an answer back that it was *impossible*. Lord Raglan was much annoyed at this, turned to the assistant adjutant-general of Royal Artillery, and said, "Adye, I don't like the word *impossible*: don't you think the guns can be brought up?" Major Adye said he was certain it could be done. Lord Raglan then sent Captain Gordon, R.A., with directions to Colonel Gambier to bring the two 18-pounders into action with the least possible delay.

At this time a splinter of a shell which had burst in the midst of the staff struck General Strangways' leg with such force as to leave it hanging by a mere shred of jagged flesh and a portion of the trousers. Without a complaint—his face as placid as though nothing had occurred—the brave old man, in his usual gentle manner, said, "Will anyone be kind enough to lift me off my horse?" Major Adye had already dismounted, and in a moment, he lifted the poor old general off his horse and laid him on the ground, and then hurried off to procure a stretcher.

As the gallant old soldier was laid on the earth, tears forced themselves from many a stout heart, for Strangways was known and beloved by every man; his snow-white hair and kind and gentle manner having rendered him conspicuous in the camp. He was removed with great care to the hospital of the right siege-train, but he had lost so much blood even before he had been lifted off his horse, that it was considered better not to torture him by an operation, which, in his weak state; would facilitate the death he was so fast hastening to. After addressing a few words to the officers of the staff and leaving his last message for those most dear to him in England, he said, "I die, at least, a soldier's death!"

Towards the close of the battle, when the Russians were retiring, Lord Raglan received intelligence that the poor old general was fast approaching his end. His Lordship immediately rode to the hospital, and going in found him rapidly sinking. He pressed the old man's hand, and told him we had gained the day. A faint smile passed over the dying veteran's countenance, but he was too weak from the loss of blood to speak. A few minutes after, and his spirit fled to rest.

The moment at last arrived when the battle was decidedly in favour of the allies, for at this instant the two 18-pounders were being brought into action. They were dragged up, not without considerable difficulty, by horses taken from the field guns which had been spiked, and by the men of Dickson's and D'Aguilar's companies, under Lieut.-Colonel Gambier.

This gallant officer was proceeding with these pieces of ordnance towards Lord Raglan, when a spent shot (comparatively speaking) ricocheted off the ground and struck him on the chest. Of course, he was knocked down senseless, and carried to the rear (as it was thought at the time) a mortally wounded man.

Colonel Gambier was many months before he recovered from the effects of this blow. Indeed, for a long time his life was despaired of, for although the shot made no open wound, it caused so great a contusion that the medical men never expected he would get over it.

His place was taken by Colonel Dickson, who brought the guns into action, and continued till the end of the battle in command of them. They had not been in action half an hour before their superiority was shown by enfeebled reply of the enemy's artillery. The loss of men encased in serving these guns was very great. Seventeen, artillerymen were killed or wounded, Captains Tupper and Ingilby being among the latter.

Several men were noticed on the field by Colonel Dickson, the most conspicuous being Gunners John Morton and Hugh Davis. The latter received a slight wound, but would not leave his post until a round-shot came and took away both his arms. He was pensioned after the war, and died at Woolwich in April, 1861.

Fresh men having been received from the right siege-train, our fire, if anything, became more accurate. There was never such beautiful practice. The greatest praise is due to Colonel Dickson for the admirable manner in which he directed his men.

The mighty duel of artillery continued for some time, the enemy drawing off their guns by fours every ten minutes or so, until but two batteries remained. These were severely knocked about by our 18-pounders, but Lord Raglan sent an *aide-de-camp* to Colonel Dickson to desire him to cease firing, as he wished to advance some infantry. Dickson begged to be allowed to have a few shots more, as he said he had the range so perfectly and to verify his assertion the guns, which were then loaded, were fired, and the shot went crashing through the Russian carriages. A minute or two later he ceased firing, an example which the Russians immediately followed.

On witnessing the decisive effect of Dickson's skill. Lord Raglan, accompanied by his staff, immediately rode up to him and congratulated him on his success. "Dickson, my brave fellow," said he, "you are your father's better." In a few moments the British had the satisfaction of seeing the last of the enemy's artillery limber up and gallop off the field.

Besides the casualties mentioned at the battle of Inkerman, Captains Morris and Baddely were wounded, while the loss in men was 13 killed and 76 wounded. Besides these the loss in horses was enormous; seven officers had their horses shot under them, of whom no fewer than four were doing duty with Wodehouse's battery.

The day after the battle a melancholy spectacle was afforded to the camp. A lofty eminence in front of the fourth division was appropriated as the burial-place of the more distinguished officers who had fallen in the battle. Cathcart and Strangways, who had first met on the field at Leipsic, when fighting for the Russians against the French, and had afterwards served together at Waterloo, had fallen in the valley of Inkerman, and were this day laid side by side, mourned not only by the whole of the army but by the English nation. Strangways was borne to the grave on a gun, escorted by the I troop of Horse Artillery, formerly the rocket troop, the only portion of the British Army which (under *his* command) had served at Leipsic.

On the 14th November occurred an event which crowned the sufferings of the devoted armies. A hurricane broke over the whole camp, scattering the tents to the winds, and a deluge of rain for more than twelve hours completed the disasters the hurricane had commenced. The poor horses were almost swept away, dying by hundreds; the camp became one huge quagmire, and the soldiers, deprived of shelter and food, cowered in wretched groups, vainly endeavouring to shield themselves from the "fierce pelting of the pitiless storm."

The siege of Sebastopol now engrossed all attention until May, when an expedition under Sir George Brown embarked at Balaklava for the Sea of Azov. The artillery attached to this division was commanded by Captain Barker. Arriving at Kertch, the place was taken without the artillery being called into action, and was quickly occupied. Anapa and the neighbouring fortresses having all surrendered to the allies, the presence of so large a body of troops at Kertch was no longer necessary. The greater number were therefore re-embarked and returned to Balaklava, resuming their duties before Sebastopol. Captain Graydon and fifty men of the Royal Artillery were left at Kertch to assist the Turks in the defence.

On the 16th August the Russian Army in the field attacked the French and Sardinians, who held a position on the River Tchernaya. None of the English Army were engaged on this, the last occasion on which the allies were attacked in the field, with the exception of Captain Mowbray's battery of 32-pounders, which was placed in advance with the Sardinian troops, and did most excellent service in preventing the advance of the enemy's artillery.

CHAPTER 15

War in the Crimea—Siege of Sebastopol

In October, 1854, the artillery destined to bombard Sebastopol was commanded by Colonel Gambler; the companies of the right attack (Dickson's, D'Aguilar's, and Strange's) being under Lieut.-Colonel Dickson, and those of the left (Young's, Freese's, and Rowan's) under Lieut. Colonel Irving.

At nightfall on the 8th October ground was broken before Sebastopol, and for the next week the trench work proceeded vigorously. The guns were then placed in position, and batteries erected, and on the evening of the 16th orders were issued to commence the bombardment.

On the 17th, at daylight, the silence was broken by such a peal of artillery as has scarcely ever before in the most famous battles or sieges shaken the earth around the combatants. A hundred and twenty-six pieces, many of them of the largest calibre, opened at once upon the Russian defences, and were answered by a still larger number of equal range and power. The din was incessant, and the smoke in the batteries so dense that after a few rounds the gunners laid their pieces rather by the line on the platform than by a view of the object aimed at.

The magazines of the right attack running short of powder, Lieut.-Colonel Dickson sent a demand to Colonel Gambler for more.

It was a difficult and dangerous operation to bring ammunition-waggons into the trenches under so heavy a fire; but the duty was most gallantly performed by the men of Wodehouse's field battery, under Lieutenant Maxwell, who galloped the waggons across the open to the trenches amidst the loud cheers of the gunners and sailors. The conduct of Lieut.-Colonel Dickson on this occasion, in directing the unloading of the waggons and personally assisting in conveying the ammunition into the batteries, was also very much noticed. (Colonel Dickson afterwards received the Victoria Cross for his conduct on this occasion. Lieutenant Maxwell died in India, January 23, 1860).

At midday the fleet approached the scene of action, and prepared to take their share in the dangers and glories of the day,

A distinguished officer of the Royal Artillery, one who in his youth had bravely sustained a terrific fire from the French batteries on the Trocadero at Cadiz, had taken part in the great battles of Barossa, Salamanca, Toulouse, etc., and had shed his blood on the glorious field of Waterloo; and who in his riper years had taught the Chinese to respect the power of England on their own shores; was, almost unknown, engaged with the fleet this day. This was Major-General the late Sir William Brereton (died in London, July 27, 1864), who was on board Admiral Dundas's ship the *Britannia*, directing the fire of the rockets against the forts and city of Sebastopol.

On the 18th the bombardment was confined to the land batteries.

On this day Sergeant George Symons volunteered to unmask the embrasures of a five-gun battery in the advanced right attack, and, when so employed (under a terrible fire, which the enemy commenced immediately on the opening of the first embrasure, and increased on the unmasking of each additional one), after unmasking them all he boldly mounted the parapet, and was throwing down the sandbags, when a shell from the enemy burst and wounded him severely. (Sergeant Symons afterwards received the Victoria Cross, and was presented with a commission in the Military Train. He is now (1865) adjutant of the Yorkshire Volunteer Artillery).

On the night of the 19th, as a gunner was returning from fatigue duty in the trenches of the right attack, he lost his way, and wandered on till he found himself among the enemy's outposts, by whom he was quickly made prisoner.

Major Young was slightly wounded on the 20th. (This officer, who had served in Spain during the Carlist war, in China in 1842, and in Kaffraria in 1847, was invalided home; and on February 24, 1865, he was killed by falling out of the window of a hotel in Portsmouth).

The interest excited by a contest of artillery without decided advantage on either side soon languishes, and in a few days the thunder of the bombardment was almost unheeded. But the troops in the trenches and batteries were hardly worked, the artillerymen not having more than five hours' rest out of the twenty-four, and exposed day by day incessantly to a tremendous fire.

On the 23rd the fire of the enemy was unusually sharp, ours having somewhat abated. Captain Childers, R.A., was killed on this day; Captain Moubray and Lieutenant Hope were wounded.

The first, a most promising young officer, the son of a captain in the 42nd Highlanders, was in conversation with Major Freese as to the progress of the enemy's earthworks; and leaving him for the purpose of taking an observation of the Russian batteries, he had no sooner looked over the parapet than a large round-shot struck him on the head, and death was instantaneous.

From this time the fire slackened on both sides, and the incidents of the siege were not distinguished by any important result: sometimes the besiegers made some apparent decided hits; then in turn the besieged effected some trifling advantage, but nothing of moment occurred.

The sufferings of our army during the ensuing; winter are, alas! too well known. It cannot be expected that the Royal Artillery fared any better than their companions in arms—indeed, it is not certain that the men of the siege train were not worse off than any other portion of the army, for the reinforcements did not begin to arrive till the season was far advanced, and the whole line of English batteries had to be defended by the remnants of six companies who were worn out with continual duty. (The men of the field batteries were occasionally sent up to assist in the trenches).

Among the heavy fatigues which had to be performed by the artillery at this inclement season, was that of bringing shot and shell up from Balaklava to the front. The process was most tedious: one man would have a 32-pounder shot in a sand-bag over his shoulder; another, with three horses, himself on the centre one, would bring four shot or shell, one being slung on each side of the two outer horses. Thus, two men and three horses, in bringing fire shot, would be occupied many hours, the said shot being hurled against Sebastopol in as many seconds.

Four officers of the Royal Artillery died during the winter, one of whom, Major Swinton, was stuffocated by charcoal which he was burning in his tent in the hope of obtaining warmth.

Many changes took place in the artillery department during this winter. The chief command, rendered vacant by the death of Strangways at Inkerman, devolved on Colonel Dacres. (Afterwards Lieut.-General Sir Richard J. Dacres, K.C.B., late commandant of Woolwich garrison).

Heavy Artillery in the Crimea

When Colonel Gambier was wounded, the command of the siege train devolved on Lieut.-Colonel Lake. This officer being shortly afterwards invalided, the command was taken by Colonel E. C. Warde. Majors Rowan, Freese, and Young having been promoted, they were succeeded in command of the batteries by Captains Henry, Grant, and Shaw. Among the reinforcements which arrived during the winter were eight companies for the siege train, commanded by Captains Broughton, H. Campbell, Wragge, Graydon, Oldfield, Dixon, Rogers, and Hawkins.

****

Lieut.-Colonel Lake died at Shooter's Hill, May 19, 1864. He was cousin to Colonel Atwell Lake of Kars.

Colonel E. C. Warde afterwards the commandant of Woolwich garrison. In July, Colonel Warde returned to England, when Colonel St. George assumed the command of the siege train, which he retained until after the fall of Sebastopol.

****

Excepting a stray shot now and then, and an occasional puff from a rifle when any of our men exposed themselves, there was very little fighting before Sebastopol until the night of the 22nd March, 1855, when the Russians, about 7,000 strong, made a sortie upon the whole face of our lines.

The attack was principally directed against the French works in front of the Mamelon, from whence, however, after an obstinate struggle with our allies, they were repulsed. They were driven from our batteries on the right by a party of the 97th, under Captain Vicars, though Lieutenant Price and his detachment of Royal Artillery in charge of the guns barely escaped being made prisoners, as they were for a time completely surrounded by the Russians. While the attention of the defenders of the trenches was thus drawn to the conflict in this direction, the enemy made another attempt to penetrate our lines farther to the left, where there was a mortar battery. Here they succeeded in gaining a footing, and the men were compelled to retire from the battery.

Bombardier Marsh, R.A., of Captain Dixon's company, was in charge of the magazine of this battery, where he remained after the enemy had taken possession. Two Russians came into the magazine, and fancying they heard somebody, probed about with their bayonets, till one of them inserted the point of his weapon into the bombardier's thumb; the other, on leaving the place, fired his piece, the bullet going into a case of fuses. Some infantry being now brought up, the Russians gave way, and a general attack was made upon the retreating masses, who fled utterly beaten.

The escape of Bombardier Marsh was most miraculous, as the magazine was full of powder; the only harm he sustained, however, was the scratch on his thumb, which did not prevent him from joining in the pursuit.

Shots now became more frequent, as if, preparatory to the next bombardment, our artillerymen were endeavouring to obtain the most accurate range.

The correspondent of the *Times*, in a letter dated March 23, says:—

> The practice of our artillerymen is splendid. Scarcely a shot fails in striking the top of the parapet just at the right place, and a black pillar of loose earth shoots up into the air from the work after every discharge from our guns.

A number of new batteries having been constructed, and connected by trenches into one entire line of attack, on April 9, the second bombardment commenced from 140 guns and mortars, and continued night and day for a week, when it gradually diminished. (140 British: the French had 360 pieces in battery:—total, 500).

If even the supply of ammunition had been unlimited, it would have been impossible, considering the way our artillerymen were worked, to have continued the bombardment much longer. The gunners passed eight hours in the batteries, then had eight hours' relief, and then returned to their guns; and out of the eight hours' remission nearly two were spent in going to and returning from their camp; so that they spent, ten hours on their legs, which caused many to suffer so much from sore feet that they performed their duties with difficulty. Added to this, during the first few days there was an incessant rain, so that the artillerymen were drenched to the skin, and standing in thick mud: nevertheless, they worked the guns with admirable vigour. ("The sappers worked in providing channels for clearing away the mud, which obstructed the artillerymen at the guns."—Conolly's *History of Royal Sappers and Miners*).

On April 11, Lieutenant Luce was struck by a round-shot in both legs, and died about two hours after his removal to camp. On the 13th, Lieutenant L'Estrange was wounded. Lieut.-Colonel Dickson had some mantelets made from cow-hides sewn together and stuffed with hay, and slung on a beam across the top of the embrasure; they withstood the rifle fire remarkably well, but the gunners could not be persuaded to use them during a bombardment. The gunners were invariably careless of their own safety, and, unless strictly watched by the officers, would sure to be unnecessarily running into danger.

On one occasion, taking advantage of the presence of a young officer new to the trenches, a party of them came across the open to the second parallel, instead of by the covered way. The Russians saw them, and at once sent a hailstorm of rifle-balls at them. One man fell, shot through his red night-cap (the dress worn by the gunners in the batteries consisted of a red worsted cap, a blue guernsey, and their regimental trousers); the rest dispersed, two lying down for shelter under a low wall. A sailor came along, "dodging" the balls; he looked at the body, seized it up, and carried it to the doctor; but the spirit had forever fled.

Disobedience of orders usually brings its own punishment. Thus, an artilleryman was told to load a gun in No. 17 "after dusk." He went in daylight, at six o'clock, took out the gabion from the embrasure, and was proceeding to load, when a round-shot came in, killed him, wounded two others, and dismounted the gun. During the 13th and 14th, the guns of the Russians were turned upon some of our advanced works in vast numbers; and in one particular instance, the injury sustained by a battery was so great that the unremitting exertions of Captains Henry and Walcot, and the gallantry and determination of the artillerymen under their orders, alone enabled them to keep up the fire and maintain themselves in it On April 15, the following order was issued:—

> Colonel Dacres will be so good as to communicate to Captains Henry and Walcot, and express to them not only my approbation of their conduct, and that of the officers and men under them, but my warmest thanks for their gallantry and perseverance in the discharge of their duty.
> —Raglan.

On the 14th Lieutenant Mitchell was killed by a round-shot from the Redan, which fractured the base of his skull.

About ten o'clock on the morning of the 16th the enemy sent a shell through one of the magazines of No. 9 battery, right attack, which caused it to explode, killing the magazine man, of whom no remains were ever found except his hands, and wounding five others. The debris of the magazine and of the parapet, a considerable portion of which was knocked down, rendered unserviceable for the moment all the guns of the battery, with the exception of one, which the officer in command—Captain Dixon—turned at once upon the Russians, who stood on the parapet of their works and cheered, at the same time pouring a heavy fire on the ruined battery.

Nothing could exceed the gallantry of Captain Dixon, whose coolness und courage excited the admiration of all. He has received the Victoria Cross.

During the month of May (with the exception of the troops despatched on an expedition to Kertch) the army was occupied in erecting new batteries, replacing the magazines, and placing additional guns and mortars in position.

At three o'clock in the afternoon of the 6th June the third bombardment commenced. The Russians replied with a heavier fire than usual all the afternoon, but during the night and morning of the 7th they scarcely returned a shot.

The Mamelon, which on the previous afternoon had fired salvos, was reduced to two or three guns, and its parapets, as well as those of the Redan and the face of the Malakoff looking towards our batteries, were little more than a shapeless heap of earth, testifying to the excellence of our artillery fire, which was probably unequalled for precision and effect. The casualties in the artillery were very heavy during the bombardment of the 6th and 7th: Captains Mortimer Adye and Alexander Gordon, with Lieutenant Keane, were wounded (the former severely, by a shell which burst between his legs); one corporal and ten gunners were killed; five sergeants, and forty-seven rank and file wounded.

★★★★★★★★★★

Captain Adye died in Woolwich, April 3, 1862, after two days illness. One of the five sergeants was Daniel Dowling, of Wodehouse's battery, who served with the siege train as a volunteer. He was noticed for his gallantry on two occasions, and at the conclusion of the war he received the Sardinian medal, and was appointed to the Military Train as adjutant. He left that corps in 1859, and soon after obtained an appointment in the Volunteers. On the cry which arose in 1860, "Help for Garibaldi," Dowling was one of the first to offer his services. Arriving in Sicily, he was appointed to the command of a battery, and on the arrival of the British volunteers in Italy, he selected a body of forty men with the view of forming them into a small and independent artillery force. The services of this body will be remembered by all who are acquainted with Garibaldi's campaign in Naples, and its members will be regarded by their countrymen as they were by the liberator of Italy—the redemption of the British Legion. Dowling is now a colonel in the Italian Army, and is the only one of Garibaldi's volunteers, being a foreigner, who was gazetted into the army. "His noble, gallant, and soldierlike behaviour throughout the campaign of the two Sicilies defies argument, while it has procured for him the esteem of Garibaldi, the admiration of Victor Emmanuel, and the gratitude of every man who takes pride in the high estimation by foreigners of the name of a British soldier."—*U. S. Magazine*, 1860.

★★★★★★★★★★

On the 7th another explosion took place in No. 9 battery, when Captain M. C. Dixon was again on duty. When the embrasure in the sand-bag battery caught fire. Gunner John Powell leaped into it, and extinguished the flame under a heavy fire. He was rewarded with the French medal. At half-past six on the evening of the 7th, the advanced works of the enemy, known as the Mamelon and Quarries, were assaulted and carried, the former by the French and the latter by the English troops.

Both works were turned against their former masters by daylight on the morning of the 8th, and in the arming of the Quarries no one was more conspicuous than Sergeant Fitzsimons, R.A., a non-commissioned officer who had been noticed on the previous evening for the manner in which he directed the fire of the 8-gun battery, while covering the French columns attacking the Mamelon. Gunner Thomas Arthur also distinguished himself during the attack on the Quarries, by carrying barrels of ammunition across the open to the 7th Fusiliers. This he did of his own accord several times.

The cannonade subsided with the capture of the Mamelon and Quarries, and trenches were pushed out from these works towards the Malakoff and Redan. A mortar battery was also constructed nearer the enemy's works, and as soon as the new works were properly armed the bombardment recommenced.

On the 17th June the fourth bombardment began, and for three hours the fire was warmly returned, and then the Russian batteries grow almost silent. In the evening orders were issued for the assault to take place on the following morning, but without a previous cannonade. This was greatly regretted by the artillery officers, who were very confident of rendering the Russian batteries nearly harmless in a fire of three hours.

Lord Raglan was at his post at two o'clock on the morning of the 18th June, a day of glorious memory to him, but which doubtless he hoped would be obliterated by the result of the coming attack. The point he had selected, though it commanded an excellent view of both the Malakoff and the Sedan, was certainly not one of security, for besides the wounds received by General Jones and other officers attached to His Lordship, the gunner stationed there for the purpose of discharging the signal-rocket had his head smashed by grape-shot.

The signal being given about half-past three a.m., the British column advanced to the assault of the Redan. Twenty men (volunteers) of the Royal Artillery, under Captain W. J. Williams and Lieutenant Ward, accompanied the assaulting column for the purpose of spiking the guns, or, if opportunity offered, of turning them round on the enemy. Of this party eleven were killed or wounded, Captain Williams being among the latter. Among the most distinguished of this party who survived were Corporal James Browne, Bombardiers John Hagan and Samuel Ewing (lost a leg), Gunners Michael O'Donohue, E. O'Brien, W. Glass (wounded), and Thomas Arthur (wounded).

The latter was the man who distinguished himself during the attack on the Quarries. He was afterwards decorated with the Sardinian medal and the Victoria Cross. Gunner Glass was wounded when about half way between the Redan and our advanced trenches. He was completely disabled, having been wounded in three places. Gunner M'Ardle crept out of the trenches on his hands and knees, and managing to get Glass on his back, returned with him to the trenches.

The attack was met by the Russians in a determined and successful manner, the allies being repulsed and compelled to retire, suffering great loss.

As our troops were retiring, Colonel Dickson opened on the Russians from the 21-gun battery, and swept them away in numbers as they crowded out to fire on our broken columns.

Though the besiegers had been repulsed, they were still resolute and determined to overcome every obstacle.

On the 6th July Captain Alexander Gordon, R.A. was killed in an advanced battery. This officer went out from England in charge of troop horses, and after his arrival in the Crimea asked permission to remain for a short time to do duty in the batteries. His request was acceded to; but his services being required at Woolwich, he was about to return in a few days. He was wounded on the 6th June, but his ardour for the service was only increased, and he returned to duty as soon as he was able, which was on the 5th July.

As he was leaving the battery on the evening of the 6th, he observed a large shell coming towards the spot where he and some of his men were, and at once gave the word to seek shelter. He himself appears to have felt a momentary hesitation as to the side of the traverse on which the missile was falling, and while looking up, the shell struck the side of his head, and he was killed instantaneously. The shell lodged near him and burst. No one else was injured, the men having thrown themselves under cover immediately the word was passed.

On the 17th August, as soon as day broke, the English and French opened their batteries for the fifth bombardment with a sweeping fire upon the whole range of the enemy's works.

It was returned almost as briskly from the Russian batteries, and the deaths in the trenches were terrible. Nevertheless, our men worked with unwearied assiduity, each day getting nearer the defences of their antagonists.

On the 17th August the conduct of Bombardier John Trotter, R. A., in clearing away the earth from an embrasure which had been laid in ruins by the enemy's fire (himself all the while exposed to a shower of bullets, as well as the fire from the guns), was noticed and recorded by his commanding officer.

Captain Oldfield, than whom no man worked harder or took more interest in the trenchwork, after being daily and closely passed by death for ten months, was on this day struck on the head by a fragment of a shell at a battery of the left attack, and, to the great loss of the service and the regret of many friends, never spoke more. On the same day Major Henry, R.A. lost his right arm.

During the remaining few weeks of the bombardment the casualties in the Royal Artillery were unusually severe. On the 19th August Lieutenant Scott was; wounded, on the 20th Captain P. Dickson (an officer who served in the batteries during the whole period of the siege), on the 24th Lieutenant de Winton, and on the 26th Captain Arbuthnot. The latter, "one of the best artillery officers in the Crimea, and one of the coolest men under fire it is possible to conceive," was wounded by a rifle-bullet which passed through the fleshy part of both his thighs. This was the second time he was struck by the enemy,

Although there were daily cannonading's betwixt the besiegers and the besieged during the closing days of August and the beginning of September, yet the fire was not anything like brisk until the 6th, when it assumed a formidable aspect.

New batteries were opened, and a fire poured upon the devoted city such as had never before shaken the earth. The British alone had in operation 114 guns of heavy calibre, besides ninety-seven mortars and two Lancasters. Our artillery practice was perfect. Every shell and bomb appeared to tell exactly where they were intended, and in the evening, as if to encourage the besiegers in their work of destruction, the flame from a line-of-battle ship in the harbour, which had been set on fire by our artillery, illuminated the whole of the Russian works, and showed the terrible effect of our fire.

Captain Snow, R.A. was killed during the day, and among the other casualties may be mentioned the death of Sergeant Morian. The circumstances connected with the fate of this most excellent non-commissioned officer are best given in the words of Mr. Conolly in his *History of the Sappers and Minesr:*—

> Two old acquaintances, who had not met for years, chanced in the early night, as the darkness was falling, to recognise each other in the Quarries. Each grasped the other's hand, and while engaged in the animated greeting, with the warm smile of welcome on their lips, a round-shot struck off both their heads! The friends were Sergeants Wilson of the Sappers and Morian of the Artillery. (Erroneously spelt Morrison in Mr. Connolly's work).

The Russians during this bombardment; replied but feebly. On the afternoon of the 7th another vessel was set on fire, and burnt all night. This was the eve of the assault, the orders for which, detailing the divisions of attack, were issued in the afternoon, and the hour fixed for noon. Accordingly, after what Gortschakoff most justly styled a *feu d'enfer*, which lasted up till twelve o'clock on the 8th, the columns advanced to the assault. In a few minutes the French were in the Malakoff, working vigorously to establish themselves securely in that fort—the key of Sebastopol. Major H. F. Strange, R.A., who was in command of the batteries in the Quarries, perceived masses of the enemy pushing forward to repulse the French through some streets of the Karabelina suburbs, which were enfiladed by only two of the guns of No. 17 battery, where he was commanding.

Promptly cutting away with his artillerymen the left faces of the five other embrasures, he brought the guns to bear in the same direction as the other two (though it threw them off their platforms), and was enabled to direct a crushing fire of round-shot and shrapnel on the Russian reserve coming up in support. The Russians came on to the open ground, but the shot and shell told on them fearfully, and arms and legs flew into the air; they retired, but again attempting to run this terrible gauntlet, they were driven back a second time. This energetic service, performed by Major Strange at so critical a moment, was most valuable.

The signal was now given for the British to advance against the Redan; twenty artillerymen, under Captain Davis, taking part in the assault. The infantry attack not meeting with success, however, the services of this party were not called for. They remained at the head of the advanced sap, under a murderous fire, until the troops retired from the Redan, and suffered heavy loss. They did not remain idle, however, but inspired by the example of their captain (who was decorated with the Victoria Cross for his bravery and humanity on the occasion) rendered great service in assisting the wounded, at the peril of their own lives.

Among those who rendered themselves conspicuous on this occasion were Sergeant William Armstrong, Corporal James Hamilton, Bombardiers John Bower and Daniel Cambridge, Gunners Robert Botfield. John M'Ardln, Charles Henderson, and Edward O'Brien. There had been two brass field-guns in the Redan when our men entered, and these the Russians, immediately after the repulse, placed in embrasures, where their green wheels were plainly risible, and began firing on our trenches and on the French on the slope before the Malakoff. Two or three of our guns were directed on them, and struck and silenced both.

****

Sergeant Armstrong was wounded in the head. He received a commission in the Military Train.

Corporal Hamilton received the French war-medal for carrying a wounded officer of the 3rd Buffs from the ditch of the Redan to the advanced trench.

Bombardier Bower received the French medal. Greatly exerted himself in bringing in wounded men until wounded himself.

Bombardier Cambridge received the Sardinian medal and the Victoria Cross. He was severely wounded when advancing to the assault, but refused to go to the rear. Later in the day he assisted in removing the wounded from the most exposed places, amid showers of shot and bullets until he was completely disabled, being wounded a second time.

****

Captain Williams, R.A., the officer who commanded the spiking party during the assault of the 18th June, served on this occasion as *aide-de-camp* to General Straubenzie; his gallantry in the Sedan was testified to both by the general and Colonel Windham.

The daughter of an artillery officer (Colonel H. Williams, who died at Barbadoes, November 10, 1852), was during this terrible assault anxiously watching from the right picquet-house the return of her husband, Colonel Handcock, 44th, whose bleeding corpse was soon conveyed to the rear; while at the same time the son of another gallant officer of the artillery, struck through the body, had moved himself into a cave to die. (The officer referred to was Lieutenant Douglas Dynely, adjutant 23rd Fusiliers, son of Major-General Dynely). Major Fyers of the Rifles, an officer who led his regiment to the assault in a most praiseworthy manner, was also the son of a distinguished artilleryman—the late Major-General Fyers, C.B.

The casualties among the artillery in the batteries were very numerous. At one gun (No. 2 of the five-gun battery) a sergeant was wounded, when his place was taken by Mr. Hayter, an officer of the Commissary Department, who began his career as a drummer in the Royal Artillery, and had served many years in the corps. He had not been long at the gun before he was struck by a shell which broke both his legs and one of his arms, and he died the same evening. Gunners W. Smith and J. Cockshoot were severely wounded while serving at the same gun—the former by a rifle-bullet, and the latter by grape-shot. Lieutenants Champion and Tyler were wounded; but the greatest loss sustained by the corps in this eventful day was that of Captain Fitzroy, who was killed by one of the last rifle-shots fired.

He was the son of Sir Charles Fitzroy, and nephew of the Duke of Richmond, and his gallantry had been borne testimony to on several occasions.

In a letter from Sir R. Dacres it is stated:—

> On the opening of the bombardment (17th August), when Captain Oldfield was killed in an advanced battery, he volunteered his services; and his bravery was the theme of admiration of all who saw him.

In another from Captain Keppel to his father:—

> There was no man in the British Army to surpass him in gallantry and coolness under fire. The last day of the bombardment, when one of his gunners hesitated about clearing the embrasure of earth that had shaken down, he shamed the man

by seizing the shovel and jumping outside to perform that dangerous service.

During the day Captain Fitzroy himself laid nearly all the guns in the battery where he was commanding, and with most signal effect. As he was leaving the battery, about six in the evening, he was struck in the spine by a rifle-bullet. He did not die immediately, however, but lingered in great agony till a little after midnight on the 10th. Firing ceased at dusk on the 8th, and a few hours afterwards it was discovered that the work of the British artillery was accomplished.

Gortschakoff, seeing he could no longer withstand the tremendous fire the allies had for three days poured into Sebastopol, and which they were prepared to continue, withdrew his troops across the harbour to the forts on the north side, sunk his ships, and blew up his forts; and thus, after a siege of nearly twelve months, the soldiers of England and France took possession of what the Russian general truly termed "a heap of bloodstained ruins."

The only other event of any importance in which the siege train was concerned, was the great explosion which took place on the 15th November.

The great magazine in the French park having blown up, the fire quickly communicated to the stores of our siege train, which were parked around a windmill near Inkerman, in which were deposited eighty tons of gunpowder. Shots, carcasses, rockets, and shells, with their myriad splinters, fell in a terrible shower, breaking up tents, burning huts and siege materials, and striking down men at a considerable distance from the scene. The only officer killed was Deputy Assistant Commissary G. Yellon, whose body was so charred that his identity was only established by a ring which remained on one of his hands. Some brass spurs, which it was remembered he had been wearing, were found near his corpse. He had been a most respectable non-commissioned officer in the Artillery, and was promoted in 1854 to the position he held at the time of his death.

Lieutenant Dawson, R.A. and a sergeant of the Rifle Brigade were carrying away a box containing combustibles, when a shell fell and burst near them. The sergeant was killed; Lieutenant Dawson escaped with the loss of his left foot. Lieutenant Roberts was severely burned and received other slight injuries.

In the meantime, the powder mill was the point on which all eyes were riveted. Between two fires, and with flaming combustibles falling all around, it seemed wonderful that the powder was not ignited. As quick as thought, however, several brave fellows, headed by Major Grant, R.A., ascended the mill, and, with wet blankets handed to them from below, covered the roof so completely that any rockets or sparks which afterwards fell upon it were perfectly harmless. One of the foremost to ascend the mill was Bombardier Angus Sutherland, R.A., who was decorated with the French medal for his brave conduct on this occasion.

One company of the Royal Artillery, under Captain Johnson, accompanied the expedition to Kinburn, but was not actively employed.

Before closing this chapter, it must be observed that several officers of the Royal Artillery were, during the siege of Sebastopol, employed in various situations, not the least important of which was the office of that valuable agent—the employment of which in the field was suggested by an artillery officer, Major-General Wylde—the electric telegraph.

****

Major-General Wylde served in Holland in 1813-14, and afterwards went with the army into France. In April, 1834, he succeeded Lord William Russell as military commissioner at the headquarters of Don Pedro's army in Portugal, and continued with them until the convention of Evara Monte; and subsequently, from November, 1834, to 1840, at the headquarters of the Spanish Army, and in all the general actions during that period, including the raising of the siege of Bilboa, for which he received the thanks of the Spanish Cortes. During the civil war in Portugal, in 1840, he was sent as British commissioner, and signed the convention of Oporto.

****

The submarine department of the telegraph was under the control of Major Biddulph, R.A., assisted by Lieutenant Holdsworth.

The office on the opposite side of the Black Sea, at Varna, was under Captain Oldershaw, who was assisted by some intelligent sergeants of the corps. (These non-commissioned officers were afterwards discharged, and are now (1865) employed on the Indian telegraph, at Mosul, in Asia Minor.

Lieutenant, afterwards Captain Fenn, R.A., served as assistant engineer during the siege of Sebastopol, and acquitted himself most honourably in performing all the toilsome and hazardous duties connected with the Engineer Department.

Lieut.-Colonel C. Morris (afterwards commander of the Volunteer Artillery), was attached to the staff of General Bosquet, of the French

Army, during the greater part of 1855, and assisted at the carrying of the lines of the Tchernaya, the assault and capture of the Mamelon and of the Malakoff. He was especially named by the French general in the official despatches.

Nothing more remains to be said of the siege train in the Crimea. That they performed their duties in a manner which could not be surpassed, was borne testimony to, not only by our generals and the officers of the French Army, but also by the Russians, who declared that nothing but the artillery compelled them to quit Sebastopol.

CHAPTER 16

The Royal Artillery in China

In the year 1792, the empire of China having been formally recognised by the British Government, an embassy, of which Earl Macartney was the head, was sent from England to the court of Pekin in the hope of effecting a treaty of commerce between the two nations.

Among the numerous presents sent to the Emperor of China by George III. were several pieces of ordnance, and for the purpose of mounting the guns and explaining the nature and management of them to His Celestial Majesty, Lieutenant Henry W. Parish and a detachment of twenty men of the Royal Artillery were sent with the embassy. (Lieutenant Parish drowned while on passage from Ireland, December, 1800).

They sailed from Portsmouth on the 25th September, 1792, and arrived at Madeira, where Lord Macartney went on shore, on the 11th October. Early in November the ships anchored off the islands of Cape Verde. Here the artillerymen went on shore to wash and dry their linen; whence they returned extremely scorched, and their legs covered with blotches from standing in the burning sands. On the 6th February, 1793, the island of Amsterdam was reached, and Sir George Staunton, with several other gentlemen, accompanied by a party of artillerymen properly armed, went on shore and made great destruction among the natives of the place, such as seals, penguins, albatrosses, etc. Great quantities of fish were also caught here and salted for the service of the ship.

Having arrived in China, the presents were examined and the guns uncased and mounted on the carriages. They consisted of six new brass field pieces, two mortars, and one wall piece, with a complete artillery apparatus. (These pieces of ordnance were taken by our army in the sacking of the Summer Palace in 1860). The report of the state of the ordnance being made to the ambassador, he was pleased to come and see the guns exercised, when several rounds were fired with great quickness, activity, and exactness. On 28th August Lord Macartney received a message that the emperor desired him to proceed to Tartary, where he wished to see him and receive his credentials. On the 17th September the embassy was presented to the emperor, and the presents delivered.

When Lieutenant Parish caused the field pieces to be exercised and fired in the presence of the Chinese *mandarins*, the latter affected to think nothing of the evolutions performed by our artillerymen, saying "their own soldiers could do it just as well, and perhaps better." On the 20th it was notified by the imperial orders that the embassy was to quit Jehol the next day for Pekin. Shortly after they had quitted the city, an artilleryman named Jeremiah Reid, who had been suffering from an attack of bloody flux, died; and the next morning his body was taken to the village of Quangchim, where it was interred with military honours.

On Tuesday, 8th October, a *mandarin* came with a letter from the emperor, expressly commanding the ambassador and all his retinue to quit Pekin the next day. The reason assigned for this conduct by the mandarin was, that His Imperial Majesty was said to be alarmed at the number of sick persons in the retinue of the embassy, and to apprehend the communication of a contagious disorder among his subjects. On the 10th they were embarked on board seven *junks*, which conveyed them to Canton; then afterwards went to Macao, where, on the 8th March, 1794 they embarked on board the fleet, and on the 17th sailed for England, arriving at Spithead on the 3rd September.

For the next half century China was, if not to England, to the Royal Artillery at least, a sealed book; unexpected circumstances then familiarised our soldiers with that portion of the world, from whom, it is hoped, the Chinese have learnt a valuable and lasting lesson. Difficulties having arisen with the Celestial Empire in 1841, two companies of the Royal Artillery, under Captains Greenwood (died at Cheltenham, September 22, 1861), and Knowles, were sent to reinforce the artillery of the army destined for service in China, which consisted of drafts from the artillery of the East India Company.

The latter were veterans inured to service in Eastern climes; but the men of the Royal Artillery were for the most part young, to whom tales of battle were as stories of the past, and who had for the first time travelled to a country previously regarded as one to be classed with those in the *Arabian Nights*. Notwithstanding these disadvantages, when called upon they nobly performed their duty.

At Chuanpee, at Canton, and at Chic-Kiang-Foo they rendered most important services, and at the storming of the last-named fortress the gallantry of Captain Knowles was most conspicuous. The gatehouse was firmly defended by Tartar soldiers, and for three quarters of an hour the efforts of the British troops were of no avail. Knowles armed himself with the musket of a dead soldier of the 55th regiment, and leading a charge at the head of the 41st Native Infantry, drove the enemy before them.

Towards the end of 1842 the expedition reached Nankin, when the Chinese acceded to all the demands made on them by Great Britain. One of the articles of the treaty was the cession of the island of Hong-Kong to the British; and among the troops detained for the occupation of this newly-acquired territory was Captain Knowles' company of the Royal Artillery. The unhealthy state of this island and the consequent mortality among the British troops are matters well known and not easily to be forgotten.

Knowles having reached the rank of lieut.-colonel, and having seen his company die one by one till reduced to a small detachment, himself fell a victim to the pernicious effects of this climate on the 2nd November, 1843. Colonel Knowles was a man of superior talent as well as of unquestionable bravery, and among the services on which he was employed may he mentioned the mission to Turkey in 1836, when, assisted by a sergeant of the regiment, he had charge of the ordnance stores presented to the *sultan*, Mahomed II.

At his death the command of the artillery in China was assumed by Colonel Chesney, on whom was bestowed the rank of brigadier-general. Immediately on the arrival of this officer he ordered the commencement of operations to ameliorate the unhealthy state of the island, and gave instructions to drain the land and build hospitals on the north or more healthy side.

Hong-Kong is now (1865) comparatively a healthy station, and undoubtedly to General Chesney is due the credit of having been the prime mover in making it so; thereby drawing upon himself the gratitude of the country, and the blessing of every soldier whose lot falls in that island.

On the 1st April, 1847, Major-General D'Aguilar, C.B., commanding the troops in the island of Hong-Kong, received a communication from Her Majesty's plenipotentiary in China, Sir John F. Davis, informing him that, in consequence of the reported aggressions of the Chinese upon British subjects in the neighbourhood of Canton, and the unsatisfactory replies of the Imperial High Commissioner to his demands for redress, it was necessary to prove to the Chinese that our forces in Hong-Kong were sufficient to chastise aggression. Without waiting for reinforcements from England or India, he at once, in conjunction with Captain M'Dougall, R.N., organised an expedition, which embarked at Victoria at midnight, and by nine o'clock in the morning of the 2nd the squadron arrived in the Bocca Tigris.

Colonel Brereton, C.B., Royal Horse Artillery, who was second in command of the expedition, at once proceeded to the forts on the islands of Wantong, accompanied by detachments of the 18th regiment, the Royal Sappers and Miners, and the Royal Artillery. The latter was under the command of Lieutenant Paterson. (He died at Quebec, February 18, 1862). The gates of the fort on the northern island were opened and possession taken, the garrison making no resistance. Lieutenant Paterson and the men of the Royal Artillery at once proceeded to spike the guns. Possession was taken of the fort on South Wantong in a similar manner, 259 guns of great calibre having been effectually spiked, the magazines destroyed, and much powder thrown into the sea during the day.

By eleven o'clock on the morning of the 3rd the squadron arrived at a reach of the river on which stand four strong forts—Pachow, Wookongtap, Napier, and Whampoa Creek. The attack on the first two was entrusted to Colonel Brereton, and that on the two others was led by Major Aldridge, R.E. Entrance being refused Colonel Brereton's force at Pachow, the gates were instantly blown open by the Royal Sappers and Miners, the work occupied, and sixty-four guns effectually spiked by Lieutenant Paterson and the men of the Royal Artillery, the ammunition being, as before, all thrown into the sea. Fort Napier was entirely disarmed. On approaching towards Forts Wookongtap and Whampoa Creek, a well-directed fire of round-shot, chain-shot, and grape was opened by those batteries upon the steamers and boats; and Major-General D'Aguilar said:

> He considered it due to Colonel Brereton to state, that but for the intelligent manner in which that officer directed the crowded boats under his command to be steered upon the salient angle of Fort Wookongtap, a very heavy loss must have inevitably ensued, as showers of grape, poured from guns of large calibre, fell thickly around the boats almost immediately after

the colonel had caused this judicious movement to be made.

A gunboat, manned by the Royal Artillery, threw shot and shell into Fort Whampoa Creek.

Brereton's force was landed, and formed for the attack on Fort Wookongtap, but the garrison escaped from the rear, and the guns were at once spiked and the ammunition destroyed. The expedition next proceeded to the French Folly fort, which, with four other batteries, were disarmed; and by six o'clock in the evening the troops had landed at the British factories, Canton, after having rendered unserviceable 879 pieces of ordnance and 150 rockets, besides having destroyed tons of ammunition. On the 8th, the demands of the British having been acceded to by the Chinese, the troops re-embarked, and arrived in Hong-Kong the afternoon of the following day, not one man having been killed or wounded during the operations. D'Aguilar says in his despatch:

> Of Lieut.-Colonel Brereton, I cannot speak too highly. His long experience, his distinguished military reputation, and his professional attainments and resources, have been apparent in every step throughout the expedition) and I cannot sufficiently express my acknowledgement for the scope he has given to all these valuable qualities, and for his perfect and most cordial support. Lieutenant Paterson, commanding the detachment of Royal Artillery, afforded me every assistance.

On the night of the 28th December, 1851, a fire broke out in the Chinese town known as Sheong-Wan (Victoria, Hong-Kong), by which nearly 500 houses were destroyed. The Royal Artillery, under Colonel Tomkyns, were soon upon the spot, rendering every assistance in their power. A train was laid for the purpose of blowing up the Nemesis Tavern, to prevent the flames from communicating with the Tapingshan, and as it did not explode within the time expected, Colonel Tomkyns, Lieutenants Lugg and Wilson, (Royal Engineers), Bombardier Whitford, and Gunner Mills of the Royal Artillery, re-entered the house to examine the fuse, and the explosion took place before they could escape. Lugg was close to the gunpowder, and no remains of him except his sword were ever discovered. Colonel Tomkyns, Lieutenant Wilson, and the men were taken up alive and sensible, but the colonel died before daylight on the 29th.

Having forgotten the lessons they had received in 1842 and 1847, as well as the treaties into which they entered, the Chinese again commenced a series of aggressive acts against British subjects, the most remarkable of which was the seizure of the crew of the *Arrow* in 1856. They also attempted to destroy the English troops in Hong-Kong by supplying them with poisoned bread. Fortunately, the plot was discovered, but not until many had felt the ill effects of the poison, among whom was Colonel Dunlop, the commanding officer of the artillery, who was seriously ill for some days. The government being determined to put down these aggressions, an expedition was organised in England, and in April, 1857, Colonel Crawford, with four companies of the Royal Artillery under Captains Knox, Barstow, Longden, and Middleton, embarked at Woolwich for service in China. They arrived at Hong-Kong just at the time when India was in danger, and accordingly Colonel Crawford, with the two last-named companies, was immediately sent to Calcutta.

The campaign in China was deferred for a time, and when it opened, in December, 1857, the artillery force consisted of three companies under Major Barstow, Captains Rotton and Knox, the whole commanded by Colonel Dunlop. The old working qualities of the Royal Artillery were not less conspicuous on approaching Canton than in any other corner of the "Ubique" nearer home. They had but to look behind them, where Artillery Island and Knowles Point had received their names fifteen years before, to be reminded that the reputation of the corps had travelled before them, and was to be sustained.

The naval bombardment of Canton began on the morning of the 28th December, and during the day the artillery were landed and placed in position.

★★★★★★★★★★

Captain Rotton and eighteen gunners of the Royal Artillery served with the fleet during an attack on Canton, in November, 1856. An entrance was effected into the city by blowing open one of the gates, in which operation Captain Rotton and four gunners were employed.

★★★★★★★★★★

The first piece to open fire was a $4^{2/5}$-inch howitzer of Knox's battery which had been run forward in front of even the most advanced battery by Captain C. W. Elgee, Lieutenant Rochfort, and a zealous gun-detachment. Two shells were fired into the Lin Fort with good effect; immediately after which the French, quite tired of long-shots, ran forward at their *pas gymnastique*, and in a most dazzling way swarmed over each other up the sides of the fort and into the embrasures; the Chinese, about thirty, scampering down the other side of the hill and into the city as the allies advanced.

The French had one or two wounded in this little affair; we were without a casualty, save a dog. "Punch," who had followed the Royal Artillery from Hong-Kong, and was shot before the foremost gun. As soon as the fort was taken, the guns from the nearest part of the city wall commenced to play upon it, but without the slightest damage. They were replied to by Lieutenant Dillon with a howitzer of Knox's battery, which was placed under the walls of the fort, exposed to the whole fire of the city. This useless cannonade was stopped, and attention turned towards making the Lin Fort habitable for the night, in the course of which, by some unknown means, a quantity of powder was ignited, and very nearly blew up Colonel Dunlop and a number of artillery officers. The night passed over quietly.

In the morning (29th December) Barstow's battery advanced to a hill on the right centre; Rotton's took the left centre, where the wall was higher and the parapet might require breaching (his guns being the heaviest of the field batteries), and Knox's occupied Lin Fort.

Rotton's battery upset the parapet and cleared the wall for a space at the centre of attack; this was done at point-blank range, with considerable accuracy, eliciting the praise of the French admiral Gerouilly. Two of Barstow's guns, under Lieutenants Hamilton and Carr, were posted within eighty yards of the wall, exposed to the very thickest of the fire, strange to say, these guns escaped without a casualty, although rockets dropped all about them, and a round-shot upset a house so close to Carr's gun that some of the bricks fell among the detachment. The gunners of the Royal Artillery were employed as sharpshooters during the bombardment, which lasted till nine o'clock, when the assaulting parties advanced.

Lieutenant Cane and Gunner M'Luggan accompanied the attacking force; and when, on capturing one of the forts, it was desirable to turn the guns upon their late owners, these two artillerymen (assisted by a motley crew of infantrymen, sailors, and Frenchmen) turned the guns round, and came into action, but with little effect, from the bad quality of the Chinese powder. Some Jolly Tars attempted to compensate for this deficiency by ramming in as many Chinese cartridges (each about twenty inches long) as the gun would hold, until the battery tottered again, and gave evident signs that the overloaded gun was as great an enemy to it as any that had been employed against it. In the meantime, orders had been sent to the artillery to come into the city by the north-east and east gates, which had been opened.

Barstow's battery took post in Mud Fort, a clay redoubt over the north gate, commanding the adjacent country to the north and west. Colonel Dunlop, with Rotton's battery, soon joined Barstow, and in about an hour the last of the enemy melted into the village beyond Canton, and the allies set about consolidating their position.

★★★★★★★★★★

A remarkably good shot was here made by one of Barstow's 3-pounders. A *mandarin* who had been particularly prominent in encouraging the men was observed coming boldly forward and waving a flag. The gun was aimed for him, and cut him in two at about 600 or 700 yards.

★★★★★★★★★

The headquarters of the artillery and Rotton's battery took up their quarters under Magazine Hill; Barstow's battery was posted at the south-east angle, and Knox's took up a position on the north-east wall, excepting a division under Lieutenant Rochfort which held Lin Fort The allies remained in the forts till the 4th January, when the troops entered the city and captured the Imperial Commissioner, Yeh, who was the chief cause of the war. This functionary was shipped off to Calcutta, where he died in 1858. The troops occupied the city of Canton till the signing of the treaty of Tientsin, which was effected by the allied ambassadors under the protection of their navies on the 26th June, 1858.

One of the clauses of the treaty of Tientsin was that France and England should each have an ambassador at Pekin. These gentlemen having been appointed, they proceeded, escorted by a number of gunboats, to be installed in their respective offices in the Chinese capital, to reach which they must ascend the River Peiho. The river was barricaded, but it was resolved to force a passage. There were forts on either side of the river, however, against which the gunboats were of no avail, and they were obliged to retire, having suffered a heavy loss.

This treachery was not to be unavenged.

As soon as the news reached England, in the autumn of 1859, an expedition was organised on a grander scale than any that had before visited the Celestial Empire, which assembled at Hong-Kong in April, 1860. The army, commanded by Sir Hope Grant, included eight batteries of artillery, two of which were armed with the Armstrong gun, a weapon that had never yet been employed against an enemy. These batteries were commanded by Major Barry and Captain Milward; the other field batteries (6-pounders and 9-pounders) under Captains

Desborough, Stirling, and Govan, were forwarded from India; while the heavy batteries under Captains Rotton, Pennycuik, and Bedingfield, were those stationed at Hong-Kong. The whole artillery force was under Brigadier-General Crofton.

★★★★★★★★★★

This officer served in Spain during the Christino and Carlist war in 1837-8, when he was taken prisoner by the Carlists; he made his escape, however, and rejoined the army after traversing the country, unknown and unfriended, for 300 miles. He died suddenly, while in command of the artillery, at Malta, June 26, 1863.

★★★★★★★★★★

On the 29th May, Captain Govan's battery was embarked on board the ship *Maldon* for transport to the north. At nine o'clock at night a detachment of this battery, under Sergeant W. Lindsay, having loaded a raft with harness, men's kits, etc., was leaving the shore, when the raft sunk three feet in the water. Having pushed off, the raft began to sink rapidly, when Sergeant Lindsay gallantly jumped over and seized the rope at the peril of his life, and with the water up to his throat, thereby saving a total wreck or loss of men.

The detachment, with the raft, etc., were then got on board the gunboats, where they remained all night.

Sergeant Lindsay served in India with Colonel Malcolm's force, and his bravery in volunteering to blow up the gates of the fortress of Murgoond, which he succeeded in doing without the loss of a single man, and to the satisfaction of all his officers, was recorded in the *Bombay Gazette*.

After a long and wearisome encampment at Talienwhan, the British Army embarked on the 26th July, and set sail for the rendezvous, about twenty miles south of the Peiho. Being joined by the French, the troops landed at Peh-tang on the 1st August, but three days passed before the whole of the artillery were landed.

On the morning of the 3rd a reconnaissance was made by a portion of the allied troops, who, after they had been out for some time, were joined by two guns of Desborough's battery, which came up at a gallop. They had received their orders but an hour before, and the horses had only been landed on the previous night. Nevertheless, they turned out as though they had been stabled in Woolwich Common instead of having passed the night in a muddy bivouac at Peh-tang, and the easy way in which the guns were moved along the filthy causeway excited universal admiration. The reconnaissance was attended with important results, the nature of the ground and the state of the Tartar field force having been ascertained before the troops returned to Peh-tang.

On the 7th Captain Govan, R.A. discovered a slow match lighted in a house occupied by the artillery, which match was connected with a large catty of powder. It was providentially found in time, for the effect of an explosion in the town, with the enormous mass of ammunition collected in every quarter, would have been something frightful.

On the 12th August the army began its march. Milward's and Barry's Armstrong batteries being with the advance. (Major Barry's battery suffered so much from sickness, that on going into action the only officers were himself and Lieutenant Phillpotts; and about one-third of the men were in hospital). After a long and tiresome march, during which the guns had to be dragged through a muddy country by men who had also to assist the horses in getting over the same ground, the troops arrived before Sinho, a place defended by about 5,000 Tartar cavalry. The Armstrongs having been inspected and found (contrary to all expectations after the rough usage they had had) quite perfect, were now ordered to open fire—for the first time upon an enemy.

****

> "Barry's and Milward's batteries were shipped in the Thames. Arriving at Alexandria, they were unshipped and conveyed across the desert by rail. Between Suez and China, they were shipped and unshipped at Kowloon and Odin Bay, and were eventually landed at Peh-tang. They had undergone that process no fewer than eight times. Milward's battery was then dragged for miles over ground all but impracticable for artillery, and yet not one gun received the slightest damage. It may therefore be assumed that the Armstrong gun is not too delicate for the rough usage of war."—*Times, Nov. 3,* 1860.

****

The first gun was fired at twenty minutes to eleven a.m., at a range of about 1200 yards. The first shot was bad, the elevation was too great, and the shell passed harmlessly over the enemy. It was the only failure. The second shell burst right in the midst of the largest group, and half-a-dozen saddles were instantly empty. "Three degrees!" shouted Captain Milward, and the range was got by every gun. For upwards of ten minutes the battery made magnificent practice. Not a shot failed, not a shell that did not burst in the exact spot to which it was directed. The Tartars stood right manfully for ten minutes, when they found the place too hot for them; so, after some wavering, they took the desperate resolution of attempting to turn both flanks of the English and so get into their rear.

Stirling's battery was now brought into action, when, to the surprise of everyone, a body of eighty or ninety Tartars rushed from their front to take his guns in flank. So unexpected was this attack that Captain Stirling had barely time to fire two rounds of case, when they were within 100 yards of the guns. They were gallantly met, however, and quickly dispersed by twenty-five of Fane's Horse, who were attached to Stirling's battery. Barry's (Armstrongs), Desborough's, and Govan's batteries now commenced a tremendous fire against the advanced entrenchment. The enemy were soon driven from this on to their second line, from whence they were quickly dislodged, and retreating along the causeway to Tang-kow, they crossed the river, leaving the allies to take possession of Sinho.

The next few days were spent in getting up the heavy guns, etc., for the siege of the Takoo forts. On the morning of the 18th a Chinese battery opened across the River Peiho upon our working parties, whereupon two of Barry's Armstrongs, under Lieutenant Hosier, were brought to bear upon it. The guns were hardly unlimbered when the Chinamen opened fire from five guns in good tine, but twenty feet too high. The first shot from the Armstrongs fell to the right and missed them; the second burst in their battery; the third dismounted a large gun, sending the carriage into the air in splinters; the fourth plumped in among the fugitive gunners, who never fired another shot.

Early on the morning of the 20th a party of officers rode to the upper northern fort with a summons to surrender. The Chinese refused, and began to throw some 32-pound shot near our troops. Milward's Armstrongs were at once brought up, and in an hour silenced the enemy's guns at a distance of 2,000 yards. Our artillery was placed in two lines for the siege of the large fort. The centre battery, 600 yards from the fort, contained three 8-inch mortars, under Major Pennycuik. In the left front battery were two 8-inch howitzers and two 32-pounders under Captain Bedingfield. In rear of these, and at about twice the distance from the fort, were two of Govan's 24-pounder howitzers, Milward's and Barry's Armstrongs, and an 8-inch gun under Major Rotton.

Desborough's battery and the remainder of Govan's directed their fire as required. About five a.m. on the 20th the fire commenced from Milward's battery, and soon after six all the batteries were in full play. At half-past six a tremendous explosion took place in the fort, followed ten minutes afterwards by another. The credit of having caused these explosions was hotly contended for among our batteries. It is more than likely, however, that they were caused by shells from Rotton's gun or moveable mortar. The whole of the English artillery were now pushed up to 500 yards from the gateway, and kept un an incessant fire, under cover of which our skirmishers advanced.

Here Lieutenant Gye and several men were wounded. At eight a.m. the Chinese guns were nearly silenced and the principal fort was assaulted, and in a short time Captain Bedingfield, with one of his officers and a dozen men (volunteers), was preparing to enter it for the purpose of turning the guns round on the other forts. This, however, was unnecessary: they were all taken without any further bloodshed. Tientsin was now occupied by the allies; and on the 9th September Lord Elgin started for Pekin, escorted, however (and, as it afterwards proved, most fortunately), by the greater part of the army. On the 13th Messrs. Parkes and Wade, the interpreters, advanced to Tungchow for the purpose of making some preliminary arrangements with the Chinese authorities respecting the advance of our army.

It having been finally settled that the main body of the army was to encamp at Changkewan (a village about fifteen miles from Pekin) while Lord Elgin, escorted by 1,000 men, proceeded to the capital, the troops advanced, and arriving at Matow on the 17th, halted for the night, while Mr. Parkes, accompanied by a party of officers and civilians, among whom were Mr. Loch, Lord Elgin's private secretary, and Mr. Boulby, the special correspondent of the *Times* newspaper, went on to Tungchow to make the final arrangements respecting the camping ground.

Judge of the surprise of our army when, in the morning of the 18th, they advanced to take up their quarters at Changkewan, they found them occupied by a strong Chinese Army in position, with a number of guns in earthworks thrown up during the night. At the same time the party returned from Tungchow, and were equally surprised. Mr. Parkes at once returned to demand from the authorities at Tungchow what the meaning of this might be; while Mr. Loch rode through into our ranks and reported the state of affairs, Mr. Boulby and the officers and escort remaining among the Chinese.

Mr. Loch announced his intention of returning to meet Mr. Parkes; and it was suggested that it might be useful if an officer of the quarter master-general a department were to go with him, as he might have an opportunity of observing the enemy's position. This was said in the hearing of Captain Brabazon of the artillery, who at once volunteered for the duty. Ever ready for service of this sort, and full of zeal in his profession, poor fellow, he started—alas! never to return. What became of him was never satisfactorily ascertained. It is generally believed, however, that he was beheaded by order of the *mandarin* who commanded the Chinese during the engagement of the 21st, and who was severely wounded by a splinter from an Armstrong shell, and that his body was thrown into the river.

Mr. Loch and Captain Brabazon had been gone some time when Colonel Walker and four men of the King's Dragoon Guards, who had gone as escort to Mr. Parkes, etc., were observed to be fighting their way through the enemy. Fortunately, they all got in, though some were wounded. It was evident that there was no time to be lost. The enemy was at once attacked, and in a short time completely routed, with a loss of above 500 men and seventy-five guns. The artillery engaged in this action were Barry's (Armstrongs), Desborough's (9-pounders), and Stirling's (6-pounders) batteries. Great anxiety prevailed all this time about the missing party, as nothing could be heard of their fate; but on the 21st the troops marched for the Tartar camp beyond Tungchow.

This force was estimated at 25,000, cavalry and infantry, the former greatly preponderating. The allies attacked them, and drove them off the ground with a loss of 500 or 600 men, of their camps, and of thirty brass guns; and then continued their march till they were within four miles of Pekin, from which they fell back to their camp, about six miles from the city. The only artillery engaged in this affair were three Armstrongs under Captain Rowley. The army at once advanced towards Pekin, and made preparations to assault that city.

On the evening of the 12th October the guns were in position, and everything in readiness for an attack the next day. About ten minutes before the appointed time, however, the Chinese troops were withdrawn from the walls, and the gate surrendered in due form, a body of infantry and Desborough's battery passing through, it, the latter immediately afterwards taking up position on the top of the wall, and by so doing commanding all the approaches.

Mr. Parkes and Mr. Loch were liberated on the 8th October; but no tidings could be obtained of the other Englishmen in the hands of the Chinese. A few days afterwards information was received that they had all died from the effects of the cruel treatment they had received; and on the 14th the bodies of Lieutenants De Norman and Anderson were brought in, followed on the 16th by those of Private Phipps

(King's Dragoon Guards) and Mr. Boulby. Brabazon alone continued missing.

The British demanded 100,000*l*. to be paid in forty-eight hours, as an indemnity for the friends of the murdered men; and furthermore, resolved on the destruction of the emperor's palace of Yuen-ming-Yuen, and the destruction of all the moveables therein, thereby inflicting on His Celestial Majesty a loss of about 2,000,000*l*. The partiality of the late Mr. Boulby for the artillery, and the manner in which he recorded even the most minute details connected with the corps, cannot have escaped the observation of those who read his letters from China.

This is, doubtless, owing to a feeling of *esprit de corps*, which it is easy to believe he conceived it his duty to exhibit; for when he was born (at Gibraltar, in 1817) his father, "Thomas Boulby," was a captain in the Royal Artillery. Having retired upon half-pay. Captain Boulby took up his residence in Sunderland, where he entered upon the business of a timber-merchant, and where his son, the above Mr. T. W. Boulby, was articled to a solicitor. He died in 1843, and a few years afterwards Mr. Boulby, conceiving a distaste for the law, became connected with that journal in whose service he lost his life.

The war was now at an end. On the 24th October Lord Elgin entered Pekin in state, the ratifications of the treaty of Tientsin were exchanged, and a convention signed. An Army of Occupation, including Govan's and Desborough's batteries, remained at Tientsin; a considerable body of troops was sent to Hong-Kong; and the remainder, including the two Armstrong batteries, returned to England.

CHAPTER 17

New Zealand

In 1845 the natives of New Zealand having shown a spirit of resistance to the queen's authority, and pulled down the flag in several places, the governor, to enforce submission, applied for troops from the neighbouring colonies of Australia.

The only artilleryman, or rather the only member of the Royal Artillery, in this part of the world was Lieutenant Eardley Wilmot, who was on the governor's staff in Van Diemen's Land. (Afterwards Major Wilmot, killed in Kaffraria).

This young officer immediately volunteered for active service in New Zealand, and, with a hastily-formed artillery from the Auckland Militia, was most invaluable throughout the operations.

At Rawitta's *pah*, at the destruction of Arratuah's *pah*, and in the various affairs which took place before Ruapekapeka, in December 1845 and January 1846, Wilmot and his *quasi*-artillerymen were most effective, and received great praise from the governor.

Twenty-three men of the Royal Artillery, under Captain Henderson and Lieutenant Yelverton, were sent to New Zealand in May, 1846; but the disturbances had ceased before they arrived at Auckland.

There has ever since been a detachment of the corps in the colony.

In 1800 fresh disturbances arose through native selling land to the government, of which the Maories declared he had no right to dispose.

By this time the New Zealanders had become an intelligent race of people, and by their conduct during the war (which unhappily is not yet ended) have proved themselves no contemptible foes, while their observance of Christian ordinances has raised them to an equal standing with ourselves.

★★★★★★★★★★

Though a few cases have occurred at which humanity shudders, such as the decapitation of Captain Lloyd and the subsequent exhibition of his head, there are many things to be recorded of the New Zealanders during the present war (1865) which prove them to be a race on whom the Gospel has come with telling effect, and who, physically and morally, are, if anything, in a very slight degree inferior to our own troops. At an early stage of the war the schooner *Louisa* was wrecked on the east coast, and the crew and the passengers were in a helpless condition, when one of the native chiefs received them must hospitably; and not working on Sunday, on Monday saved spars, sails, and running gear from the wreck, and thirty sacks of wheat, and sent in canoes the crew and passengers to Auckland. They never fight on Sunday unless compelled by our troops, and latterly they have not only refrained from killing our wounded, as was their custom, but they have not even plundered the dead, whom they bury according to the rites and ceremonies of the Church of England.

****

On the 28th February, 1860, a force including a detachment of the Royal Artillery under Lieut. Macnaughten, embarked at Auckland for Taranaki, the district of the rebellious Maories, and at mid-day on the 17th March the artillery fired their first shot against a strongly-defended *pah* which the Maories had erected in the face of the British camp on the Waitara.

Although good practice was made, the shells bursting on the stockade, and the shot going through the outer defences, the natives showed no disposition to surrender; and by the evening, all our ammunition being expended, the troops were obliged to lie down among the fern till more should be brought up.

Early on the following morning the guns again opened fire, tearing away a large portion of the stockade.

Lieutenant Macnaughten went forward, and was immediately followed by several of his gunners and some of the 65th regiment; and rushing into the *pah*, they found it empty, the defenders having made their escape by a gully leading to the river. This, the first engagement of the war, is known as the capture of the Te'kohia, or L. pah.

On the 16th April a reinforcement of forty men of the Royal Artillery, under Captain Strover, arrived from Sydney, and at once joined the army.

Tall flagstaffs and yards for signals were now erected at the Bell Block, Omata Stockade, and Marshland Hill, and a code of signals was arranged under the direction of Sergeant Marjouram, Royal Artillery, by means of wicker balls by day and lanterns by night, forming words,

This worthy man and excellent non-commissioned officer did good service during the early part of this war, commanding the artillery in the absence of Captain Strover and Lieutenant Macnaughten; while his services in a higher cause, that of advancing the truths of the Gospel (both by example and precept), were recognised and acknowledged by Archdeacon Govett and all the officers under whom he served.

He was invalided home early in 1861, and died at Woolwich in June of the same year. His *Memorials*, published by Nisbet and Co., has been widely circulated and productive of much good.

About the middle of June Major Nelson, 40th regiment, commanding at the Waitara, determined to attack a *pah* the enemy had erected at Puketakauere, about a mile distant from our camp.

There were eighteen artillerymen under Lieutenant Macnaughten engaged, of whom two died of their wounds. They did their work well, especially when our infantry were repulsed, checking the advance of the enemy, who made several attempts to follow them.

The attack was a failure, but the retreat was conducted in an orderly manner, the troops returning to camp with a loss of sixty-five men, thirty-two of whom were killed.

Major Kelson remained before the *pah*, however, and continued to harass the enemy by shelling them, especially by night.

General Pratt now arrived from Melbourne and assumed the command. Lieutenant Forster, R.A. attended as his *aide-de-camp*.

Another expedition was at once prepared to assist Major Nelson at the Puketakauere *pahs*, when they were suddenly found to be evacuated.

About the end of July, a settler named Hurford, with three artillerymen from the Omata stockade, had gone into the bush to visit his farm. The natives came upon them in force, and the party separated, and two of the artillerymen made their way back reaching it at sunset, and the other arriving at midnight. Neither could give any account of the fate of those they left behind, and the following day a party was sent in search. They discovered the artilleryman, a fine strapping; young man of Captain Strover's detachment, quite dead and hideously tomahawked. The farmer's body was not recovered, but there was no doubt about his death.

On the 10th September a large expedition was organised at New Plymouth, under Major-General Pratt, to advance as far as possible into the country.

The force was told off in three divisions:—No. 1, commanded by Major Nelson, having a detachment of the Royal Artillery, with two 24-pounder howitzers, under Sergeant Marjouram; No. 2, under Major Hutchins, 12th regiment, with Captain Strover's detachment, two 24-pounder howitzers, and two 3-pounder guns; and No. 3, commanded by Colonel Leslie, 40th regiment, to which the remainder of the Royal Artillery under Lieutenant Macnaughten was attached.

Several *pahs* evacuated by the enemy were destroyed, and an engagement took place in which a brisk fire was kept up on both sides, the Maories replying to the round-shot, grape, canister, and musketry with volleys from the bush and the rifle pits, and wounding a few of our men, including; a bombardier of the Royal Artillery, who was severely injured in the foot.

The order was then given to retire to the Waitara camp.

The artillery, under Captain Strover and Lieutenant Macnaughten, took part in all the subsequent engagements—Mahoetahi, Matorikorika, etc.,—and worked with the greatest zeal in their important arm of the service, in a long and arduous struggle against a brave and determined foe, when Captain Mercer arrived from England with a battery of Armstrong guns, which in four days compelled the Maories to surrender or disperse, thus suddenly closing the campaign.

On the 4th March, 1861, Captain Mercer, R.A. arrived at Auckland in the *Norwood*, after a prosperous voyage, with the Armstrong battery and 10-inch and 8-inch mortars. That day week he had cleared the ship of the battery, mortars, shell, and other stores, in all amounting to 700 tons: notwithstanding the extra labour of discharging by lighters, as the *Norwood* lay out at some distance in the harbour, being unable to go alongside the pier to discharge, officers and men worked with a will, all being desirous of taking part in the Maori war in the Taranaki.

On the 12th March half of the Armstrong battery, with the mortars, embarked on board the colonial war-steamer *Victoria*, Captain Norman, for the seat of war. Lieut. Hunter, R.A., was left behind in charge of the other half battery, and was to follow on the arrival of Captain Watson, R.A., with 180 horses from Australia. Captain Mercer's party arrived at the Waitara River on the morning of the 13th March, and commenced landing at once in surf-boats.

The same afternoon the Armstrong guns were taken out of their cases, cleaned and mounted, the ammunition, etc., examined, and the whole found to be complete and in perfect order. Major-General Sir T. S. Pratt, K.C.B., then commanding, directed Captain Mercer to

AN ARMSTRONG GUN

proceed with Mr. Parris, the native commissioner, the following day, and select a favourable position for shelling Mataitawa, the stronghold of Wiremu Kingi, but the distance of the nearest spot from whence it could be seen over the tops of the trees of the forest was (by calculation) beyond the range of the 12-pounder Armstrong gun.

Whilst Captain Mercer was absent. Lieutenant Pickard had the men drilled and exercised at laying the guns, in order to see that they had not forgotten during the long voyage the instruction they had received in England. The artificers were at the same time busily employed in making poles, etc., for bullock draught. Three poles were completed during the day, thus enabling the guns to start for the front at six the next morning, Friday the 15th of March,

On arriving at No. 7 redoubt, the white flag was flying from the Te Arei *pah*; but about midday, when Captain Mercer was in the advanced trench with the late Lieutenant E. C. Macnaughten, R.A., examining the position, etc. of the Maori rifle-trenches, it was hauled down, and in place of it a large red war-flag was run up, A single defiant shot was then heard, which was immediately followed by volleys from the Maori pits; these rattling against the gabions of the sap showed that the natives were recommencing hostilities in right good earnest. Captain Mercer immediately returned to No. 7 redoubt, and opened fire from the Armstrong guns and mortars on the lines of the enemy's rifle-trenches, there being nothing else to fire at except the open stockading of Te Arei *pah*.

There was no heavily-timbered stockade to breach to enable the troops to take Te Arei by assault, for a broad roadway led right over the crest of the hill into the centre of the position of the Maories through open picketing. The extraordinary occurrence of finding oneself in front of enemy with apparently nothing for artillery to fire at, struck the newly-arrived artillery officers, and remarking the same, they were told if the white flag was hauled down, the rifle-trenches of Te Arei, as well as those of the neighbouring hills, would be alive with natives, as far as their fire was concerned, but they themselves would be all but invisible.

Captain Mercer then attentively considering these lines of pits or rifle-trenches along the crest of the hills all around, coupled with the peculiar mode of Maori warfare, and also being informed that their trenches were generally constructed in the following ingenious manner:—First a narrow deep trench is made, then on the side fronting their assailant it is dug out in the form of a shoe, the earth so excavated being thrown outside on the top to the rear, rough woodwork, beams, etc. arranged so as to support the earth above the excavation, thus forming a secure place where they immediately retired after delivering their fire,—it appeared to Captain Mercer that he had before him in these rifle-trenches a target of about eight feet in height, counting from the top of the trench to the bottom of the excavation, and running laterally some distance; and he calculated that, by aiming at the centre of this target, some three or four feet below the earth thrown on the top rear of the trench, the shell penetrating just below the crest of it, and meeting with the resistance of the rough wooden support of the earth in the trench, or any other body momentarily to arrest the flight of the shell, it would burst inside and deal destruction around.

To increase the chance of unearthing some of these wily natives, planks were procured for gun-wheels and trails to rest upon, so as to adjust the gun to the greatest nicety of level. After a trial shell on each of their positions, and the range having been accurately obtained, the Armstrong guns were loaded and laid on certain points of the lines of the enemy's rifle-trenches, and the gunner, with lanyard in hand, waited for the word to fire from the officer who was watching the trench with glasses, until some heads appearing above, or a puff of smoke from the discharged pieces revealed their presence in that direction, when the gun was instantly fired, and the shell was observed from the battery to enter just below the crest of the trench, carrying destruction to any Maories in that portion of the pits.

The natives were also in the habit of firing volleys when the working parties or any number of men were going to or returning from the head of the sap. On these occasions the guns were laid on the lines of the pits, and the shells fixed with both time and concussion fuses, and before the parties marched, the gunners were ready waiting for the word, which was given directly the natives opened fire, and the Armstrong shells at the same instant burst amongst them.

Lieutenant Pickard and Acting Sergeant-Major R. Hayes made some excellent shell practice with the Armstrong guns. Colour-Sergeant J. Moran, Royal Engineers, whilst at the head of the sap, and Bombardier T. Singer. Royal Artillery, whilst working the Cohorn mortars (with the late Lieutenant E. C. Macnaughten, R.A.) have both given satisfactory evidence of their having personally observed the action of the Armstrong shell, its entering just below the crest of the rifle-trench in front of Te Arei and bursting inside.

On Saturday, 16th March, an attack was made on our extreme right.

A 9-pounder gun, accompanied by a detachment of the 40th regiment, commenced firing some rounds of common case into the bush to drive out the natives; and subsequently, on their retiring to the trenches on the edge of the wood, some shrapnel shell were sent amongst them. Soon after the firing ceased, and the men returned to camp.

It had been the practice to place every night behind the sap-roller, and sunk in the earth in its box, an eight-inch naval shell, with a friction-tube fixed through the fuse, and a cord attached to it and the sap-roller, so as to explode should the natives attempt to capture the roller. This was suggested by the Royal Engineers, and carried out at their request by the Naval Brigade, in consequence of one sap-roller having been carried off by the natives; conceiving that, in the event of their trying to do so a second time, the main rifle-trench in front of Te Arei, not far from the head of the sap, would be lined with natives watching the operation, as well as at hand to help to secure the roller and drag it up the hill to the *pah*.

The Armstrong guns were loaded and laid on this trench the last thing before dark; each night also the mortars were laid on different parts of Te Arei. On Saturday night the trap of the shell succeeded; the Maories endeavouring to capture the sap-roller, the shell exploded, and immediately afterwards the enemy got the benefit of both the Armstrong and mortar shells from No. 7 redoubt.

Sunday, 17th March, was a sad day for the artillery, for they lost poor Macnaughten. He was killed whilst in the act of laying a Cohorn mortar in the extremity of the advance demi-parallel, the ball passing through the wrist and entering the chest. He died almost immediately firing his last shot on the anniversary of his firing his first one in this war. He had ably conducted the fire of the Cohorn mortars since the advance of the sap from No. 8 redoubt, and had been in every engagement throughout the whole war.

Lieutenant Macnaughten's death was thus recorded in the *Taranaki Herald*, Sunday, March 17th, 1861 (St Patrick's Day):—

> The first anniversary of a war that has for twelve months cursed New Zealand, and desolated the province of Taranaki, has been marked by the irreparable loss of as brave an officer as ever fought and fell on flood or field, —as devoted a soldier as ever gained lustre for the British flag at the price of his blood. Lieutenant Macnaughten of the Royal Artillery is, alas! numbered with the dead. This intrepid soldier was stooping over a mortar,

in the act of adjusting its elevation, when a musket-ball struck him in the hand which held the plumb-line, and then pierced his breast. An officer who was near him exclaimed, 'Macnaughten, you are hit!' but the lieutenant smiled, and, with his usual calmness, replied, 'Oh, never mind, 'tis but in the hand!' They were his last words. He stood up, turned pale, staggered backwards, fell, and died.

The sorrow of the troops of all corps for the loss of this officer is inexpressible. Every soldier knew and appreciated his worth; all admired his unsurpassable valour, his uniform coolness, and his skill in gunnery; while his undeviating affability and kindness endeared him even to the most-thoughtless. His presence at the guns was the inspiration of confidence in the troops, for no one doubted the accuracy of an aim taken by Lieutenant Macnaughten. He walked up to the sap today full of ardour, full of confidence, full of every quality that constitutes a perfect soldier. Alas that the green shamrock which he so proudly wore on his manly breast should be so soon dyed red with his life's blood!

Many a stout heart sighed, and many a stern eye dropped a tear, as they beheld the noble soldier borne past them a lifeless corpse. When the ambulance which bore him from the field arrived at No. 6 redoubt, the officers and men of the 65th regiment mingled round the vehicle to get a last glimpse of the honoured and beloved dead. The brow even of the most thoughtless wore a sad gloom, and rough hands endeavoured in vain to conceal the big tears that rolled from the eyes that could not restrain them. The memory of Lieutenant Macnaughten will be ever pre-eminently dear to our hearts.

Sergeant J. Christie, R.A., an excellent non-commissioned officer, was wounded in the shoulder in the advance demi-parallel early on Monday morning, whilst Captain, Mercer was arranging with him about carrying on the practice with the Cohorn mortars.

On Monday afternoon an attack was made on our extreme right in the wood. During this attack the Armstrong guns were used against the main rifle-pits just in front of the *pah*, to keep down the fire of the natives on the head of the sap. A 9-pounder gun and a 24-pounder howitzer were taken down towards the wood, the former under Captain Strover, and the latter under Lieutenant Pickard. The practice with common and shrapnel shell was with good effect, after the natives had been driven from the bush to their rifle-pits by a few rounds of common case. Gunner T. Selford was wounded in the leg.

At four o'clock on the morning of the 19th March, Captain Mercer, with an escort of the guard, went outside the redoubt and fired the last two mortars at Te Arei, and within two hours afterwards white flags were flying from all the Maori positions.

It is beyond our province to enter into the events of 1863, but the Royal Artillery have so signally distinguished themselves in New Zealand during the present struggle, that passing notice must be given of their services.

The Maories having, in May, 1863, waylaid an escort of the 57th regiment and killed the greater number of them, the government determined to uphold its authority, and, if needs be, exterminate the rebellious people. A number of additional troops were therefore despatched to Auckland, including another Armstrong battery under Lieut.-Colonel Barstow.

A series of engagements with various results have taken place, in all of which the Royal Artillery have rendered important services. Not only have they exhibited their usual courage and ability in the working of their guns, but have acted as cavalry and also as infantry. Captain Mercer's battery rendered great service at the taking of the Katikara *pah* on the 4th June. The Maories were driven from their hiding places by the guns, when they fled inland pursued by the infantry and by Lieutenant Rait and his detachment of artillery armed with sword and revolver.

At the capture of Rangiriri (20th November) the assault was most gallantly led by Captain Mercer, R.A., who was followed by about thirty of his own men armed with revolvers. A great number of this detachment were struck down, the first being Captain Mercer, who received a bullet in his jaw. By his side fell his servant, Gunner Culverwell, upon whose corpse the captain rested his mangled head till he was removed on the following morning.

Lieutenant Pickard, who bravely followed his captain to the assault, scaled the parapet, and, lying flat on the top, fired his revolver at whoever showed. Finding himself alone, however, and hearing that Captain Mercer was wounded, Lieutenant Pickard descended, and, the assault being impracticable, collected the few remaining men and drew them off in safety. Assist.-Surgeon Temple, R.A., hearing that Captain Mercer was wounded, determined to go to his assistance, although warned that to go over was almost certain death. He succeeded in reaching the spot in safety, however, and stayed there attending to the wounded all the evening, until, a trench being dug, the dead and wounded were removed.

Captain Mercer died on the 25th November, and was buried with military honours at Auckland on the 27th.

Other engagements have since taken place in which the corps has sustained its high reputation, and special mention has been made of Lieutenant Rait and his mounted detachment (acting as cavalry); of Lieutenant Larcom, who commanded a detachment at the capture of Kaitaka, and who, although severely wounded, remained with his gun until the detachment retired; of Sergeant M'Kay, a "stalwart Scot from Sutherlandshire," who rendered great service at Orakau by pitching hand-grenades into the midst of the enemy "as coolly as if he had been playing a game of quoits;" of Lieutenant A. Grubb, who, with a battery of six mortars, drove the enemy from their rifle-pits; and of Assist.-Surgeon Manley, who, under a heavy fire from the enemy, went to the assistance of the wounded at the disastrous assault of the Gate *pah*.

Lieut.-Colonel Barstow and Captain Betty have both been mentioned as having directed the fire of their batteries with good effect.

ALSO FROM LEONAUR
AVAILABLE IN SOFTCOVER OR HARDCOVER WITH DUST JACKET

THE FALL OF THE MOGHUL EMPIRE OF HINDUSTAN *by H. G. Keene*—By the beginning of the nineteenth century, as British and Indian armies under Lake and Wellesley dominated the scene, a little over half a century of conflict brought the Moghul Empire to its knees.

LADY SALE'S AFGHANISTAN *by Florentia Sale*—An Indomitable Victorian Lady's Account of the Retreat from Kabul During the First Afghan War.

THE CAMPAIGN OF MAGENTA AND SOLFERINO 1859 *by Harold Carmichael Wylly*—The Decisive Conflict for the Unification of Italy.

FRENCH'S CAVALRY CAMPAIGN *by J. G. Maydon*—A Special Correspondent's View of British Army Mounted Troops During the Boer War.

CAVALRY AT WATERLOO *by Sir Evelyn Wood*—British Mounted Troops During the Campaign of 1815.

THE SUBALTERN *by George Robert Gleig*—The Experiences of an Officer of the 85th Light Infantry During the Peninsular War.

NAPOLEON AT BAY, 1814 *by F. Loraine Petre*—The Campaigns to the Fall of the First Empire.

NAPOLEON AND THE CAMPAIGN OF 1806 *by Colonel Vachée*—The Napoleonic Method of Organisation and Command to the Battles of Jena & Auerstädt.

THE COMPLETE ADVENTURES IN THE CONNAUGHT RANGERS *by William Grattan*—The 88th Regiment during the Napoleonic Wars by a Serving Officer.

BUGLER AND OFFICER OF THE RIFLES *by William Green & Harry Smith*—With the 95th (Rifles) during the Peninsular & Waterloo Campaigns of the Napoleonic Wars.

NAPOLEONIC WAR STORIES *by Sir Arthur Quiller-Couch*—Tales of soldiers, spies, battles & sieges from the Peninsular & Waterloo campaingns.

CAPTAIN OF THE 95TH (RIFLES) *by Jonathan Leach*—An officer of Wellington's sharpshooters during the Peninsular, South of France and Waterloo campaigns of the Napoleonic wars.

RIFLEMAN COSTELLO *by Edward Costello*—The adventures of a soldier of the 95th (Rifles) in the Peninsular & Waterloo Campaigns of the Napoleonic wars.

AVAILABLE ONLINE AT **www.leonaur.com**
AND FROM ALL GOOD BOOK STORES

ALSO FROM LEONAUR
AVAILABLE IN SOFTCOVER OR HARDCOVER WITH DUST JACKET

AFGHANISTAN: THE BELEAGUERED BRIGADE by G. R. Gleig—An Account of Sale's Brigade During the First Afghan War.

IN THE RANKS OF THE C. I. V by Erskine Childers—With the City Imperial Volunteer Battery (Honourable Artillery Company) in the Second Boer War.

THE BENGAL NATIVE ARMY by F. G. Cardew—An Invaluable Reference Resource.

THE 7TH (QUEEN'S OWN) HUSSARS: Volume 4—1688-1914 by C. R. B. Barrett—Uniforms, Equipment, Weapons, Traditions, the Services of Notable Officers and Men & the Appendices to All Volumes—Volume 4: 1688-1914.

THE SWORD OF THE CROWN by Eric W. Sheppard—A History of the British Army to 1914.

THE 7TH (QUEEN'S OWN) HUSSARS: Volume 3—1818-1914 by C. R. B. Barrett—On Campaign During the Canadian Rebellion, the Indian Mutiny, the Sudan, Matabeleland, Mashonaland and the Boer War Volume 3: 1818-1914.

THE KHARTOUM CAMPAIGN by Bennet Burleigh—A Special Correspondent's View of the Reconquest of the Sudan by British and Egyptian Forces under Kitchener—1898.

EL PUCHERO by Richard McSherry—The Letters of a Surgeon of Volunteers During Scott's Campaign of the American-Mexican War 1847-1848.

RIFLEMAN SAHIB by E. Maude—The Recollections of an Officer of the Bombay Rifles During the Southern Mahratta Campaign, Second Sikh War, Persian Campaign and Indian Mutiny.

THE KING'S HUSSAR by Edwin Mole—The Recollections of a 14th (King's) Hussar During the Victorian Era.

JOHN COMPANY'S CAVALRYMAN by William Johnson—The Experiences of a British Soldier in the Crimea, the Persian Campaign and the Indian Mutiny.

COLENSO & DURNFORD'S ZULU WAR by Frances E. Colenso & Edward Durnford—The first and possibly the most important history of the Zulu War.

U. S. DRAGOON by Samuel E. Chamberlain—Experiences in the Mexican War 1846-48 and on the South Western Frontier.

AVAILABLE ONLINE AT www.leonaur.com
AND FROM ALL GOOD BOOK STORES

ALSO FROM LEONAUR
AVAILABLE IN SOFTCOVER OR HARDCOVER WITH DUST JACKET

THE 9TH—THE KING'S (LIVERPOOL REGIMENT) IN THE GREAT WAR 1914 - 1918 *by Enos H. G. Roberts*—Mersey to mud—war and Liverpool men.

THE GAMBARDIER *by Mark Severn*—The experiences of a battery of Heavy artillery on the Western Front during the First World War.

FROM MESSINES TO THIRD YPRES *by Thomas Floyd*—A personal account of the First World War on the Western front by a 2/5th Lancashire Fusilier.

THE IRISH GUARDS IN THE GREAT WAR - VOLUME 1 *by Rudyard Kipling*—Edited and Compiled from Their Diaries and Papers—The First Battalion.

THE IRISH GUARDS IN THE GREAT WAR - VOLUME 1 *by Rudyard Kipling*—Edited and Compiled from Their Diaries and Papers—The Second Battalion.

ARMOURED CARS IN EDEN *by K. Roosevelt*—An American President's son serving in Rolls Royce armoured cars with the British in Mesopotamia & with the American Artillery in France during the First World War.

CHASSEUR OF 1914 *by Marcel Dupont*—Experiences of the twilight of the French Light Cavalry by a young officer during the early battles of the great war in Europe.

TROOP HORSE & TRENCH *by R.A. Lloyd*—The experiences of a British Lifeguardsman of the household cavalry fighting on the western front during the First World War 1914-18.

THE EAST AFRICAN MOUNTED RIFLES *by C.J. Wilson*—Experiences of the campaign in the East African bush during the First World War.

THE LONG PATROL *by George Berrie*—A Novel of Light Horsemen from Gallipoli to the Palestine campaign of the First World War.

THE FIGHTING CAMELIERS *by Frank Reid*—The exploits of the Imperial Camel Corps in the desert and Palestine campaigns of the First World War.

STEEL CHARIOTS IN THE DESERT *by S. C. Rolls*—The first world war experiences of a Rolls Royce armoured car driver with the Duke of Westminster in Libya and in Arabia with T.E. Lawrence.

WITH THE IMPERIAL CAMEL CORPS IN THE GREAT WAR *by Geoffrey Inchbald*—The story of a serving officer with the British 2nd battalion against the Senussi and during the Palestine campaign.

AVAILABLE ONLINE AT **www.leonaur.com**
AND FROM ALL GOOD BOOK STORES

Ingram Content Group UK Ltd.
Milton Keynes UK
UKHW010754270323
419227UK00001B/169